Pounding
Praying
Playing

Pounding
Praying
Playing

A personal account of boarding school in St. Pat's Cavan

Liam Mc Niffe

Distribution: **www.mcniffebooks.com**

Also by Liam Mc Niffe:

A History of the Garda Síochána (1997)
Meath Studies in Local History (ed.)(1999)
A History of Williamstown Kells (2003)

Dedicated to all staff and students
past and present
of
St. Patrick's College Cavan
and
To my wife Mary and to my sister Valerie

ISBN 0-9546269-1-5

Designed by
Raymond Fadden

Printed by
Turner Print Group,
Convent Road,
Longford.

Contents

Doorway...

1974

Dr. Liam Mc Niffe was born in Ballinamore, Co. Leitrim in 1957. He studied at Maynooth University where he was awarded an M.A. and PhD in history. He taught in Eureka Secondary School in Kells for 26 years. Having completed an M.Sc. in Educational Management in Trinity College Dublin, he was appointed principal of his alma mater, St. Patrick's College Cavan in 2005. He retired in 2013. Liam has published numerous articles and a number of books on history. He lives in Kells and is married to Mary. They have three grown-up children, Aisling, Ruairí and Shane. He is now a grandad as Ruairí and his wife Ciara have a son, Darach.

... St. Patrick's College

2014

Acknowledgements

Two previous publications on St. Pat's were of enormous benefit to me in writing this book. Despite being written forty years ago, *St. Patrick's College Cavan, a Centenary History*, by Rev. T. Cunningham and Rev. D. Gallogly, has stood the test of time as an excellent history of the college. The more recent, *The College Boys*, by Bishop Francis Mac Kiernan and Raymond Dunne, was of incalculable help to me. My book would not have been possible without it.

Reading every week's issue of *The Anglo-Celt* from July 1972 to September 1974 brought me right back into the world of that decade. The staff of Johnston Central Library, Cavan facilitated me in every way with this research. Rev. Donal Kilduff, Diocesan Chancellor, was of great assistance while I accessed the photographic collection of the college in the Diocesan Archives in the Bishop's House. The help of my former class mate, George Cartwright, was invaluable in the section devoted to the careers chosen by our class.

A number of people read every chapter and suggested amendments: Frank Cogan's critique allowed me to see my work more objectively; Mentor and friend Vincent Comerford's insightful remarks were of great assistance; Friend and colleague from St. Pat's, Leon Lynch's encouragement and advice were of immense help; Friend and colleague from my Eureka days, Leonard Noone's support and incisive comments were greatly appreciated.

A finished book is content and style. The author provides the content but the designer is responsible for the style. It was an education to watch Ray Fadden at work. Practically anything is possible with a talented craftsman who sets himself very exacting standards.

Were it not for my mother, most of the memorabilia from my time in St. Pat's would have been discarded. Her personal diaries were crucial to the writing of this book and I appreciate her giving me unlimited access to them. Within a few weeks of her ninetieth birthday it is great to see her in very good mental and physical health.

My son Ruairí copy-edited the work with precision and insight. Aisling gave very pertinent suggestions having read the twelve chapters. Shane gave very constructive criticism on key chapters.

The support and encouragement of my wife Mary and sister Valerie were of inestimable help to me. Mary read each chapter 'hot' off the printer, proof-read them all numerous times thereafter and as usual was my sounding board. Valerie's interest was so great that she usually read each e-mailed chapter on her phone rather than wait to view them on her PC.

As a indication of my debt, this book is dedicated to them.

Foreword

This is an unusual and fascinating piece of writing, combining a very personal memoir of adolescence and schooldays in St. Pat's, with a wealth of detail on Irish life in the period of the early 70s, so that it has a strong overlay of social history. It evokes a stage of human experience which has now almost entirely disappeared from the Irish human landscape - that of the no-frills boarding school in a diocesan seminary in "middle-Ireland", at a time of very significant transition in the educational and social spheres in the state.

This is also an extremely well-drawn picture of the meeting of the traditional Catholic Ireland of the 50s and 60s with the new, questioning Ireland in the early days of the communications revolution, the transition from single black and white channel formula for living in Ireland to the more complex and multi-layered modern society.

It is not so much a portrait of rebel youth (with or without a cause) but more a faithful reproduction of what life was really like for the majority of Irish teenagers, who were beginning to push against the traditional constraints but not concerned to rock the boat excessively - it was also a time when parental restraints were becoming less strict, though still determined by traditional values. Set in the border midlands, the Northern Troubles are present as menacing backdrop to the life of the students, breaking through occasionally to the foreground of awareness, even if the self-contained world of the boarding school was largely insulated from the external world.

The intertwining of the themes of the loneliness of the young student away from parent and family, the awakening of the adolescent mind in facing up to the challenges of the educational and personal path before him and the accompanying changes in the broader society around him is skillfully developed and portrayed in a series of episodes covering the period of the Leaving Cert cycle. The process of character formation in the rigid - though slowly loosening - structures of Church and school in the context of preparing for the great watershed moment - the final exam, which would (or so it seemed at the time) irrevocably shape one's destiny - is handled very well through an engaging combination of humour, irony and sensitivity.

Those who remember growing up in the '70s will be filled with nostalgia induced by the multiplicity of contemporary references to music and fashions of the time - from the lists of hits on 'Top of the Pops' to the kind of 'duds' which the kids of Ireland, in emulation of their 'flower-power' counterparts across the trans-Atlantic cultural space, chose to wear to social gatherings,

principally the thronged Saturday-night dances to the music of showbands in barn-like halls across rural Ireland.
All in all, this story of one boy's experience in St Pat's becomes an absorbing study of teenage life at a very interesting period in Ireland.

It is a very entertaining read.

Frank Cogan
Former pupil of St. Pat's, 1959-64.
Retired Irish diplomat - former Ambassador to Iran, Italy and Austria.
Dublin
November 2014.

Preface

The no-frills boarding school experience of forty years ago is totally unknown to a whole new generation of Irish people. Very few factual accounts have been written on the subject, apart from Patrick Kennelly's *Sausages for Tuesday* published in 1969. My primary aim in writing this book was to ensure that the boarding experience, lived by tens of thousands of boys in Ireland in the latter half of the last century, be recorded for posterity. In particular I wanted to record what life was like as a boarder for all the pupils who passed through my alma mater, St. Patrick's College Cavan.

This book is fact, not fiction. The names are the real names of pupils and of staff. In so far as is possible, it is an accurate, honest and realistic account of my time as a boarder. I have not sanitised, nor sensationalised, anything about my time there. Boys were sent to St. Pat's for an education. One chapter looks at the origins of boarding school in general and the record of St. Pat's in particular in providing an education for all its pupils.

It is impossible to understand what life was like in St. Pat's at that time unless it is seen in the context of Irish society in the 1970s. As a result I have tried to capture that world, its music, fashion, Northern troubles, education system and clerical influence.

This is a very personal book. It is my experience of St. Pat's. I am very conscious that some others had not nearly as positive a time in the college as I enjoyed. I did not really suffer from homesickness, and did not have to start at the bottom of a very hierarchical system, as I only came to the school as a Fourth Year. I was not bullied and I enjoyed the responsibilities and privileges of being a prefect in my final year.

Reading about one individual's experience of his boarding days, makes little sense unless something is known about where he is coming from. My experience of the college was to some extent influenced by the type of person I was before I went, what I wanted from the two years I spent there and what happened members of my family during that time. Hence, while most of the book is devoted to life in St. Pat's, there are a number of chapters dealing with the summer holidays and other events that helped shape me as a person.

In conclusion, I hope I have written an authentic account of boarding school and of what it was like to be an adolescent in 1970s Ireland. You are the ultimate judge.

Liam Mc Niffe
Williamstown
Kells, Co. Meath
18 November 2014

mcniffeliam1@gmail.com
www.mcniffebooks.com

Pounding

A pupil with two elbows on the desk, head down and hands over the ears,
in a pose of grim determination, eliminating all distractions,
to transmit and absorb knowledge, from the printed page into
the stubborn brain.

Chapter 1

Life before St Pat's

Try having a decent fight in a car, especially if you are in the front seat and your two opponents are in the back. There was no reason for the fight, nothing malicious, just young lads enjoying themselves, but that did not mean the brief encounter was any less intense. Two of my friends, Kielan Logan and Peter Mc Caffrey, and myself were all on our way to Cavan in my father's car[1]. It was March 1969 and my Dad who worked as a car salesman for Smith's Garage in Cavan town had briefly left us alone while he called en route to see a customer in Aughawillan. The car rocked with the movements. My street cred took a bashing when Dad hastily returned and gave out to me in front of my friends.

I was excitable and impatient at the best of times, but the advertisement a few weeks previously in the local paper, *The Anglo-Celt*, had left me in a state of ecstasy and feverish expectation[2]:

ST. PATRICK'S COLLEGE, CAVAN

All Prospective Entrants will be required to do

APTITUDE TEST

IN IRISH, ENGLISH and ARITHMETIC

On SATURDAY, 15th MARCH

Candidates who secure the First Twenty-five or Thirty Places in the above-mentioned Test will be invited back to compete for Six Scholarships after Easter.

The Subjects for the Scholarship Examination will be Two out of the following:—

ALGEBRA, GEOMETRY, HISTORY, GEOGRAPHY

For the purpose of awarding Scholarships the marks obtained in this latter Examination will be added to those scored in the Aptitude Test in order to determine the order of merit.

Boys who apply for admission after 15th March will do an Aptitude Test in September before they are assigned to the Classes which suit their attainments.

For further particulars apply to:—

THE PRESIDENT (1353)

Saint Patrick's College Cavan, known as 'St. Pat's' or just 'Pat's', depending on the degree of familiarity claimed by the speaker, was the Catholic diocesan boys school for Kilmore diocese. Free second level education covering tuition costs and free bussing had been introduced in September 1967 by the Minister for Education, Donagh O' Malley[3]. Each of the college scholarships (referred to above) paid the cost of boarding and was worth approximately £90 annually (€1,226 in today's terms and over three weeks of my Dad's pay at that time)[4]. It was paid for three years. Some parents wanted their children to do an entrance exam to a college like St. Pat's to see how well they were doing academically and on the off-chance that they might get a scholarship[5]. Others did the exam because they intended going to St. Pat's. I wanted to do it because a number of lads in my class in Ballinamore Boys National School were doing it and it seemed exciting. The application form and a letter of recommendation from my parish priest as required was returned with my birth certificate attached.

In an attempt to familiarise me with the format, my mother had written for past papers to a friend whose son had done the exam the previous year. The papers duly arrived with a covering note which opened with the sentence, 'Enclosed are the papers which you expressed a desire to secure'. The elaborate phraseology forever stuck in my mind. On the night before the exam, my mother was trying to make sure I was presentable for the next day[6]. 'Liam, you can't wear those brown shoes, there's a hole in the sole of one of them. Get your good black pair'. To her consternation she discovered that they had a hole in both[7]. The shoes had been multipurpose in my eyes, their primary function being playing football. The next day I had to put my best foot forward.

One other lad from my class in Ballinamore, Leo Plunkett, also took the exam, as well as his brother Micheál. Their father, Tony, had gone to St. Pat's as a boarder. The boys stayed the previous night in the college in order to taste the experience of boarding[8]. It was a mild, damp, drizzly morning. When we arrived, I remember meeting Micheál outside the ref. (refectory) and cracking some puerile joke about a quick escape as we viewed these enormous wicker baskets for laundry, parked opposite the door that led to the kitchen area. Clouds of steam were billowing from the kitchen below. The noise was phenomenal as one hundred and fifty young lads made their way downstairs to the study hall for the test[9]. The boys from Cavan town, whose brothers had told them all about the college, shouted familiarities across to one another. I was seated near the back of the study hall. We had exams in Irish, English essay and comprehension as well as Arithmetic. My memory of the actual papers, except the English composition, is hazy and my results proved this. We had free dinner in the ref. and there was some type of farola or semolina pudding with a very small amount of tinned fruit salad on the top of each pudding. Kielan, Peter, Leo and I decided to skip the dessert, bolted out and gave ourselves a guided tour of the college. The boarding students were not there, having gone home for St. Patrick's weekend. The exam resumed in the afternoon. I was finished early, but we were not allowed hand up the paper. However I was bored and when the supervising priest, (Fr. John Murphy I think), had just walked past my desk, I hopped up and following quietly in his footsteps went up three or four desks to Leo Plunkett. The priest swung around and in a fairly loud voice asked, 'where do you think you are going? I replied, 'I was just seeing was my friend done'. When I returned to my seat I remember thinking that my mother, who was a stickler for proper English, would be annoyed that I had said 'done' rather than 'finished'. For some reason I thought better of informing her about the incident.

A few weeks later when I arrived to school, Kielan Logan informed me that he had got sixth place in the aptitude test and Peter Mc Caffrey eleventh, both being recalled to do the further scholarship exams in History and Geography. Leo Plunkett got fifty-seventh place. I got permission from Master Joyce to go home and see if the post had arrived. (Those were innocent times, no obsession with health and safety issues as I flew through the town). I got seventy first place, with quite poor results in most areas, except English composition where I scored 45/70. I do remember choosing to do an essay entitled, 'An imaginary city under the sea'. I had a good imagination, if nothing else. As it happened, none of us went to St. Pat's, with all four starting St. Felim's College, our local diocesan day school, in Ballinamore the following September[10].

My knowledge of boarding school was very limited and naive at that time. Michael Leydon from Swanlinbar, who attended St. Pat's in the mid-sixties, had regaled me as an eight year old, with stories of robbing orchards and general high jinks. It seemed great craic. In retrospect I realise it was very fortunate I did not go to St. Pat's as a First Year boarder. I was always a rebel, refusing to take anything lying down, never keeping my mouth shut and always ready to stand up and indeed fight, if I was treated, (as I perceived), unfairly. Boarding school operated on a hierarchical system; traditions were very strong, First Years were expected to keep their heads down and say nothing. St. Pat's would not have suited me as a hot-headed twelve year old. I would have been eaten alive. One incident that subsequently happened in St. Felim's illustrates my point. In 1969 a pupil who had attended St. Pat's as a boarder for three years, came as a Fourth Year to Ballinamore, the same time that I arrived as a First Year. Many of the lads played soccer at lunch time, and there was a limited number of hard courts available. The Fourth Years, headed by this former St. Pat's boarder, took possession of the court on which we, mere First Years, were playing. In an act of defiance I grabbed their ball and kicked it away as far as possible, and then ran off. The next day the Fourth Year in question dragged me into his classroom, and got some of his class mates to help him hold me down, while he wrote "Class Two" (his class name) in biro on my stomach. I was humiliated and secretly swore revenge. Physically he would have chewed me up and spat me out, so subtlety was required. I waited a week and then got a classmate and friend of mine, Gerry Greene, to stand guard at lunchtime outside the Fourth Year classroom. If anyone approached he was to knock on the door and I would escape out the window. I entered the room and scattered all my inscriber's books around the room. I did the same the next day and felt my dignity restored.

Another anecdote shows me as a non-conforming junior pupil. On our first day back as Second Years in Ballinamore, one teacher, Padraig Griffin, who had never taught us in First Year, stuck his head in our classroom door and publicly warned Kielan Logan, myself and I think Pat Flanagan, that he had heard all about us and we were marked men. Notwithstanding that introduction, that teacher never treated me unfairly. Ballinamore let me mature in my own way. St. Pat's being a boarding school, with a strong tradition of seniority among pupils, would have made me grow up the hard way.

I spent three happy years in St. Felim's. There was a very nice atmosphere, no bullying that I was aware of, great craic, and much slagging between the lads from West Cavan (Swanlinbar, Ballyconnell and Killeshandra) and ourselves. In addition the rivalry, against our fellow Leitrim classmates, as we togged out at weekends in spring and summer to play for our respective clubs, was intense. The staff was all young with a good sense of fair play, despite the reality that there was corporal punishment, a fact of life that we just accepted.

At the end of First Year, I got a summer job in Logan's, a local supermarket at £3 (€41 in today's terms) per week. I continued part-time when school reopened. Class finished at 4.20, I raced home, grabbed dinner and was at work at 5.00 until 7.00 four evenings per week. I also worked all day Saturday, 9.30 am. until 10.45 pm. One Saturday night, as I was crossing the street carrying groceries for a woman to her car, I impertinently put up my hand, like a garda points-man on traffic duty, to stop the oncoming traffic, while

we crossed the street. As the car I had made stop drew alongside me, to my horror I realised it was driven by Fr. Mc Kiernan, president of my school, accompanied by Fr. Keogan my Science teacher. The look from Fr. Mc Kiernan was not one of approval. My pay was £1.10 shillings per week (€21 in today's terms), rising to £1.16 shillings (€25) the following year, a very fair amount at the time. My parents let me keep all my earnings and continued to give me 2/6 (€1.75) pocket money, which I lived on, while saving my pay in the Credit Union. I was working on the Monday (evening) 15 February 1971, when the new decimalisation currency was introduced. An elderly man held out a mixture of the old shillings and pence with some new pence and stated, 'Sonny, take what you need there, I haven't a clue'. I worked full-time during Halloween, Christmas, Easter holidays and all three months the next summer. I was always treated very well and the job gave me a great sense of self-worth. The owner's son, John Logan, was a newly appointed teacher to the vocational school in Carrigallen. Despite our age difference we got on very well and he always talked to me as an equal.
After Christmas in Third Year, I reduced my work to just Saturdays during term, as I wanted to concentrate on the upcoming Inter Cert[11]. I always loved English, due in large part to my mother's interest in reading and in knowledge in general. Joe Prior, an excellent English teacher further cultivated the love of the subject in me. My other love was History, greatly helped by my teacher Brendan Burns. Another teacher, Gerry Brady, greatly broadened my education, when he got our class to look up answers to general knowledge questions as well as doing our ordinary Commerce homework each night.
I had decided by Inter Cert year (1971-2) what I wanted to do, study English and History at university, but with no thought of becoming a secondary school teacher. If I got four honours in the Leaving Cert there was a County Council grant available to fund university. That was my aim. So I wanted to start by doing well in the Inter Cert. I was nothing if not focused. In addition to doing homework in the evening, I started getting up circa 6.30 am. in February of that year and revising until 8.00, when I had breakfast. I then got a lift with my father who, on his way to work in Cavan, dropped me at school to play soccer until class began. On the advice of our History teacher, I ordered exam papers by post and started analysing the trends so as to study as efficiently as possible. The idea of boarding school, where study was an integral part of the day, began to appeal to me.
Why St. Pat's? My Dad had worked for many years in Cavan town and we frequently shopped there. It was also the local diocesan boarding school. My mother's family, the Kelly's had strong ties with it. Her uncle, Michael Kelly,

had been a student there from 1902-06[12]. He had returned as a priest and was college bursar for a while[13]. Two of my mother's brothers, Seán and Micheál, were pupils in the 1930's[14]. Four first cousins of mine attended in the 1960s, and early '70s[15]. Some lads from Ballinamore were boarders at this time. Furthermore my older brother, Micheál, had repeated his Leaving Certificate in St. Pat's, 1970-71, and had done well as a result. My mother and father were in favour of the idea. For the most part, St. Pat's attracted the more academic pupils from much of Cavan, large tracts of Leitrim and many other counties. The standard was inevitably higher, fuelled by the scholarships, and the boarding school ensured that study was not a problem. I never felt my parents would object, even though it would cost considerably more than day-school.

On 27 July 1972, a few weeks before I started St. Pat's, my father was made redundant[16]. It was a mark of the man that he told none of us until late that night, so as not to spoil the small family birthday party for my older sister Valerie. It was an awful blow to him, as he could not understand it. We subsequently discovered that a routine medical report for work had rung alarm bells for his superiors, something we did not know at the time. He didn't drink or smoke, his family was everything to him and he worked very hard all his life. He had been promoted from car salesman, to sales manager and eventually overall manager of Brittain Group garage (formerly Smith's) in Cavan town. We had always enjoyed a new free car, free insurance, tax and petrol as part of his job. He worked all the hours that God gave him, with one man actually calling to buy a car on Christmas day. Although we as children were amazed by this interruption, Dad thought nothing of dealing with him on that day. I never questioned for a moment that Dad's being without work for the first time in his life, might prevent me from going to St. Pat's, even though my sister, Valerie, was also at boarding school in Bundoran.

Like most teenagers, I was obsessed with my own life that summer of '72. I worked in Logans, went to football practice three, sometimes four times, per week with my local club, Seán O'Heslin's. I was on the Under 16 and Minor teams. Football was everything, well not quite everything. Getting to the odd dance in 'The Slieve' (local Slieve an Iarainn hotel) on Saturday night, was almost everything. Getting 'going with' a girl would have been everything. My parents, especially my father, totally trusted us and expected we would act responsibly. My mother, a nurse, was nursing an elderly neighbour at night time for a number of months that summer. If I really wanted to go to the dance in the Slieve, I would not ask permission until I came home from work late on a Saturday night. Mam wasn't there and Dad always allowed me to go, with the caveat 'Mam won't be too pleased'. The prospect of 'facing the music' from my mother in the morning did not deter me from facing a good band that night. Having got to the dance, the next hurdle was actually getting a dance. It wasn't easy at just fifteen years of age, with only a small number of girls your own age there. The girls lined up on the left hand side of the hall, security in numbers for them. They could not ask the boys out to dance, their only option being to accept or refuse when asked to dance. Fellas lined up along the wall opposite the girls. For my few friends and I who were relatively young, it was high stakes. There were a few self-preservation rules you followed. It was social suicide to cross the floor and approach the girls on your own as you were bound to be refused and very publicly humiliated. Only the very confident or the very naïve did so. The modus operandi was to move forward like the Roman phalanx of soldiers, and in the general melee hope that the victim you asked accepted to dance with you. If a girl refused to dance, you never asked the girl beside her, because if she accepted, she was admitting that her standard was lower than her friend's. What really frustrated me was that girls my age were always asked by, and accepted to dance with, lads two or three years older. You danced girls whom you knew and it was an unwritten rule that they would not refuse you. On one occasion one such girl did refuse me. I did not pass much heed as she was only one of a long list of refusals I had received that night, albeit not from neighbours. She met me the next day and apologised and told me that her mother had pointed out that she should have danced with me. I was very impressed with her telling me. My friends and I did get dances, but also refusals. So we employed less than chivalrous defence tactics. If refused a dance, I retorted, 'You are fussy who you dance with'. Somewhat taken aback the girl replied 'well I am', and I replied with the cheap shot, 'Well, I'm not, so that's why I asked you'. Being fair the dances in The Slieve were usually fairly civilised affairs, there was no drink served at the dance and most were sober. If a girl was drunk it would have been the talk of the town the next day.

This was still the era of the big show band. The signs of its demise were beginning to make their appearance with some venues advertising John Dee Disco Show and some hotels having got bar extensions (until 12.30 a.m. usually), with supper provided. (The supper was frequently inedible parts of a chicken or weird looking sausages, but in order to get the longer opening hours officially food had to be provided). However most venues hosted show bands and drink was not sold at them. There was only a mineral bar in the ordinary dance halls and in the marquees. The latter dotted fields all over

Cavan and Leitrim in the summer months, with the following typical advertisement appearing in the Celt on 1 September 1972:

Carnival
Spacious 5 Pole Marquee in Belturbet
Saturday 2 September
Music by Brian Coll and the Buckaroos
Dancing 9.30 to 1.30, admission 50p.

The 50p (€0.63) admission was one ninth of my weekly summer wage of £4.50 at that time. The following were the bands scheduled to play at carnivals, and dance halls that were advertised in a massive two page spread every week in the Celt[17]:

Ray Lynham and the Hillbillies
Jimmy Swarbrigg and the Fabulous Times
Corrida and the Country Style
Rory Daniels and the Green County
Big Tom and the Mainliners
Sahara Showband
The Indians
The Blossoms
Mary Lou and the Highwaymen
Mattie Fox and the Country Boy Blues
Des Wilson and the Big Country
Gene Stuart and the Mighty Avons
The Cotton Mill Boys
Seán Thompson and the Everglades
Dermot Henry and the Virginians
Dermot Hegarty and the Plainsmen
The Nevada
The Big 8
Rio Grande
The Dixie's.

For many of us teenagers, there were only two types of music at this time, Pop and Country and Western. The latter was seen as somewhat old fashioned but there were some great bands who just played Country and Western and in any event they played more slow sets. In order to appear 'with

it' officially you had to be seen to complain about Country and Western and harp on about preferring Pop, regardless of your actual preference.
The Ballinamore Festival, held the second week of August each year, was an incredible event. It is impossible to exaggerate the anticipation beforehand, the sheer enjoyment during it, and the sense of desolation on the Monday after it finished. On that Monday it appeared that the evenings had suddenly shortened dramatically and the reopening of school was now on the horizon. During the Festival the carnival atmosphere was fantastic, everybody was in great form as returned emigrants thronged the town. The Festival Marquee had a dance, with a major show band, each night of that week. It was always packed. If you didn't get to the dance, the next day you invariably asked a friend who had attended, was it any good, hoping against hope that it wasn't and that you had missed nothing. On one memorable occasion I asked a fairly hefty, very solid built fellow, two years older than me, how 'The dance went', to which he replied, 'It was a great night's pushing, we pushed up the marquee and we pushed down the marquee, it was horrid craic'. The same lad must have changed tack, because I saw him out dancing the next year and he got married shortly afterwards[18]. He was not joking, a very small minority of lads never danced but spent the night ensuring that there was a continuous melee as fellows attempted to ask girls to dance. In fact occasionally, you would have asked a girl to dance, and before she got the chance to refuse or accept, you were swept along by a tsunami of bodies in the opposite direction. The floor never extended totally to the perimeter of the marquee tent. Consequently if there was a melee, some poor unfortunate could be pushed off the actual timber floor and fall on to what was at best wet grass and at worst muck. The result was not a pretty site.
In August 1972 I was at a Festival dance, my last outing before I headed off to the seclusion of boarding school for two months. In addition it had been announced this this was the last dance of the night, which always resulted in an even greater rush to get a partner as if the lads' lives depended on it. In the melee, I saw my opportunity. Right beside me, with her back to me, was a lovely girl, a little smaller than I was (at that age you never asked a girl taller than you to dance, as you'd look a right eejit in everyone's eyes), with beautiful shoulder length blonde curly hair. I tipped her on the shoulder and asked her to dance. She turned round, and faced me with the greatest look of resentment I have ever witnessed. I mumbled something about wanting to know what time it was, while HE told me to f**k off, which I speedily did. I can honestly say without doubt that this incident was the most embarrassing moment of my entire teenage years.

Like most teenagers, I felt if I was not in fashion I might as well be dead. The early '70s saw the continuation of the androgynous hippie look from the 1960s. Jeans remained frayed, cheesecloth shirts and Mexican peasant type blouses were popular[19]. In addition to the miniskirt, mid-calf length dresses called 'midis' and ankle length dresses called 'maxis' were also worn. Vera Brady's shop in Cavan town advertised ladies trouser suits at £6 (€82 today's terms) and maxi dresses at £4.99 (€68), while miniskirts were on sale starting at 25p (€3.40) each[20]. In 1971, extremely brief, tight-fitting shorts, called hot pants, were a fashion craze for girls and young women. We young lads could only commend the fashion designers. Trousers for both sexes, flared at leg bottoms, were very tight and revealing from the lower thighs up. Fitted blazers for both sexes with buttons covered and very wide lapels were also popular[21]. Platform shoes appeared in 1971, and often had soles two to four inches thick. Both men and women wore them. Mullins shop in Cavan advertised ladies platform shoes reduced from £4 (€55) to £2.50 (€34) and gents' shoes at £2.75 (€37)[22].

At this time every home did not have a television[23]. While colour television came into Ireland in the early seventies, the vast majority of homes had black and white sets for another ten years[24]. There was just one Irish television channel, R.T.E. It only broadcast for about six hours daily during the week and for about ten hours daily at the weekend. The following is the R.T.E. schedule for Friday 15 September, 1972[25].

Transmission began at 5.30 in the afternoon:

5.30 Cartoon
6.00 Angelus
6.01 News Headline
6.06 Encyclopaedia
6.15 Gunsmoke
7.15 An Nuacht
7.25 Sports final
7.30 The Ray Stevens show
8.30 Marcus Welbey MD
9.30 The News
9.50 Minority report
10.20 Mannix
11.20 Outlook
11.25 Late News
11.30 Closedown

Many homes in Cavan and Leitrim, including ours, also had access to Ulster Television. On that same Friday in September 1972, UTV started transmission at 1.45 with racing, followed by Romper room, Crossroads at tea time, with Sale of the Century afterwards, followed by the cartoon, The Flintstones, finishing the night's viewing with a film ending at approximately midnight[26]. There was only one English speaking Irish radio station, Radio Éireann, with no local stations[27]. However most of us listened to Radio Luxembourg 208, many on our transistors (small portable radios). If you possessed an ear phone for your transistor you looked really modern. Radio Luxembourg with its non-stop Pop music and trendy D.J.s, was our staple diet.

While we teenage lads worried about how we looked, who looked at us, what music was 'in', who we were playing next in the Under Sixteens or Minors, our parents had to come up with the £120 (€1,632 in today's terms) it cost to board in St. Pat's for the year[28]. This did not include books or laundry. As was common in most boys' schools, there was no uniform. The £120 covered our total keep for 228 days, working out at about 52 pence (€7.20) per day[29]. This was very reasonable mainly because it was subsidised by the salary of the priests who taught there. They just received a stipend, while the remainder went towards running the boarding school. In effect our boarding fee was subsidised by our priest teachers. However the £120 was still a substantial amount of money for most families at that time. The position of an experienced general assistant for a hardware shop was advertised at £25 (€340) per week[30]. My father, when manager of Brittain Garage in Cavan, received £40 (€544) per week plus the free car. However he was now redundant. The new job that he was to take up shortly was at the reduced pay of £28 (€381) per week. This meant that my fees cost my family over four week's pay. All women and single men teachers received from £22-£38 (€300 - €517) and married men £38-£47 (€517 - €640) per week[31]. Many of the pupils in St. Pat's came from farming backgrounds. There were marts in Cavan, Cootehill, Kingscourt and Bailieboro as well as Carrigallen in South Leitrim. Mc Carren Meats were offering farmers £17.25 (€236) per hundredweight for Grade A pigs delivered to their factory[32]. Farming incomes had not yet received the fillip they were to, following entry to the Common Market that was due to happen in January 1973. It took real sacrifice from most families to send one, or frequently two, sons to boarding school. I was part of a privileged group, although I did not appreciate it sufficiently at the time.

On 5 September 1972 I was to enter St. Pat's as a Fourth Year pupil. Little did I know the drama with which that particular day was to begin.

College with Intermediate and Junior pitches in the background

No. ____________

Received from Willie Mc Niffe

the sum of £120-00 Pounds ____________ Shillings

and ____________ Pence sterling.

One hundred & Twenty pounds.

Dated this 5th day of Sept. 1972

£ Rev. P. Brady.

ST. PATRICK'S COLLEGE, CAVAN

Author's receipt for boarding fees for 1972-73, signed by dean, Fr. Patrick Brady

Chapter 2

Daily Routine

September - Halloween 1972

'Did ya hear the news?'
'Yea, a whole lot dead and hostages taken, I'd say the West Germans will storm the village and try to release them',
'Na, they'll negotiate',
'Bet ya they won't',

Two fifteen year olds, animated by dramatic breaking news, anxious to outdo each other with the copper-fastened certitude that only fifteen year old lads possess. Peter Mc Caffrey and I were standing outside my house at midday on Tuesday 5 September 1972, discussing what was to be known as the Munich Massacre. We had all been following the Olympics, and were in awe of Mark Spitz, the United States swimmer, who had won seven gold medals in total. However on that Tuesday morning Palestinian terrorists, known as Black September, had broken into the Olympic village and taken Israeli athletes, coaches and officials hostage, with terrible consequences[1]. The world was in the throes of the Cold War, and we saw everything in terms of black and white. We had regarded the recent World Chess Championship between Bobby Fischer of the United States and Boris Spassky of the Soviet Union as a war and rejoiced when Fischer became the first American to win the title five days previously. Peter, Leo Plunkett and I, had completed the Inter Cert in Ballinamore the previous June. That September evening we were due to go as boarders to St. Pat's. As it happened, the same three of us had done the entrance exam to St. Pat's three years earlier[2].

That day was also my Dad's forty-sixth birthday. My parents had bought a new red leather writing-set case, on which they wrote the date, as a gift for me going to boarding school. Dad, Mam and I went to Cavan, in Auntie Anne's car, an Austin 1300. The previous December Anne had suffered a subarachnoid brain haemorrhage and had to give up her position as theatre sister in the Surgical Hospital in Cavan. She could not return to driving and kindly gave Dad the use of her car, while he was making arrangements to set up his own garage. It was a beautiful warm evening, with the sun shining and Cavan town bustling with mothers, no doubt making last minute purchases for children returning to school the next day. We went to the Central Café on Bridge Street to get something to eat. I was conscious that prior to this we had always eaten in the Farnham Hotel any time we were in Cavan. I didn't mind as my taste buds at fifteen were basic enough, (burger and chips), but I was conscious that it hurt my father, although nothing was said. There were lots of fellows of secondary school age around the town and I wondered were any of them going to St. Pat's. I saw one red haired lad who later turned out to be a Third Year boarder, Kevin Colton from Belturbet[3].

As we drove up to the long winding avenue, it never struck me that I might be lonely or homesick. I didn't think of missing my friends in Ballinamore as Leo Plunkett and Peter Mc Caffrey were coming with me to St. Pat's. In any event I loved adventure, something new and exciting beckoned and I was animated. I was however slightly taken aback as we came into full view of the impressive college façade. I had been there a handful of times previously, but this was different. I was not a visitor, this would be home for the next two years. We were met with a flurry of activity. Cars of all descriptions, Cortina, Viva, Escort, Anglia, Minx, Capri, Renault 4, Oxford, Cambridge and the ubiquitous Volkswagen Beetle were parked in all areas, with doors and boots open. Big cases of all colours, sizes and ages were being carried, dragged, or drawn towards the large open main double brown doors. There was much noise as returning pupils shouted familiarities across to each other. Such camaraderie and somewhat exaggerated bonhomie, I soon learned, was part and parcel of boarding school life, when parents were present. A small table was in the entrance lobby, where the fees were paid and we were just marked off the list as having arrived.

I was assigned a room on the top corridor of the new wing. It had two single iron beds, with light mattresses. I made up my own bed as everyone supplied their own bedclothes. It was somewhat eerie as there were no curtains on any windows. There was a small cupboard for belongings and the case went under my bed. I was surprised to realise I had a sink and hot and cold water in the room. It was clean and adequate. I had no roommate yet. I don't remember nearly anything of the rest of the evening, except as I was going to sleep noticing the fanlight above the bedroom door. I was looking forward to the next day. There were lots of other lads I knew from Ballinamore apart from Leo and Peter; Thomas Mc Tague and Mel Mc Kiernan were in Inter Cert, Thomas's brother Seamus had just arrived as a First Year, Dermot Prior was in Fourth Year and Cathal Sharpley was in Leaving Cert.

Everything burst into life the next morning with deafening noise. A loud hand bell was rung to get us up, and down to Mass, not in the college Chapel that was being refurbished but, in the assembly hall where the chapel seats had been temporarily installed. We were assigned seats for the year by the Dean,

Rev. Paddy Brady. We had school Mass twice a week in Ballinamore. You could sit where you liked and with whom you liked, so long as you were not at the back of the Church. It was very different here. Seniority was everything, dependent on what year you were in and how bright you were perceived to be. Each year was divided into three classes, according to academic ability. So Leaving Certs were classes 1, 2, and 3, Fourth Years were classes 4, 5, and 6 and so on, down to the new First Years, whose entrance test meant they were already streamed. Class 1, the brightest lads in Leaving Cert, were assigned seats at the back of the chapel, back of the study hall and at the top of the ref. The First Years sat at the top of the chapel, top of the study hall and bottom of the refectory. Consequently everyone knew how good you were academically by the number of your class, and by how near the top of your year group you were seated. This was all new to me. The First Years were the last to be seen to. Even then, I felt a bit of a cheat as I knew I was benefiting from being a Fourth Year without ever having had to earn it from First Year up. I had always believed very strongly that being younger was not a crime so why should you be penalised.

The prefect system was an integral part of running the boarding school. The prefects, who were Leaving Cert students, (chosen I assume by the president, dean and some priests on the staff) had great responsibility and were given privileges as a reward. Tom Flynn from Killinkere was head prefect[4]. Liam Tuite (Oldcastle, Meath) was second prefect and Paddy Gilroy (Ballyconnell) was third. Peter Callaghan (Kilnaleck) was sacristan, this included preparing the vestments each day in advance for all the priests, as each one said Mass on a daily basis. Charlie O' Gorman, (Cavan) was the fourth prefect. As prefects they helped maintain order in the study hall, the refectory, the Church and the First Year dormitory, as well as being role models.

After Mass we all rushed to the ref. congregating outside until the double doors opened. Again we were assigned our seat with our class mates. Each table in the ref. seated eight pupils, except the First Year tables that seated twelve. The dean, Fr. Paddy Brady, had a pulpit-like podium opposite the main door to the ref., allowing him to ensure order. He said grace before meals. There was a large jug with creamy milk from the college farm on each table. The delph was light and white. There was one square of strong tasting and very yellow butter, for each pupil. The reverberations of almost two hundred lads devouring cornflakes from silver aluminium-type breakfast bowls echoed throughout the refectory. Large catering aluminium teapots, sat waiting in a big trolley to be collected by one pupil (on daily rotation) from each table. The tea came with milk and sugar already added. Most fellows liked sugar and to be fair, the tea was always very sweet. In fact the sugar was added by the kitchen staff, using a cup and in the rush to get it done, sometimes the top and sides of the pot were sticky with the melted sugar that spilled. You could eat all the bread (sliced pan) you wanted. I was fussy. I liked very weak tea, with no sugar and lots of milk. Previously I had toasted all bread that ever passed my lips. My real education had begun. Many lads were well stocked up with jam and other food that they had brought back with them. We had lockers in the ref. near the dean's pulpit, for storing such food. No one was allowed to leave until grace after meals was said.

When we emerged from the ref. the day-boys had arrived, adding another two hundred and forty voices to the shouts of us, one hundred and eighty boarders[5]. We were all directed to assemble in the area bounded by the study hall, the five new flat-roofed classrooms and the entrance to the assembly hall, to hear a rallying of the troops from the college president, Rev. Terence Mc Manus. Standing behind the railing and above us, Terry as he was commonly called by pupils, delivered his state of the college address to us. He was a small man who had a very distinct, high pitched Fermanagh accent, coupled with a deep and very audible intake of breath, before each sentence. He also had the idiosyncratic habit of an involuntary chicken-like movement, whereby he continually drew his elbows in to his sides, quite like that practised by some soccer professionals today. As a result he was easily caricatured, with every pupil believing that he alone was the best mimic of the college president. Terry told us about how he had synchronised the timetable to allow certain subjects run concurrently, thereby allowing any senior pupils who wished to do honours in English but pass in Irish etc. Many of us pupils had no idea what 'synchronised' meant, let alone the obstacles Terry had overcome to produce this timetable. However we were all out in the lovely sunshine, listening to the college president and clapping when we thought it was a good idea and in the hope that he might prolong his address, and so postpone our going to class.

Alas, all good things must come to an end, and we were dismissed and reluctantly streamed back to class. Streamed being the operative word as everyone knew the class to which they were assigned, based on academic ability. I was assigned to Class V, the second stream of Fourth Years. I was disappointed as I had come to St. Pat's to achieve and wanted to be in the top class. On enquiring I was informed that pupils would be reassigned class depending on the Inter Cert results, which were due out in a week or two. Our classroom was in the New Wing, fifth down the green-tiled corridor.

It seemed very small and somewhat dilapidated to me, coming as I was from Ballinamore where the school was less than ten years old. On closer inspection the dark wainscot revealed former pupils' names and the date of the inscription. The furniture consisted of individual small tables with formica-type tops and chairs. Each classroom had a raised platform or dais on which the teacher stood. In reality the size of the room mitigated against the teacher moving around. I was in Ray Dunne's Latin class and I distinctly remember his energy and enthusiasm as he referred to us as 'gentlemen' and continually used the lip on the dais to remove the back of his slip-on shoe and then slip it on again.

Class started at 9.00 and lasted forty five minutes. The five morning classes were punctuated by a fifteen minute break commencing at 11.15. Lunch was from one to two. I was surprised that dinner consisted of three courses. The logistics of distributing the food was obviously the result of a long tried and trusted formula. The big wooden trolley was wheeled alongside the table, with those pupils nearest lifting the soup filled bowls and passing them along the line of their table, receiving their own food last. The dinner consisted of meat with gravy, mixed vegetables, (carrots and parsnips, turnips or cabbage) and jacket potatoes. The designated pupil from each table went down to the serving area and collected the silver tray with the meat. This was then rotated around the table, with a different pupil having first choice each day. Similarly with the silver round container of potatoes, and vegetables. While it seemed very regimented to me at first, I soon realised it was totally fair and just. Some fellows had Y.R and Chef Sauce of their own in the lockers. When Grace after meals was said by the dean we all trooped out of the ref. I thought it peculiar that we boarders did not seem to play football at lunch time as we had done in Ballinamore. However I soon realised that there were two aspects to life in the college, the school day with the influx of day-boys, and the evenings and weekends with just the boarders. The three afternoon classes of forty minutes each finished at 4.00, the day-boys raced home and the college resumed a quieter level of noise.

We boarders went to the ref. for afternoon tea, which consisted of tea and all the bread you wanted, with the one square of butter each. Occasionally one of these squares had a long hair attached to it. If it was someone else's butter that was so endowed, you could crack the joke that you thought that you could see dandruff on the hair. Some lads supplemented the afternoon tea with jam, cheese and bananas. Not all the fellows bothered going in for this food. We had recreation for an hour and a half from 4.00. At 5.30 evening study commenced. Everyone raced down to the study hall as you could get punishment work for being late. The hall held nearly one hundred and eighty pupils, seated two to a desk, in four rows of twenty two. One of the four Leaving Cert prefects sat at a podium at the top, facing pupils and keeping an eye on the First Years. One of the teaching priests, occupied the podium strategically placed at the back of the hall, so pupils had their back to him. If I was amazed by the decibel level of the ref. in the morning, I was astonished by the deafening silence that descended on the study hall in the evening. If you needed a book or details regarding homework given from a classmate, you wrote a short note on a scrap of paper and put the recipient's name on it. It was passed hand by hand to them and you duly received the item requested. Of course occasionally the note got added to as it travelled, but usually its integrity was respected. A note landed on my desk after a few days, my first connection with the pupil express, and I felt really chuffed, I had 'arrived' in St. Pat's. The top of each desk lifted to reveal quite a large storage place, where we boarders kept our books. I was enthralled that first evening, as many lads started drawing up a calendar from 6 September until the week before Christmas. I subsequently discovered that at the end of study each night, fellows ritually crossed off that day, like a convict awaiting release.

For about the last fifteen seconds before seven o'clock on the study hall clock, lads started to fidget as they waited impatiently for the bell of release. One hundred and eighty desk lids banged down almost simultaneously as fellows raced to the ref. for evening tea. This consisted of the tea with milk and sugar added, as much bread as you wanted and the square of butter. The main course consisted of one of the following on separate evenings: beans, burgers, sausages, fried eggs, hard-boiled eggs, chips on their own, and fish fingers occasionally. There was one Leaving Cert lad who would have been quite capable of eating the entire week's main courses in the one evening. In fact he used get any meat left over from dinner or tea from the tables around him. Tea was over relatively quickly and we had about twenty five minutes free time until we went to the Church for the rosary at 7.45. This was followed immediately by a resumption of study from 8.00 until 9.30 for the First Years who then went to bed. The rest of us remained studying until ten o'clock. Lights were centrally controlled and went off at about 10.30 each night.

The routine of that first day was repeated, with just a few changes, every week day until the end of Fourth Year the following June. After two weeks, the refurbishment of the college Chapel was finished and we vacated the assembly hall. For the first few weeks there was absolute bedlam, each morning before class, at the school bookshop as hundreds of pupils fought

to gain access to buy their text books. The shop was located between the ref. and the stairs to the dean's corridor in the New Wing. A half-door protected the pupils who were the shop boys, Greg Cornyn (Dowra) and Eamonn Gorman (Ballinalee, Co. Longford) who tried to remain calm as pupils jostled, roared and tried to get their attention. Again the more senior you were the quicker you were served. That was just the way it was. A week or two after we had settled back, morning study was reintroduced. We had Mass at 7.30 each morning, breakfast at 8.00, followed by morning study, from 8.40 until 9.00 when class started. The idea behind morning study was to refresh homework done the night before. For a number of weeks in September, on numerous mornings, prior to study starting, seated pupils would spontaneously break into the St. Pat's football anthem. The exploits of the victorious college senior team were recalled in lyrics accompanying the air of Molly Malone, that included periodic outbursts of 'St. Pat's' followed by rhythmic hand clapping[6].
For the first time in its history, St. Pat's had won the Hogan Cup the previous April. I had followed their fortunes closely as many of us in Ballinamore were interested in their progress in the competition, but nothing prepared me for the pride felt by St. Pat's, until I got there as a pupil. This was the Holy Grail, the All-Ireland Senior G.A.A. Colleges competition. As I walked around the grounds my first day I was awe struck as I saw the wall of honour, one of the handball alleys with the winning team outlined in clear writing as follows:

A. Elliott.

P. Mc Gill. E. Gillic.

J. Sweeney. O. Brady. G. Smith

K. O'Keeffe. S. Leddy.

C. O' Donoghue. N. Brennan. B. Brady.

H. Reynolds. M. English.

The panel included M. Rudden, G. Mc Intyre, B. Crowe, F. Costello, A. King, P. Brady, B. Mc Dermott, C. Maguire, O. Martin, and M. Mc Keown[7].

The following Monday afternoon, I received my first letter (my mother) and was reading it during recreation when someone told me I was 'In Recep.', the college shorthand for being in reception, in the sense that someone was visiting you. My Dad and brother Micheál were in Cavan on business regarding setting up the new garage and had called out to see me. My father wanted to know if I were happy, and had I enough money. I was somewhat nervous as we had just heard that the Inter Cert results were due out the next day. Dad assured me that it did not matter how I did in the Inter Cert as I was now in St. Pat's, a boarding school with supervised study, and would do well in future. Later I remember at evening prayer, asking God that I would get four honours in the exam as that was the minimum requirement for getting assigned to the top class.

The next day, Tuesday 12 September, was a beautiful sunny day. The three of us from Ballinamore spent the morning at the pay phone right beside the main front door, trying to get through to Ballinamore school to get our results. Unknown to us they had left the phone off the hook until they had told their own pupils the results. The anxiety was increased as our new classmates in St. Pat's emerged having gotten their results, George Mc Keon (Drogheda) getting six honours, Noel Barrett (Cavan town) receiving five honours, Tom Fitzpatrick (Ballyhaise) and Cathal Maguire (Bawnboy) getting honours in all seven subjects. And still we waited. Making a phone call was an event in those days. We had to ring the handle on the phone and wait for the telephonist in Cavan exchange to answer us. We then 'booked' the call. We listened while she tried to get through to the Ballinamore exchange who then tried to get through to the school. We must have attempted to phone seven or eight times. In fact we were startled when we did actually manage to make contact. Gerry Brady, our former Commerce teacher answered and informed me I had passed with 'flying colours'. I had got a B in honours English, D in honours Irish and D in honours Maths. (There was only honours and pass in these three subjects nationwide, all the remaining subjects were at honours level only). I got a D in Woodwork, C in Latin, D in Science, C in Commerce, B in History and C in Geography (these two latter subjects were regarded as just one at that time). I had gotten the magical four honours and in the subjects I liked. The other two lads got their results and we all double checked with our former teacher that we had the grades correct. Even at the time, it crossed my mind that he was very gracious considering that quite a number of lads from the town of Ballinamore had in effect turned their backs on the local school to go to St. Pat's. There was an air of celebration as we Fourth Years swanned around, the centre of attention, while some of last year's veterans, the Leaving Certs, informed us that the Inter Cert was child's play compared to the Leaving.

Second level education, in terms of numbers attending, range of subjects taught, organisation of class groupings, level at which state exams were set and especially grades awarded, was very different in the early seventies, than that which exists today. In the early 1960s, the majority of pupils finished their education after national school or only spent a year or two at a second level school[8]. The introduction of free second level education in 1967, saw the numbers attending second level schools in Ireland increase dramatically[9]. However participation rates were still much lower than they are today. It was only in 1972 that the Government raised the school leaving age from fourteen to fifteen. Prior to this a small number of pupils who were fourteen leaving national school, did not continue to second level at all. I remember one lad from my school in Ballinamore going straight from 6th class to work. A number of pupils who attended Vocational Schools finished their education having done the Group Cert state exam after two years. Some continued on to do the Inter Cert. The secondary schools, like St. Pat's, tended to attract the more academic pupils, the majority doing at least the Inter Cert and most of these continuing to complete the Leaving Cert. However the attrition rate was still high, compared to today. Of the 102 pupils who entered St. Pat's in 1969 as First Years, 28 had left by the end of Second Year[10]. Some may have transferred to local schools, but some just dropped out of education. Just over 70% of those who entered in 1969 completed the Inter Cert in 1972. A further 15 did not return to start the Leaving Cert course. So by the start of Fourth Year only 55% of the original First Year lads were still in the College[11]. Of course new pupils had joined from other schools, including the three of us from Ballinamore. Kilnacrott Abbey outside Ballyjamesduff had closed as a boys secondary school and so a number of their pupils came to St. Pat's. The following lads came from Kilnacrott as Fourth Year boarders; Brendan and Leo Flood (Corlurgan), Philip Magee and Ray Slowey (Ballyjamesduff).

The Inter Cert course was very different from the Junior Cert that has been in existence since 1989. In general pupils studied fewer subjects, usually seven or eight. In St. Pat's all pupils did seven subjects. As already mentioned all subjects were at honours level, except Irish, English and Maths, which had honours and pass. A minimum of five passes was required to pass the Inter Cert. Not only was it compulsory to study Irish, but you had to pass it in order to pass your Inter Cert. In other words if you got six honours but failed Irish, you did not pass your Inter Cert. *The Anglo-Celt* newspaper of September 15 ran an article commenting on the different performance of boys and girls in this State exam nationally. More girls (54%) than boys (46%) did the exam. While there was a very high failure rate generally, fewer girls (23%) than boys (26%) did not pass. Religion was studied but was not an exam subject. There was no S.P.H.E. Neither was there any C.S.P.E., although civics was taught in most schools, one class per week, in First and maybe Second Year. History and Geography were taught as two separate subjects, you got two separate results in the Inter Cert, but they were only regarded as one subject. I got B in History and C in Geography, but my average mark for the two was C, so that counted as just one honour at C level. The curriculum in St. Pat's was typical of all diocesan schools, and fairly typical of most boys secondary schools, with few, if any practical subjects. Woodwork, Metalwork, Technical Drawing, Art and Music were not on the curriculum for the Inter Cert class of that year. Science was compulsory for all pupils.

Strict streaming was the norm in most schools. An entrance exam decided what base class you were assigned to in First Year, and if you performed extremely well or poorly you were moved up or down at the end of term. This was the exception however. St. Pat's had three class groupings per year. In Junior level, the top class did honours Irish, English and Maths. The second class did honours Irish and English, but pass Maths. The third class did pass Irish, English and Maths. All other subjects were at just one level, honours. Latin was compulsory for all pupils in the Inter Cert in St. Pats. Only nine got an honour in Latin, while two out of every three fellows failed it. The top two classes did French, while the third did Commerce.

In 1969 grades replaced the actual percentage awarded in subjects in State exams. The grades awarded in the 1970s were light years away from what we have become accustomed to in recent times. An analysis of the Inter Cert results for St. Pat's in 1972 will demonstrate this[12]. It is important to bear in mind that the college attracted the more academic pupils, including the best and brightest in the surrounding counties via the scholarship scheme, had boarders who studied over twenty seven hours per week all year, and a dedicated teaching staff.

Intermediate Certificate Results 1972
Number of pupils doing exam: 72

Subject	No. doing honours	No. getting an honour	No. awarded grades		
			A	B	C
Irish	45	9			9
English	43	22		2	20
Maths	19	16	2	5	9

Most pupils in the top two classes did honours Irish and English. Only a handful got honours in Irish and half got honours in English. Most of those in the top class did honours Maths, with the vast majority getting the honour.

Inter Cert results were talked of in terms of honours achieved, not grades awarded. All other subjects were common level, so a C or higher in any other exam counted as an honour. The maximum result was seven honours in St. Pat's as all pupils did just seven subjects.

Intermediate Certificate Results 1972 Number of honours achieved by pupils							
Honours	7	6	5	4	3	2	1
No. of pupils	2	4	8	5	11	15	5

The total number of As, in the entire Inter Cert, awarded in St. Pat's in 1972, was six. One really exceptional pupil achieved four of these. In the three subjects with a higher level paper, Irish, English and Maths, a total of only two As was achieved. A different world to today. Twelve pupils passed the exam without any honours. Another ten pupils did not pass the required five subjects, one actually having achieved two honours, but failed to pass the requisite five subjects. The results in St. Pat's were actually very good at the time.

In Ballinamore the highest result was six honours, one lad got five honours and another lad and myself got four honours. Only six of us had done honours Maths. You had to have a third language to get to University. Most boys schools did Latin, many girls schools did French. In Ireland in general, a significant indicator of shift in curriculum balance was the steady decline in classical studies, with Latin plummeting from its position of prominence[13]. In Ballinamore the top class of two classes studied Latin. When we started Third Year in Ballinamore, fifteen of the twenty eight pupils petitioned to give it up, and were allowed to do so. Consequently only thirteen did Latin in the Inter Cert and I think only one got an honour in it.

After dinner on that day of our results, we, the Fourth Years, were allowed 'out town' for the afternoon as a reward. I remember going out with a group of lads and we all went for burgers and chips in some takeaway, an obligatory event whenever we were out town. I left the fellows to call into the Farnham Hotel where my Mam and Dad were attending the wedding reception of Michael and Celine Leydon from Swanlinbar. I felt very proud of my results, but realised that they already knew how I had done, having phoned the school themselves. After I left them, I met a fellow student with whom I had become somewhat friendly in the past few days. I needed to buy a big folder to hold the A 4 pages for our History notes that the teacher, Fr. Dan Gallogly, had suggested. As we approached Whelan's shop, opposite the Surgical Hospital,

I remarked to my friend that the two old ladies in the shop would follow you like hawks as you looked around. I had spent many hours on Saturday mornings, after dental appointments, as a youngster killing time, visiting shops in Cavan, as I waited for my Dad to finish work. When we exited the shop with our folders, my friend who had a slight stammer, stated 'they didn't watch too closely, did they'? With a wry smile, from under his folder he produced a book, 'Virgin Soldiers' which he had obviously stolen. I was incredulous and in shock. All types of scenarios crossed my mind as we walked back to St. Pat's. I was only there one week and I thought what happens if the college becomes aware of this and I am implicated. I also thought how terrible Dad would feel if I were in anyway associated with theft, as he had instilled honesty and telling the truth in all of us. Furthermore it was Cavan town and rumours could fly that Willie Mc Niffe's son had stolen from a shop. Having expressed my disbelief to my friend, I had to maintain a pretence of being cool and not appear to be a wimp. The book had a very bright blue cover, with young male soldiers on it. As I regained my equilibrium, the testosterone teenager in me realised that 'virgin' could apply to male as well as female. I certainly was being educated. I realised what 'irony' meant when that same lad was put in charge of lost property the following year as a Leaving Cert student. He subsequently went to work in a bank, and in the 1990's he was found guilty of embezzling money and spent time in prison. What is puzzling is that he was a very decent nice fellow, more mature than many other lads. We came back down to earth when we returned to St. Pat's as we had to attend study that evening as normal, although we had no homework to do as we had not had class that day.

The next morning Fourth Year pupils were reassigned class, some being demoted, some promoted, depending on their Inter Cert results. There were 30 in the top class, 33 in the second and 16 in the third class. There were twenty three teachers in St. Pat's, with fourteen priests, one nun and eight laymen. The top or more academic classes were usually taught by the priests. I was moved up to the top class, called Class 1V. A number of pupils, including Eddie Mc Govern (Ballyconnell) and Owen Martin (Templeport), astutely worked out whom they considered to be the better teachers, and declined the offer to move up to the top class. They knew they would have two very good teachers for Science and Maths in the second stream. Fr. Fintan Mc Kiernan from Templeport taught Physics and Chemistry, one subject at that time, and Fr. Leo O'Reilly taught Maths. Fintan was of farming stock and loved the land. He transferred his straight talking and straight action of the farming world to the classroom with great effect. There

was no nonsense, rules were clearly set out or understood before the year began. His reputation preceded him, so no one dared cause trouble. Definitions had to be learned off by heart, loudly pronounced in triplicate by him as 'Dafinitions', 'Dafinitions' Dafinitions". He drove lads to success whether they wanted it or not. By sheer force of personality and hard work, he got lads to work, some possibly through fear, but there was more than a grudging respect for him and lads wanted to be in his class if they wished to do well. As a teacher Fr. Leo O'Reilly (later Bishop of Kilmore) was very different in personality. He had a fairly low voice that commanded respect, a presence that meant there was serious work in hand and was very methodical, logical, and explained the Maths perfectly. Two men, two subjects, two totally different approaches and one result, very good grades at the end.
Weekends were relaxed, if somewhat boring. The day-boys departed at 4.00 on Friday and we, the boarders, had the school to ourselves until Monday morning. Friday evening was the same as any weekday evening, except that we had an extra thirty minutes of recreation until 6.00. Saturday saw a lie in, we did not have Mass until the late hour of eight, followed by breakfast. We were then supposed to return to our bedrooms to sweep and tidy them, with a number of brushes being provided. There was a general bustle and loud chat as most fellows were in and out of their rooms talking and acting the eejit as the mood was light hearted due to it being the weekend. Study started at 10.00 until 11.00 and resumed at 11.30 until 1.00, followed by dinner. We were then free until study at 5.30, with afternoon tea on at 4.00 as usual. There was no formal structure for recreation. Fellows strolled around the grounds, walked around the 'half', a walk circling the Inter (intermediate) pitch or others walked the 'whole' (a walk circling both the Inter and the Junior pitch) which was much more arduous. As you strolled around the Inter pitch the question invariably arose, 'are we doing just the half or the whole'? Nobody did this walk on their own, except one fellow who earned the nickname, 'The Lone Ranger' for his efforts. Some played soccer or basketball on the hard courts running parallel to the ambulatory (long concrete shelter). Sometimes lads togged out for a game of Gaelic. Those on college teams, especially the Rannafast competition, had competitive games on Saturdays at this stage of the year. Others played push-penny. It was a game played by two people, each armed with a comb, on a windowsill. The objective was to propel the penny with your comb, past your opponent's defence (his comb) to score a goal. We played it with greasy, dandruff speckled combs on the broad window sills that abounded in the college. Others hung around classrooms, in the study hall or played table tennis in

the basements. Some played handball against the many walls around the college. Study resumed for everyone at 5.30 until 7.00, and from 7.45 until 9.45, followed by night prayer.
Sunday started with morning prayer at 8.30 followed by breakfast and Mass at 10.00. This Sunday Mass was accompanied by hymns, such as 'Mary of Graces', 'Soul of my Saviour', 'Be thou my vision', 'Now thank we all our God' and the Irish/Latin hymn 'Deus meus adiuva me'[14]. Charlie O Gorman (Cavan town) played the organ and the hymns were sung by most pupils. The Mass also involved a sermon. The priests said the weekday Mass and Sunday Mass for us on rotation. Some Masses were obviously longer than others, and Fr.Dan Gallogly's street 'cred'. with pupils received an enormous fillip, when he was noticed surreptitiously glancing at his watch as he said Sunday Mass. We were hugely impressed. There was no talking at weekday morning Mass as we were all half asleep. However the later Sunday Mass was different and very occasionally a murmur might be heard. The dean, Fr. Paddy Brady, was once known to have positioned himself on the gallery above, not visible in the centre but at the extreme right as we looked up, wedged between the organ and the wall. A number of Second Years, oblivious to his presence, who were not paying attention to Mass were noted and punishment followed. On one occasion, Fr. Seán Reilly, celebrant of the Mass was preaching. As he did so he calmly walked down the aisle, (there were no altar rails) still giving his sermon, and stopped at the end of one seat, beckoning a particular student to come to him. You could hear a pin drop in the Church as all eyes turned to see what was happening. Fr. Reilly gave him a slap across the face and told him not to be talking at Mass. There was a general snigger, natural teenage boys' reaction to a contemporary being caught out. However I think most of us felt it was unfair to publicly humiliate a pupil like that. We were free after Mass until study that took place from noon until one. Dinner followed and like Saturday we were free until 5.30. Lads from nearby who boarded were frequently collected by their parents at one, going home to enjoy good family Sunday dinners. I remember envying Paul and John Kelly as they returned in time for 5.30 study, loaded down with goodies of all sorts to last them for the coming week.
Sunday evenings were lonesome. If you were anyway homesick, I believed this was the time you would feel it most. To add to the sense of despondency, the evening tea was always a cold meal. On the first Sunday there I thought the lads were having me on when they said there would be Tayto crisps for tea. In fact we all made crisps sandwiches, a first for me. Other Sunday evenings produced a banana each, so we made banana sandwiches and other

Sundays produced a half-pound of Calvita cheese among eight of us, so we made cheese sandwiches. To be fair, the girls in the kitchen who worked from very early morning until 8 pm. most days, usually had Sunday evenings off, hence the cold tea. Going from this tea back to face evening study from 7.45 until 9.45 was somewhat dispiriting. However the authorities soon began showing a film in the assembly hall on a Saturday night and it was repeated on a Sunday night. We had the choice as to what evening we attended, which meant not having to do study from 8.00 until 10.00 on one of the nights. I chose Sunday as it was a treat and something to look forward. One film that made a big impression on me was 'Z', a political thriller presenting a thinly fictionalised account of the assassination of a democratic Greek politician in 1963. It was very potent as it captured the outrage about the military dictatorship that was ruling Greece at this time in 1972. On Sunday nights, we were in a magical world of drama, idealism, courage and escapism, and then... the film ended. Chairs screeched on the timber floor as we trudged out of the assembly hall. Reality struck as we exited the hall and were hit by the cold autumn night air.

One Sunday night as we emerged from the film, someone in our group shouted: 'Double Dan, Irish f***ing grammar in the morning.' The reference was to Fr. Dan Gallogly, who taught the honours Irish class in Fourth Year. There was method in his madness, hammer the grammar into us right at the start of the year and thereby avoid silly mistakes when doing essays, literature etc. in the rest of the Irish course. The bright blue, deceptively attractive, Irish grammar book, '*Nuachúrsa Gaeilge na mBráithre Críostaí*', had become the bible of Dan's pupils. A double-Irish class, devoted solely to grammar on a Monday morning was sobering to say the least. Corporal punishment was normal in Ireland at that time, mostly in boys schools. Senior pupils were rarely slapped in St. Pat's. In fact I saw less than a dozen senior pupils slapped in my two years there. However Dan did lift us up by our locks or sideburns when we did not know the answer, or clattered us on the head. This may seem terrible by today's political correct standards, but was mild enough at that time. In Ballinamore secondary school, one Thursday morning, a lay teacher gave twenty four of us First Years, four slaps with the cane for not knowing our homework. He had warned us the day before but we simply did not understand what was being taught. We bore no grudge, it was a different time, and that was the way things were done. We compared the marks left by the cane, and it was a source of pride the longer they remained on our hands, with one lad still showing faint marks the following Tuesday week.

In the middle of September two slightly peculiar incidents happened, late at night, both involving phantom girlfriends. After study, Liam Tuite, the second prefect, told me there was a phone call for me in the infirmary. I hurried over to hear a female voice, calling herself Sylvia and wishing to talk to me. In the background I could hear others singing, 'Sylvia's mother says Sylvia's too busy to come to the phone', lyrics from Dr. Hook's massive hit at the time, 'Sylvia's Mother'. I knew immediately it was a joke as I had mentioned to Dermot Prior, from Ballinamore, that a girl called Sylvia was the heart throb of a number of lads at home. He obviously got some of the day-boys to get a girl to impersonate her, with a backing group. I had no romantic entanglement whatever with the girl, but I was secretly chuffed that some might think I had a girlfriend. Dermot and I were in the one class although he was a bit older than me. He had been in St. Pat's since Second Year and was a great friend and support to me for my two years in the college.

I had been told that my letters might be opened by the president to ensure nothing untoward was contained therein. Unfortunately I had nothing to worry about on that score, as any letters were from family and there were no epistles from forlorn girlfriends pining for me. The letters were distributed each afternoon at 4.00 tea in the ref. by a prefect. However one night after 10.00 pm. the head prefect, Tom Flynn, gave me a letter which he said he was told to by the president. I thought to myself this was a bit naïve of Terry the president as it was obvious that he had checked it. He was innocent in the best sense of the word and just wanted to ensure I got the letter as soon as possible. I would not impute the deviousness to Terry of him purposely letting me know that he had checked my mail. I did not mind in the least and thereafter I knew of no other letter ever been checked. It was from my friend and first cousin, Raymond Mc Hugh, congratulating me on my Inter Cert results. I didn't write letters on a regular basis. We were allowed to use the phone when we wished. I phoned home on the 18 September to wish Mam and Dad a happy twenty first wedding anniversary[15]. Mam wrote letters now and again with a note always inserted from Dad. In early October, I had an unexpected visit one Sunday afternoon from Dad and my brothers, Micheál and Christopher who were delivering a garage car to Mel Doherty for panel beating[16]. I never felt cut off and did not expect my parents to visit me on a Sunday. If Dad were in Cavan any day he'd call out and if I needed to contact home I'd phone.

We had a Parent Teacher Meeting in early October. As pupils, we accompanied our parents as they went to each teacher in the assembly hall. It turned out to be a social occasion. Dad knew most of my teachers, having worked for many years in Cavan. As all of them were priests, they knew my mother was a brother of Fr. Micheál Kelly. Fr. Dan Gallogly was from Ballinamore and knew both my parents well. I was anxious to see what my physics and chemistry teacher would say as I knew I was struggling. However it transpired that Dad knew Fr. Carney well, having sold him cars in the past. They talked about everything but my 'progress'. At the end Fr. Carney stated that I was doing fine and always asked intelligent questions. I remember thinking that is not going to alter the Christmas exam result. Dad and Mam were very pleased with the feedback and I walked them out and up the steps to the car.

In mid-October a rumour swept through the college one morning that we had a new bishop of Kilmore, Rev. Francis Mc Kiernan. Those of us from Ballinamore felt particularly chuffed as not only was the new bishop a Ballinamore man (well, an Aughawillan man) but he had been president of St. Felim's, our former school. A few weeks later he came in to visit all the classes in St. Pat's. I was a bit anxious as I knew he was none too pleased that a number of us had left his Ballinamore school to attend St. Pat's. However I need not have worried as he recognised and acknowledged all of us ex-Felim's lads, and we felt six inches taller among our peers.

The first six weeks or so of my time in St. Pat's were characterised by an Indian summer. There was so little rainfall that we did not have showers during that time as the college relied on its own well. As teenage boys we were not too concerned, anyway we had sinks in each room and the First Year dormitory had a large adjacent room full of sinks. My memories of that first term is of lovely autumn dry evenings, sunshine and we lads playing soccer, walking around or hanging around during recreation. On my second Sunday there in September we were allowed out to Breffni Park to see the Senior Championship final between Crosserlough and St. Brigid's (Laragh-Stradone). While I was fanatical about Ballinamore football, I felt no great affinity with Cavan Club football, and so with about ten minutes to go Dermot Prior and I left. We wanted to be ahead of the other lads from the college who would be crowding into chippers and cafes. We went to the Bridge restaurant, and suitably stuffed, sauntered back. As we meandered up the front avenue we saw the soon-to- retire Bishop Austin Quinn, out strolling towards us. (His house was very close to the college and used the same avenue). I had only met this kindly man once in my life as he administered Confirmation to me. Dermot and I passed ourselves off, mumbling something about the weather as we were not in the habit of addressing bishops. However he enquired were we at the match and alas asked who won, to which we had to admit that we had exited early. We should have stayed as that match saw Crosserlough win their famous seventh senior title in a row, 3.8 to 2.6[17].

In 1972 my home club, Ballinamore (officially Seán O'Heslin's), contested five championship finals at different levels, in Leitrim, winning four of them[18]. I had been right half back on the Under 16 and Minor teams, the only two teams that didn't at least reach a final!. We usually trained three times a week that summer as there was little else to do. However I had never made it on to St. Felim's College team as I was not good enough. When training for St. Pat's Rannafast panel began, I togged out. I remember tackling Donal Donohoe (Laragh), only a Second Year at that stage, and he brushed me aside as I got in his way. I got a whack on the mouth (not deliberate) that left me unable to use my two front teeth for a day or two. Despite this I enjoyed the football training although it was not the same craic and camaraderie as playing with my club mates with whom I had grown up in Ballinamore. In any event I soon realised I was out of my depth. At this stage I had a roommate, Gerry Mc Govern (Dowra), who was in the same year. Gerry was a very good footballer but did not want to play. I remember Fr. Seán Brady (later Cardinal) begging him to participate which he duly did. I would have given anything to have been in his boots.

Rannafast was the Ulster Junior Colleges top division Championship, second only to Mc Rory, the Ulster Senior competition. The team got off to a good start at this early stage of the year despite being behind in the first match, 2.2 to no score, St. Pat's rallied and beat St. Mary's Belfast, 2.9 to 3.4[19]. Fr. Benny Maguire gave me a lift to the match, even though I had not made the panel. He was quietly pleased that I knew so much about the Hogan Cup All Ireland victory, and his training of the team. We easily beat our namesakes, St. Pat's Maghera at Irvinestown, 2.14 to 2.04[20]. We then beat old rivals, Abbey C.B.S. Newry, in a peculiar game. At the interval St. Pat's were leading by fourteen points, and increased this to eighteen in the second half. Abbey made a spectacular recovery and the game ended, 5.6 to 4.9, a four point victory for St. Pat's[21]. The winning margin didn't matter, we were now in the Rannafast final for the first time in a decade[22]. This was played on Saturday 28 October against St. Mary's Belfast. Pupils were allowed attend the game at Knockbridge, Dundalk. As we would be absent for dinner, we had a great feed of bacon and sausages at about 11.00. Shortly afterwards many buses pulled up on the basketball courts directly behind the Old Wing. I was again somewhat taken aback, that boarding the bus was on a seniority basis, not a first come, first served. However it did remove pushing and shoving. Our lads looked set for success in the early stages of the game, but were unable to last the pace and the Belfast boys came out with a late rally to force a draw[23]. The replay was fixed for the same venue ten days later, interrupted by our impending Halloween break. I assume the team had to train over the break. As the game was on a Wednesday, I don't recall any supporters going. In any event, the team didn't need us, as they outclassed their opponents in every phase of the game. This lead to frustration among some St. Mary's players, resulting in the Belfast team finishing with only eleven men instead of thirteen. The final score was amazing considering it was a replay, St. Pat's 5.12, St. Mary's 0.3[24]. This was only the second time that our college had won the Rannafast competition, the previous time being in 1945. The team on the day of the final was as follows: Myles Mc Entee, Gerry Mc Govern, Lee O' Connell, Cathal Maguire, Thomas Fitzpatrick, Martin Brady, Matthias Rudden, Hubert Conaty, Seán Kilkenny, Pat Bradley, Thomas Conaty, Jimmy Fox and Owen Martin. The panel included many who had played pivotal roles earlier in the campaign: Padraig Martin, Percy Seagrave, Brian Rahill, Bernard Donohoe, Eugene O'Reilly, Robbie. Mc Dermott and Paul Mc Evoy[25].

The footballers used to get a special tea on occasions when they missed ordinary meal times due to training or matches. We envied them their sausages, beans and chips. On one occasion when the lads were doing exceptionally well in the Rannafast competition, I had the temerity, in class on front of Fr. Ray Brady, to state that 'at least they got good food'. Fr. Ray asked me what I had said and a kick from Dermot Prior alerted me to the unwritten convention that you did not criticise the food in public statements. The food was not appetising in St. Pat's, but it must be seen in the context of the time. St. Pat's, like most diocesan schools, had its own farm that provided much of the food for the college. It had two full-time men, brothers Tommy and Paddy Walshe, running the farm. Breakfast was fine, with cornflakes and as much bread as you wanted. At this time in Ireland, many homes did not have cereal for breakfast. Occasionally we got porridge, which most lads loved, but I had never liked porridge, my loss. I remember one morning at breakfast, a few pink wafer thin biscuits, being pushed out to us, through a minute crevice in the closed hatch that divided our ref, from the priests' ref. No other biscuits would have fitted. They were being given to us, by 'John the Bawn'. John Brady was college steward from 1927. A lovely man he always wore a white coat like a doctor's. We always assumed that was the reason why he was called 'John the Bawn'. We got a three course dinner every day of the week, unheard of in practically all of our homes at that time. The soup was fine. The vegetables were ok. The 1972 potato crop must have been very poor, as my memories of much of that year is of extremely soggy potatoes that disintegrated into nothing when peeled. A good idea was to put them in the soup which most of us did. The meat tended to be greasy and quite fatty. We got two sausages each on Tuesdays, laid out on a flat aluminium type tray, with one tray for each table. Tuesday was the dean's day off and another priest, Fr. Peter Casey, who was sub-dean supervised the refectory. One Tuesday, the fellow at our table whose turn it was to bring the food to the eight of us, arrived with not one, but two trays of sausages, one neatly concealed under the other. I was taken aback as this pupil had appeared to be a 'goody goody' and was always licking up to the priests. However I swallowed my disgust at his hypocrisy, along with my two extra sausages. We also got dessert every day. It was usually a milk type pudding, semolina or tapioca. During a retreat, some priest mentioned 'wet dreams'. At lunch that day one pupil, (who shall remain nameless) put his spoon into his dessert and then getting our attention by shouting 'wet', let the white fluid-like dessert roll off his spoon into the bowl. None of us who witnessed this, ate any more of the dessert that day.

I do remember leaving the ref. hungry after dinner a number of times, but that was my choice. I did not eat all put in front of me, as I had money from home and from my summer job to visit the school sweet shop. I frequently raced up the stairs, situated as it was opposite the Second Year dormitory, and fought my way through to the hatch. Fran Treanor (Bailieborough), always served me quite quickly, as his brother Damien and my brother Micheál had been friends in Pat's a few years before[26]. I horsed into bars of Tiffin chocolate and Smarties, frequently filling a void that I should have filled in the ref. The feeling was lovely however and I felt buoyed up for the afternoon classes. There was as much bread as you wanted at afternoon and evening tea. The absence of my favourite 'toast', the tea complete with milk and sugar, as well as the Sunday evening cold meal, meant that I didn't miss the food when I left the College. While there was always enough to eat, I shudder to think what the food might have been like had our fees not been subsidised by the salaries of the priests.

Boys love competing. Some pupils, for diversion, wanted a competition to see who could eat the most slices of pan bread at afternoon tea. Two lads, Jim Sheridan (Carlow) and Declan Mc Kiernan (Corlismore) agreed to compete, on the shrewd condition that someone would provide jam and have the slices ready as well as acting as referee. The real winner ate twenty three slices, while the runner up ate a mere 19. However the referees were friendly with the runner up, and purposely miscounted, so that he was declared the winner. I also remember a Second Year pupil, Dermot O'Flaherty, (Castlerahan) eating eleven burgers for a bet. He was a good footballer and on the Corn na nÓg winning panel later that year. While feeding up to two hundred teenage boys was a mammoth undertaking, most of us saw eating as a necessity to get out of the way before returning to more important matters like football or recreation of some type.

The dean, Fr. Paddy Brady had responsibility for discipline of all boarders. It was a thankless job, as his main point of contact was frequently with pupils who had done something wrong, usually Second Years. Human nature has not changed and teenage boys have not changed that much. Today the problem age for ill-discipline in teenage boys is Second Year and maybe up to Christmas in Third Years and it was no different in 1972[27]. The problem was exacerbated then however, as it was a boarding school and boys were under school rules, twenty four hours a day, seven days a week and for uninterrupted stretches of eight weeks. Fr. Brady was on duty from seven in the morning to 11.00 at night, (and afterwards if there were any disturbances) seven days a week, except when he left the college on a Tuesday at 11.00 and was not on duty until Wednesday morning. During our class periods and study times he had respite from his work as dean. He was on duty in St. Pat's at all meal times, (morning, dinner, afternoon and evening tea) recreation, (after breakfast, lunch time, 4.00-5.30, 7.15-7.45 and 9.30-11.00 pm.), morning Mass, night prayer, bed time, almost all day Saturday and all day Sunday. Like most boarding schools, the system was strict to allow one dean supervise and maintain order among two hundred or so teenage lads. Pastoral care as we understand it today was not a feature of that system. Fr. Brady was a strict disciplinarian and enforced the system quite rigidly. I regarded him as tough but fair and never had any problems. Corporal punishment was a feature of school life and frequently a handful of pupils, stood outside the dean's door after 10.00 pm. waiting for his return from checking the corridors, to be slapped with the cane for misbehaviour around bedtime. It was usually the same handful of fellows, invariably Second Years, with a few third Years. Life in St. Pat's must not have been too pleasant for these fellows, although some, (outwardly at least) seemed not to be put out too much. I remember a group of them on one such night, discussing the breaking news, that Gordon Banks, the brilliant Stoke and English goalkeeper, had been involved in a very serious car crash. Their misdemeanours were frequently just high jinks. Second Years from the twelve bed small dorm. racing up the back stairs to attack the First Year dorm. Attack meant to wreck their beds by pulling off the clothes. There was a number of famous pillow fights on that stairs between the few valiant Second Years trying to fight their way up and a posse of First Years defending their own homestead. Lines and punishment essays were beginning to replace slapping in some instances. Sometimes Leaving Cert pupils, to while away an hour on a Saturday afternoon, would call out an essay in very convoluted language to a Second/Third year who had got such a punishment assignment.

Although things were beginning to change, the rights of young people were not part of Ireland in the early 1970's. Corporal punishment was administered in many homes and in practically all boys schools. Allocation of resources frequently put intolerable and unreasonable workloads on the few who were given the task of keeping order and tight control in schools. The system inherited for running boarding schools was regimented, demanded conformity, and punished offenders. For most of us this posed no problem. We were discreet if we wanted, occasionally to circumvent the rules for our own benefit. For a small number of lads however, especially those 14/15 year olds who were exuberant and not too discreet, life was tough and unforgiving. For most of us life was not unduly harsh, it was fine, if we had any complaints it was of boredom.

In the Preface to *The College Boys*, Ray Dunne, brilliantly captures the daily routine of boarding at St. Pat's:

> The camaraderie of a cloistered community, the clang of the regulating bells, the reluctant rising for morning Mass as well as the monotonous grind of a stuffy study hall and of course the excitement around college musicals and football games… the hungry dash from chapel and study hall to refectory, of raucous rooks squawking from treetops and of days spent in meditative silence on prayerful retreats. Reminiscences of classes six (five) days a week and of the clack of flopping study hall desk lids, of boring strolls and of the joy of the rare visit or the long awaited news or letter from home… 100 day terms, push penny games on window sills, potatoes picked, football socks and togs dries stiff on radiators, the snatched smoke or game of cards and the relief of a dayboy's sandwich…[28].

The official routine and the boredom were sometimes disrupted by high spirits, pranks, dysfunctional phones and 'brave acts' as I was soon to find out.

The Ultimate: All Ireland Hogan Cup Winners, 1972

Back (L-R) Fr. Patrick Mallon, Brendan Crowe, Fergus Costello, Charlie O' Donoghue, Adge King, Pat Brady, Oliver Brady, Fr. Benny Maguire, Hugh Reynolds, Michael English, Brendan Mc Dermott, Seán Leddy, Owen Martin, Micheál Mc Keown, Mr. Patsy Lee and Fr. John Murphy.
Seated (L-R) Aidan Elliott, Cathal Maguire, John Sweeney, Kieran O' Keeffe, Eamonn Gillic, Fr. Terence Mc Manus (college president), Niall Brennan, Paddy Mc Gill, Brian Brady, Gerry Smith and Gerry Mc Intyre.

Leaving Cert Class 1972-73

Back standing (L-R) D. Donoghue, ----- -----, L. Callan, B. Tully, W. Fleming, N. Mc Evoy, G.O' Brien, A. Kenny, G. Cornyn, J. Gallagher, M. Rudden, L. Bouchier, C. Brady, M. Cahill, R.O' Connor and H. Cusack.

Middle standing (L-R) ----- -----, ----- -----, P. Monaghan, D. Murray, T. Flynn, P. Sexton, J. Murphy, ----- Cusack, D. Smith, J. Boyd, P. Gilroy, H. Smith, G. Murray, J. Mc Cann, O. Mc Cabe, C. Sharpley, G. Dunne, H. Conaty, B. Tully, F. Costello, E. Molocco, E. Gavin,

Sitting (L-R) J. Reilly, J. Smith, C.O' Gorman, E.O' Gorman, A. Mc Goldrick, F. Fitzpatrick, J. Murphy, M. Kelly, J. J. Rudden, F. Treanor, M. Smith, M. Smith and L. Tuite.

Front row (L-R) ----- -----, P. Callaghan, A. Elliott, L. Blessing, H. Sheridan, F. Mc Nally, G. Sheridan, M. Brady, B. Wray, O. Denning, J.O'Dowd and J. Smith.

John Brady, college steward from 1927

***Playing:* Rannafast Champions 1972-73**

Back (L-R) Fr. Mallon, Pat Bradley, Bernard Donohoe, Tom Conaty, Gerry Mc Govern, Paddy Sexton, Myles Mc Entee, Jimmie Fox, Paul Mc Evoy, Pauric Martin, Owen Martin and Fr. Seán Brady.

Front (L-R) Mr. Patsy Lee, Brian Rahill, Percy Seagrave, Donal Donohoe, Tom Fitzpatrick, Matt Rudden, Cathal Maguire, Hubert Conaty, Martin Brady and Seán Kilkenny.

Chapter 3

Out of Routine

Halloween - Christmas 1972

As a First Year boarder in 1962, my first cousin Frankie Kelly remembers asking the then dean, Fr. Seán O'Reilly, for special permission to go home for Halloween, 'but he dismissed me abruptly'[1]. Until the late sixties, pupils, including twelve year old Frankie, away from home for the first time, remained in the college for over one hundred days before getting holidays. Fortunately this had changed by the time I was a boarder.

There was a palpable air of expectation in the days leading up to our Halloween break. The decibel level increased, pupils appeared to tread with a lighter foot and everyone seemed to be in good humour. The night before we got home, evening study saw a restless, fidgety bunch of lads, champing at the bit, mad to be set free. The bell signalling the end of study was greeted with a loud cheer, and the desk lids were banged down with a finality that reverberated well beyond the confines of the stuffy study hall. Unless you have been in boarding school, it is difficult to understand the feelings that we experienced. As a day pupil, holidays just mean a few days off from class. For boarders it was incomparably more. It was twofold, being free from class, but mainly it was the idea of getting home, rest, good food, no bell, no evening study, no strict routine, seeing former school friends and family (some of whom we had not seen in eight weeks). It was the first time for me to really understand freedom. There is no gain without pain, there is no sense of freedom unless you have been deprived of it. It is not that St. Pat's was a prison, I actually enjoyed it, but like all boarding schools at that time, by its nature it was much more restrictive than living at home. The night before we were due home dusty cases were dragged out from under beds. As teenage boys we were indiscriminate when it came to packing clean and dirty clothes and frequently threw them all in the one bundle into the case. Despairing mothers usually located the case, sometimes by aroma a few days after we arrived home. It was not easy to sleep the night before, anticipating all we were going to do in the next few days.

On Tuesday the last day of October, we had a half day of class, finishing at 1.00. As the day-boys headed home, we raced up to our rooms and dormitories to collect our cases, lug them down the stairs, and out to the fleet of waiting cars. Most lads had arranged for a few to travel home together. My brother Micheál collected Cathal Sharpley, Dermot Prior and myself.

Cathal was a Leaving Cert who like me had come to St. Pat's to do the final two years. A very solid, sensible fellow, the authorities thought butter would not melt in his mouth. We knew differently. He wore glasses. One lens was actually a bit loose. On one occasion when he hadn't his homework completed, he loosened this lens, so when the teacher clouted him on the back of the head, it fell out. The apparently split second reaction of Cathal, catching the falling lens in his hands, won admiration from all. Furthermore this teacher apologised to him, and thereafter Cathal's head was a no-go area. Game, set and match to Cathal, and the teacher did not even know he had been outwitted. We dropped Cathal off at his farmyard in Aughayoule outside Ballinamore.

Arriving to my own house was surreal. I didn't know the term 'spatial relations' at the time, but that probably is what was so different. Everything at home seemed so tiny, I was like Gulliver in Lilliput. The absence of noise was deafening. Floor covering jumped up at me, as if I had never seen it before. In some ways it reminded of when I was a child and sick. After a few days of pyjamas and bed, I would be allowed up wearing ordinary clothes and moving around. It felt great, feeling taller, like you were new or something. I am not sure whether we had actually yet studied the poetry of Patrick Kavanagh that was on our Leaving Cert course. However his line:

And the newness that was in every stale thing

perfectly captures my state of mind[2]. I was a minor celebrity at home, as everyone was delighted to see me. Almost immediately I headed down to Logan's shop to 'check in' with my work mates. I was greeted like a long lost friend. I soon realised that the first question everyone asked was not how you like it, but 'When are you going back?', and me only home thirty minutes. My memories of that first break from boarding school are all very happy ones. It exceeded my expectations. Being able to eat what you liked, (especially my lovely toast) when you liked, and as much as you liked, made me so appreciative that I started saying grace before and after meals at home. At dinner time at first I just took one potato, as was customary in St. Pat's until everyone had their first choice. My mother initially thought that I had lost my appetite. I was somewhat taken aback that the protocol from boarding school was so strong, in such a short space of time, that I was unconsciously following it. My mother also had to try to get me to slow down while eating, another college habit. To stay glued to the T.V. late at night was another treat. going to bed late and knowing I could sleep as long as I wanted to, was fantastic. The bed was so comfortable.

'Trick of the loops', (amusements) as my mother called them, had arrived in the vacant lot very near my house for the Halloween break. They had bumping cars which I adored. My cousin Raymond met me that Wednesday evening and we spent hours, and hours racing in those cars. Between us we spent a little over four pounds in total that night, almost one full week's pay from Logans. At that time there was no sense of health and safety so you could go in any direction you wished, attack anyone at whatever angle you decided would do most damage. We got very proficient, as was to be expected after three hours, never leaving the arena. We soon worked out the two fastest cars. The key was to get a good clear run, away from everyone else, and then pounce with maximum effect. I felt exhilarated as we each tried to inflict maximum damage on the other. Occasionally our personal vendetta was put aside, as some other young lad, a relative novice, had the audacity to hit one of us a right wallop. We then made sure to get a really long run at him, hitting his car from behind for ultimate shock effect, or better still hit him at the side towards the back, thus spinning his car around numerous times. We showed no mercy and I can honestly say I remember that night as one of the most enjoyable of my teenage years. Interestingly, recently talking to Raymond about this evening, he has no memory of it. Obviously being out for a few days from St. Pat's added to my sense of fun and enjoyment and marked it indelibly on my consciousness.

School-breaks were not standardised, so that my sister Valerie, who was off from the Louis School in Bundoran before I was, had to return earlier. Micheál and I drove her back to Bundoran for class, early on the Thursday morning. When we returned Dad and Micheál had to go to Dublin for garage business and I went for the spin. Micheál drove. We were in a large Opel Estate car, and the engine started to smoke and then went on fire. It quickly died out, the car was fine and we were able to continue. It did cross my mind that this was very tough on Dad as he had been used to a brand new, middle to upper range car, as part of his job for the previous few years. On the following Sunday, the three of us went to see Ballinamore seniors beat Gortletteragh in the League. Ballinamore were doing so well in football at this time, that I more or less took it for granted that we should win.

On that Sunday evening, having been off from the previous Tuesday, I returned to the college. I had stocked up with a whole lot of perishables, bananas (green from Logans, as I wanted them to last), the least ripe tomatoes I could lay my hands on, Y.R. sauce and strawberry jam, as well as miscellaneous other items that would, I believed, transform my diet. I also was now the proud possessor of a new outfit, a corduroy-type bright jacket, with a felt collar, pockets and collar of a different hue, with a zip up the front. I also had a new shirt. I felt a new man. I was not upset returning, as I felt buoyed up with the comfort food. The next term was shorter followed by the Christmas holidays.

The return was quite different from the shouting and exuberance of the return after summer. Fellows had seen each other only a few days earlier, and what really struck me was the darkness and dampness. Summer time had given way to winter time, in every sense. Michael Keville was the general handyman and he looked after the boiler. With the heating off for a few days there was an air of dankness along the corridors. The college wasn't cold but it had a dark, wintry feel to it. The darkness seemed to have increased the pungency of the smell from the toilets. The brilliant Indian summer was just a faint memory. My education continued, when I realised that keeping bananas and tomatoes in a dark, warm iron type locker was not the same as refrigeration. After a few weeks or so of feasting myself on these, the tomatoes, just like the blackberries in Heaney's poem, developed:

A rat like fungus…the fruit fermented, the sweet flesh would turn sour[3].

I could have replenished my stock with supplies from out town, by getting one of the day- boys to buy some for me, but I don't know why I never did.

While daily routine went on as usual, there were a number of incidents that helped break the monotony. A 'Brave Act' was anything that required daring or neck. A junior pupil going up to a senior and calling him by his nickname would qualify as a brave act. The president, Fr. Terry Mc Manus had recently introduced formal P.E. It took place after school and was only for boarders. While lots of us thought Terry was very old fashioned, he actually was quite progressive with this initiative, especially when the P.E. teacher, was Frances O' Sullivan, a young woman in a very male preserve. If we thought we would have things our way, we were mistaken. We were not too impressed with having to forgo recreation time one afternoon a week to do P.E. in the assembly hall. Frances was the perfect choice for a boys school. She brooked no opposition and took no hostages. As a result the classes were busy, tiring and very effective. I was very friendly with Joey Mc Govern from Ballyconnell, and knew his brother Eddie quite well. Both were in Fourth Year. One afternoon, Eddie and I found ourselves talking in the basement of the New Wing. The mats for P.E. were stored there and Eddie had the brilliant idea that we would hide them and thus at best there would be no P.E. and at worst we would have to go outside to do our exercises. I was impressed with the plan. We carefully folded them up and managed to push them into pallets that were stacked nearby. They were invisible. Were we proud of ourselves and luckily told nobody of our 'Brave Act'. We could not wait for P.E. the next Thursday. Upon finding out that the mats were missing, unfazed, Miss

O' Sullivan, calmly announced we would have to lie on the hard floor for the hour and just do our routines as normal. Thank God we had told nobody. Talk about a plan backfiring. Eddie and I now had the problem of sneaking back to the basements and returning the mats to their normal place of rest, without been seen by anyone, especially fellow pupils. Somewhat dispirited we managed this, but it was not to be the last of our joint brave acts.
We were allowed watch Top of the Pops on a Thursday night at 7.30, in the assembly hall. The British T.V. dance troupe, Pans People, were a regular feature on the show. Their gyrations accompanying the songs, caused testosterone levels to rocket. It was great escapism, and enjoyment. Some of the most popular songs at the time were[4]:

1. Lieutenant Pigeon - "Mouldy Old Dough"
2. Don McLean - "American Pie"
3. The Move - "California Man"
4. The New Seekers - "I'd Like To Teach The World To Sing", "Beg, Steal Or Borrow", "Circles", "Come Softly to Me"
5. Donny Osmond - "Puppy Love"
6. The Osmonds - "Crazy Horses"
7. Gilbert O'Sullivan - "Clair"
8. Cliff Richard - "Jesus", "Living In Harmony", "A Brand New Song"
9. Clodagh Rodgers - "You Are My Music"
10. Roxy Music - "Virginia Plain"
11. Slade - "Look Wot You Dun", "Take Me Bak 'Ome", "Mama Weer All Crazee Now", "Gudbuy T' Jane"
12. Strawbs - "Lay Down"
13. T.Rex - "Metal Guru", "Solid Gold Easy Action"
14. Mary Wells - "My Guy"

The show was in black and white on a small family type TV set. There was seating for about thirty pupils, the rest stood and watched. The Leaving Certs religiously went down earlier, during afternoon recreation, and chalked individual chairs with their names, in prominent positions in front of the T.V. Eddie and I, (again Eddie's brainchild), moved the actual chairs around, leaving the names intact. After tea all those wishing to watch Jimmy Saville (innocent times for us) and this week's top hits, raced down and the Leaving Certs ran to their pre-booked seats. For the first few minutes the rest of us stood and watched, not Top of the Pops, but bedlam as the Leaving Certs argued, (in the dark as lights were off to appreciate TV), as to who should be sitting where. Eddie and I silently withdrew.

We could phone anyone we wished during recreation time. The public pay phone was to the right of the main front door as you exited, in full view of all staff entering and exiting. When the operator finally got you through to the number you requested, she told you to insert the money and press Button A, which was followed by a noise that told her the money was paid. However someone realised that if you pressed Button A very strongly, the money actually returned, into a little slot for rejected coins. The giveaway however was the noise of the dropping coins and so the operator requested you to reinsert the money. Some genius told a few of us that if you put tissue paper in the reject slot, it muffled the noise of the returned coins and the operator knew nothing and we would get free calls. We kept this business secret to a few of us and did a 'feasibility study' for the next week or two. In fact we made phone calls which we really had no interest in making, except that we knew they were free. I rang my sister in school in Bundoran. At that time everyone was charged from the time the call went through. So I would be charged from the time I got through to the school, even though someone would have to go and locate Valerie. So I went upmarket and booked 'a personal call', whereby you paid an extra 5p but were then only charged for the time you were actually talking to your nominated person. It gave us a great sense of conspiracy, of getting something for nothing and we convinced ourselves that we were really doing nothing wrong as it was costing nobody anything. We were wrong. The president, Terry, announced one evening that there was something wrong with the phone and that the bill presented to the college was larger than the money in the coin box. The phone was repaired and we realised that there was no such thing as a free phone call.

The seventh son of a seventh son is reputed to have healing powers, sometimes in his hands. While we were all aware of this, we did not know that one of our classmates, was such a son until his photo appeared in the local Celt newspaper, with his hands looming much larger than life. As a result he was greeted by an outstretched palm almost into his face for a number of days. Luckily for him he was more mature than those around him and took it in his stride.

There was one pupil who was quiet, never misbehaved and always tidied his room perfectly. Every morning he got up at the first bell and had his bed made with his pyjamas folded neatly across the bottom rail of the bed, before he went down to Mass. We were in a phase of giving and receiving French beds. (The bottom sheet is doubled-back, so that you meet a cul-de-sac with your feet, half way down. From the outside the bed looks perfect, but you can't get your feet to the bottom of it). A number of us decided to give him a French bed and then that night we all piled into a friend's room after ten and waited. There were no curtains on any pupils' windows so we could see his room clearly from our vantage point in the Old Wing. Most pupils did not put off their light until it was centrally turned off around 10.30. However we had his roommate tipped off, and he had purposely got into bed before lights off. Out unwitting victim got ready for bed and put off his light. We waited, and counted. Next second the light went on and we could see him pulling back the bedclothes and having to make his bed anew. We burst our sides laughing and saw nothing wrong with our prank.

Football was going very well. Fresh from winning the Rannafast final on Wednesday, 8 November, five or six of that team were again on duty three days later, in the first round of the Mc Rory (Ulster Colleges Senior Championship) against St. Michael's Enniskillen in Clones. We were not only reigning Ulster, but also All-Ireland champions. Despite the fact that we had only two of last year's All-Ireland team, Aidan Elliott and Brian Brady, we were confidently expected to beat St. Michael's, and at least reach the quarter finals. However a late rally saw St. Michael's win, 2.9 to 1.8[5]. The following Saturday we lined out against Omagh C.B.S. at Irvinestown, a win being essential if we were to retain any chance of reaching the quarter finals. However, Omagh, bolstered by six All-Ireland minor finalists in their ranks, beat us 1.10 to 1.8, thus ending our Mc Rory Cup hopes for that year. The team included: Aidan Elliott, John Costello, Martin Brady, Liam Bouchier, Matt Cahill, Paddy Sexton, Peter Callaghan, Matthias Rudden, Cathal Maguire, Owen Martin, Brian Brady, Ciaran Brady, Seán Kilkenny, and Hubert Conaty[6].

For a number of weeks after Halloween on Friday evenings from five thirty to seven, (instead of study) Fourth Year boarders attended First Aid classes, given by Ms. Maloney. We then undertook an exam in Junior Red Cross. We all passed with Pat Bradley (Maghera) getting the maximum one hundred and sixty marks. There was a tradition that Fourth Years, on a Sunday morning went out to visit patients in St. Felim's, the Old People's Home, directly opposite the college main gates. We all went out the first Sunday wondering what it would be like. My mother had trained as a nurse in England and had worked for a summer or two in St. Felim's in the late sixties. Nothing however prepared me, and indeed many of the lads I talked to, for what met us. The building was Dickensian and impersonal, with very large wards and single-iron type beds, reminiscent of boarding schools of the nineteenth century portrayed on television. The smell was all pervasive. The air not only reeked of stale urine, but had an overpowering sickly smell, as windows were closed to keep the wards warm. The obvious liberal use of disinfectant, vied with the smells of nature. The nurse and other staff could not have been nicer and more cheerful to us, and more importantly to the patients. The old wooden floors were spotless as was the hospital in general. Considering that there was only one hand basin in most thirty bed wards, for everyone's use, adds to the incredible work done by the staff. Sister Mercy was the Matron and treated us like family members. I remember feeling very awkward trying to approach some beds and initiate a conversation. What soon became obvious was that some patients were there much of their lives, or it seemed that way to us. Some were a little strange, others appeared just to have no home to go to. One little bald man, sat up in bed continually rocking forward and backward all day long, saying nothing to anybody. It was a chastening experience. My friend Leo Plunkett admitted to me that he had difficulty eating Sunday dinner back in the college when we returned. Likewise I felt no appetite for lunch.

In retrospect it was a great initiative from the authorities. It made us aware of old age, of loneliness, or disability, of people much less lucky that we were. However it posed a problem for me. I knew visiting was the right thing to do, but it meant missing the one hour of study from 12.00 until 1.00. So I used to study on my own from 10.45 - 11.45 and then make my way out to St. Felim's. The dean met me one Sunday at 11.50 on the front avenue, and berated me for only heading to the hospital now, in order to avoid study, instead of leaving at 11.00 as was expected. Uncharacteristically I did not explain my real reason for being late. Dermot Prior and I met one patient, an English man who was very articulate and learned. I remember he explained that the ancient Greek language had at least four words for different types of love. The only one that stuck in my mind at the time was 'eros', the term for sexual love. After a few visits he told us he was hoping to convert to Catholicism from Anglicanism and would we tell some priest in the college of his hopes. We returned and approached Terry the president, partly I suspect as we thought he being the more conservative of the priests and being president, it might make a bigger impression on him and reflect well on us. He thanked us and about three months later, quietly took Dermot and me aside and explained that he had helped prepare the man for Baptism and just that day had returned from St. Felim's and the man had been received into the Catholic Church. I thought it was considerate of Terry to remember to let us know what happened.

We got an unexpected break in early December. The episcopal consecration of the new bishop, Francis Mc Kiernan, was scheduled for 10 December in Cavan Cathedral and St. Pat's was chosen as the venue for the meal afterwards. The college received somewhat of a spring cleaning, not easy with almost two hundred lads living permanently there and another two hundred-plus in and out every day. One morning, leaving the college Chapel after Mass, someone remarked on a continuous white line, not on the road, but on the recently painted wall of the red-tiled corridor. It was done in white chalk, ran the entire length of the red-tiled corridor and continued, unabated on to the wall of the green-tiled corridor. The dean, Fr. Brady, caught the culprit, a Second Year who frequently had come to his attention. To be fair to the dean, having realised that it was an absent minded act, not a deliberate one, he merely got him to get a bucket and cloth and clean it all off. We got an extended weekend off to facilitate the bishop's reception. It was great as it was unexpected. Mam, Dad, Micheál and I went to Bundoran to my sister Valerie's Christmas concert on the Friday night. Micheál drove, as my Dad was not feeling too well. On Saturday the doctor came to see Dad and prescribed some different tablets. My brother Micheál drove a number of us back to St. Pat's on Monday night 11 December[7]. Christmas dominated the remaining eight or nine days of school: Christmas exams, Christmas concert, Christmas dinner, and then the Christmas holidays.

There was unexpected drama one morning, when news spread like wildfire that two pupils, day-boys from Cavan town, whom we knew well, had been involved in quite a serious car crash the night before. When one of our teachers was checking absences and the name of one of the lads came up, another pupil interjected, 'absent due to circumstances beyond his control', to which the teacher replied in no uncertain terms, 'It was entirely within his control', and gave us a lecture on the folly of the lads taking a father's car, crashing it and endangering their own lives and others. Inexperience had led to hospitalisation and the two boys returned a little sheepishly and with fairly serious facial cuts a few days later. Many of us had an ambiguous attitude towards them, envy of these 'men of the world' and their obviously exciting lives, coupled with a sense of superiority at their immature behaviour.

Various fads would hit the school now and again, such as firing elastic bands, playing push penny or water bombs. The latter involved filling plastic bags or balloons with water, tying the top and then waiting until some poor innocent walked three or four stories beneath your room, when you dumped the bomb on him. Its big advantage over the conventional throwing of a cup of water on someone, was that the bomb remained intact until contact with the victim, thus ensuring a thorough drenching. Darkness was essential as the recipient could not identify you. A few of us were experimenting with the weapon. We were in my room and watching unsuspecting pupils walking below.

When they were between the assembly hall and the study hall, we would strike. However after we let go a perfect shot, we heard a very angry growl, followed by a string of curses and oath of vengeance. We immediately froze as we recognised the voice. We had inadvertently hit one very strong, decent but obviously not very happy, Leaving Cert, Greg Cornyn (Dowra). We dispersed with incredible haste as he tore up the stairs to the scene of the attack. We were gone.

Fourth Years usually put on a concert for the rest of the boarders. Numerous talented lads provided a variety of music. Dermot Prior played the quirky hit from Lieutenant Pigeon - "Mouldy Old Dough", on the tin whistle. A number of us did a classroom skit, where various pupils, mimicking teachers, took us for class. Pupils are the best for taking off the idiosyncrasies of teachers, as they are in effect a captive audience, seated before the same performer, day in day out, for approximately one hundred and seventy days per school year. I don't know how good we were, but we enjoyed ourselves immensely and so did the audience. At the interval, some Second Year lads burst out of the side door of the assembly hall towards the senior pitch to 'have a fag'. Unfortunately there was a car parked directly outside the door and one lad ran straight into it, breaking his leg. A few days later we performed the concert for the patients in St. Felim's. They were delighted, though the content was geared specifically for teenagers. The Matron, Sr. Mercy rewarded us with, believe it or not, ten cigarettes each. Different times. We returned early to the college and night study was still in progress. We worked out our official excuse for not going into to the study hall, if we were confronted. It was that we did not want to disrupt those already studying. In reality we were high after the concert and wanted some craic. Someone suggested dumping (pulling all the clothes off) the priests' beds. The priests each had a sitting room and an adjoining bed room. None were locked and pupils did not enter the rooms, unless sent from class by the teacher to retrieve some forgotten textbook from the sitting room. We entered the sitting room and then into the bedroom and in the darkness pulled all the clothes off and strew them around the floor. I can't remember exactly whose rooms we dumped, around three or four. I do remember distinctly dumping Fr. Dan Gallogly's room. Even in the dark, we were amazed by the number of old newspapers there. As someone who loves history, I now shudder when I look back and remember that we scattered many of those old papers. They were probably part of Fr. Dan's research for the upcoming college centenary book. Luckily for us there was no inquiry.

The Christmas exams were serious business in St. Pat's. I needed four honours in the Leaving Cert to qualify for a County Council grant for university. I was not good at Irish. In Second class in national school, I had queried my teacher, Mrs. Gannon, as too why it was 'dinneár Nollag', rather than 'Nollag dinneár', the direct translation from English. I always thought in English and then tried to translate into Irish. After a few weeks of Fr. Dan's grammar, I sensibly dropped down to pass Irish with Fr. John Murphy. We were studying Seosamh Mac Grianna's short story book, *An Grá agus An Ghruaim*. Meanwhile the lads doing honours had to read, in their own time, a number of Irish books and have summaries ready for Dan to correct. Every weekend these pupils trudged valiantly through one of the following: *Rothar Mór an tSaoil, Tóraíocht Dhiarmada agus Ghráinne, Scothscéalta and Dialann Deoraí*. In contrast, we in the pass class got an essay on 'Sonas' in September, a much easier prospect[8]. This was followed by an essay on 'An Teilifís: Is mór an crá croí í '.

Honours Maths was incredibly difficult at that time. It counted as two full honours in the Leaving for university entrance and for a County Council grant. It was important for engineering, a highly regarded course. Not all schools actually provided Maths at honours level[9]. Although sixteen pupils had got honours in Inter Cert Maths, including 2 As and 5 Bs, only six opted to do honours for the Leaving. Fr. Leo O'Reilly taught them. I was in Fr. Torlac O' Reilly's pass Maths class. It was made up mostly of those lads who had done honours in the Inter Cert but were now doing pass. Torlac was a gentleman. He did not demand quiet in his class and as a result he certainly didn't get it. We talked among ourselves and assured him we were working out the question in hand. He came around and explained if we were stuck and he could not have been more accommodating. Noel Reilly, (Cavan) was very good at Maths and always had the problems solved before many of the rest of us. On Fridays he frequently brought in the Celt newspaper, and started reading it where he sat at the front of the class. Torlac was going around helping others with their Maths. Dermot Prior and I, just to cause some diversion, alerted him in very loud childish voices, 'Please Father, look at Noel Reilly, he's reading the Celt'. Torlac simply asked Noel had he his Maths question done, which of course he had. Whereupon Torlac stated, 'Well that's ok, you can continue reading the Celt'. A broad education!. Our mock horror rouse had fallen flat on its face. On another occasion, Dermot Prior was put out of class, on to the corridor, for acting the eejit. Seamus Mc Enroe who was doing honours Maths in Fr. Leo's class, was for some reason also out of his class on the corridor. Dermot hoisted Seamus up on his shoulders and the latter started waving into us through the fanlight above the classroom door. We could see him but Torlac couldn't. Naturally laughing erupted, as it was like a Punch and Judy show, with Seamus appearing and then disappearing. Eventually Torlac copped what was happening, opened the door and told Dermot to get back into class. One day I threw Dermot Prior's copy and book out the window. We were on the second floor. He had to sneak out of the room, down the stairs and retrieve them. Torlac noticed nothing and in fact Dermot was quietly returning unnoticed, when we alerted him with the shout, 'Father, Dermot Prior was out of class without permission'. Dermot tried to explain but of course I denied everything. We knew Torlac would let it go.

I looked on my ordinary level Maths and Irish as much less important than my honours subjects. Fr. John Murphy hit the exact right note in pass Irish, he pushed us hard enough to get the best from us, while realising it was not our priority. He had a droll sense of humour and nothing fazed him. At that time there were no points for university, so the grade you got in a pass subject, by and large, was of no consequence. It was the number of honours you achieved that mattered, (and in the required subject for your chosen course). You also had to pass at least five subjects including Irish. Pass Maths for the Leaving should have been a doddle for me, having done honours for the Inter Cert. I took it easy during Maths class, seeing it as somewhat of a break from the pressure of the other subjects. I assumed I would have no problem with maths, so much for assumption!

Fr. Dan Gallogly had forty one pupils in his History class. We were stuffed into seats in Room 1V on the green-tiled corridor in the New Wing. It was taught at an honours level. We started with Irish history using The Making of Modern Ireland by J.C. Beckett. He called out to us what to underline in this large book, so that we got the key ideas and events. Dan lectured, he couldn't do anything else with that number in such a confined space. He was brilliant. His passion and knowledge for his subject were infectious, at least for me who liked History to begin with. We all had to buy these A4 folders, in which to keep our History notes. Dan explained the topic very well, then wrote the notes on the board which we transcribed roughly into our copies. That evening we transferred them, in neater handwriting and correctly, into our red folders. Between Dan underlining the history book, lecturing, we transcribing and rewriting, it just seemed to go into our consciousness, at least it did for me. Soon we managed to transcribe directly from the board to our red folders, thus obviating the need for rewriting that evening. You dare not mess in his class, but the banter was great. He always referred to Myles Mc Entee (Cavan town) as 'Myles the Slasher', after Myles the Slasher O' Reilly, (who died on the Bridge of Finea in 1646, fighting English and Scots forces)[10].He also referred to the imperturbable George Cartwright (Crossdoney) as 'Wheelwright'. He also reminded the Cavan town boys that the extent of their contribution to Irish Independence was that one of their ancestors threw a tin of red paint over the local landlord, Farnham. He kept hammering home key concepts like that the 1881 Land Act made 'the landlord and the tenant, 'dual owners', 'the abandonment of laissez-faire', that the Conservatives believed that what Ireland wanted 'was Good Government, not Self Government'. One of the weekend exercises was to write an essay entitled, 'What were the weaknesses of Issac Butt's Home Rule Party?'

Fr. Ray Brady taught the honours English class, with about 38 of us packed into Class 1V. You did not mess in Ray's class, although he never raised his voice, never threatened, he just looked at you or made a comment in a controlled, ominous voice. He was a terrific teacher. I had always loved English and he was interesting, knowledgeable, organised and I always looked forward to the class. We started in September with Chaucer's poetry, from the book *Soundings*. We always had to learn off some verses of each poem, (a very good idea for exams and for later life) such as the third stanza of Keats's, Ode to a Nightingale:

Fade far away, dissolve and quiet forget… The weariness, the fever and the fret[11].

He made English relevant by relating it to everyday life. Our first essay was, 'The Problem of Reading', followed by 'Friendship', 'Mass Production, a Mixed Blessing', 'Should Eighteen Year Olds have a Vote', 'The Miser', 'Trees' and 'A Nightmare'[12].His corrections were very detailed, commenting on style, rephrasing my poor expression and suggesting areas for improvement as well as an overall comment. Once I wrote 'introducement', instead of 'Introduction'. Ray circled it with an accompanying caption, 'Take it away'. I used the latter comment for many years as an English teacher myself. I am amazed at how many essays he gave us, a lot of work. He also taught the Leaving Cert honours class. The essay regarding eighteen year olds having the vote, has lingered long in my memory. It was given to us in light of the forthcoming referendum on this issue on 7 December 1972. I was adamant that they should get the vote and my essay started with (in retrospect a not very logical beginning)[13] 'A Government is a group of responsible people who make rules of conduct to govern people's lives. The question now is, 'Are our eighteen year olds responsible people,' '. I wrote over seven pages of a copybook on the topic and waited patiently for the day it would be returned. There was always an air of expectation on a Friday afternoon when Ray returned with the essays. However a murmur of discontent rumbled across the classroom, as each of us on opening the final page of our essay to see the mark awarded, realised that they hadn't been corrected. We were fuming but when I mumbled something, Ray asked me was there a problem, to which I replied in the negative. I do realise that shortly afterwards, he handed out to all of us, a very comprehensive and typed A4 stapled set of great notes, that he had prepared for us himself, on the newly introduced Shakespearean play, Coriolanus.

I had Fr. Seán Brady for honours Latin. There were 26 of us in the class. He did not demand quietness, but he got it because he was a very good teacher, as well as being a thorough gentleman, and very unassuming by nature. His punctuality was legendary. He would be seen prancing up and down outside classrooms, waiting impatiently for the teacher to emerge, so he could shoot in and begin work. One day, after morning break, he was so anxious that he arrived in to class before the bell signalling the end of break had gone. We naturally objected to our break being shortened. For a learned man, he carried his knowledge lightly. He was very well respected. We started the year doing sentences, using a small grey/blue hard backed text book, *Latin Prose Composition*. Our homework was to translate English sentences into Latin, such as the following which incorporated consecutive clauses: 'The soldiers are so brave that they always conquer the enemy'; 'He has done this in such a way that we do not praise him'[14]. This was the core of the course, but unfortunately it was also the area in which I was least proficient. While I had gotten an honour in Inter Cert Latin, it was based on my knowledge of Roman History, and a reasonable ability to translate unseen Latin passages into English. Sentence construction was definitely my Achilles heel and was exposed in that first term in St. Pat's. I struggled to come to grips with grammar that I should have mastered in First Year. One day in class, as we were doing the cases of nouns I wondered aloud was the appropriate answer, the 'vocative', to which a very bright pupil who sat immediately ahead of me for the previous two months, turned around and quietly told me it was the 'accusative'. We had never exchanged words prior to this, although I sat behind him for four subjects each day since 6 September. He was a very nice fellow, but we just never engaged in conversation. I suppose that is how the dynamic of St. Pat's was different from my old school, St. Felim's, where everyone knew everyone, and the atmosphere was more relaxed. We began studying the *Aeneid, Book 6*, an epic poem written in Latin by Virgil. For the Leaving we had to be able to translate all 901 lines into English. The translation of the opening lines has remained with me always:

> Thus weeping, he (Aeneas) speaks and gives the fleet its head
> And at last glides to the Euboean shores of Cumae

The curriculum offered in most Irish second level schools at that time was much more limited than it is today. In St. Pat's, the six lads doing honours Maths, had ten Maths classes per week, and only did a total of six subjects for the Leaving. Everyone else studied seven. The top and second stream classes ran simultaneously for English, Irish, and French. This meant that there was an honours and a pass class in each subject. It was progressive as it allowed pupils to do the level that best suited them, without being locked into an all honours or all pass class. History and Geography were also timetabled at the same time so that fellows could choose which to do, regardless of their base class. Everyone in the top two classes did English, Irish, Maths, French, Latin, and Physics and Chemistry (one subject). In addition all but the honours Maths lads did either History or Geography. The pupils in the third stream did ordinary level in Irish, English and Maths. They studied Accounting/Business, Art, Geography and Agricultural Science. A small number of them did French instead of Geography.

I had chosen not to do French in Ballinamore. Luckily in St. Pat's, when my class had French, the third stream did Geography, so I, with a number of other pupils new to Fourth Year, was able to study it to make up my seventh subject. Fr. Ray Brady also taught that class. The atmosphere was very different from the top stream. The class was made up of day-boys mostly and in general was friendlier and more relaxed. I got a lot of very good natured banter from some of the friends I had there, regarding me being so keen to do honours, when most of the class were content doing pass. It reminded me most of my old class in Ballinamore. When teaching about weather, cloud formation, Ray frequently referred to one very strong, robust and determined footballer, Paddy Bradley, in our midst, to explain what happened when a light and heavy air mass collided. Peter Mc Caffrey with the help of a few others, made a papier-mâché map, showing the mountain ranges of the United States. Although I worked hard, I felt relaxed in the Geography class, perhaps too much so, as one afternoon I hit someone a friendly clout when Ray's back was turned. He caught me and I was put outside the open door. I was afraid the president, Terry, might come along, but fortunately he didn't. After class Ray, in a low calm voice told me no such behaviour better recur. I had no hesitation assuring him it never would.

There was no Biology on offer in St. Pat's. It was the only part of the Inter Cert Science that I had found interesting. I was in the top class of 30 with Fr. Larry Carney for honours Physics and Chemistry. The standard was high, my interest was low, and the teacher was good if you had a reasonable standard, which I hadn't. I did my best to make some sense of Abbot's text book. Fr. Carney tried to help me with anything I asked, but it was useless, as I was so far behind. The atomic table and the refraction of waves just did not appeal to me[15]. Around mid-November I stopped trying. I remember we had a double first on a Wednesday morning in the laboratory beside the study hall. The tiered seating was very uncomfortable when you were as lost and bored as I was.

A typical evening's homework in September included: two questions on Milton's poem Lycidas, to know translation of that day's work on Virgil's Aeneid, History notes in folder, summary of pages read in *An Grá agus An Gruaim*, Chemistry definitions in copy, warm climate page in Physical Geography, and two questions in Maths[16].

The Christmas exams were very well organised and there was a very studious air around the place, at least among most seniors. All exams went well for me except the infamous Physics and Chemistry. I wrote six to seven lines and then ran out of knowledge. I sat for what seemed like an eternity for the rest of the exam. In retrospect I realise I learned a great deal in those two hours: the feelings of pupils who find some, or indeed all, subjects very difficult, powerlessness, frustration, and inadequacy. At least I knew what grade I would receive in that exam.

A beautiful aroma wafted its way from the kitchen to our nostrils from lunch time on one particular day. We all waited impatiently for the best meal of the year. The Christmas dinner did not disappoint. The atmosphere was vociferous with two hundred fellows dying to stuff themselves with turkey, ham and pudding, followed shortly by Christmas freedom.

We headed home at dinner time about one week before Christmas day. While I was really looking forward to three weeks holidays, it was tempered by the fact that Dad had been admitted to the Bons Secours Hospital in Dublin, the previous day. We expected he would be out in a few days. I started work the next morning in my old job in Logan's supermarket. I worked every day, starting at 9.30 am. and finishing late each night, around 10.45 pm. as we drew nearer to Christmas. It was great. We were so busy the time flew and everyone was in high spirits. Mam was very upset when I came home for lunch four days before Christmas Day. Dad had just phoned to tell her the doctors would not be letting him home for Christmas. It cast a dark shadow over everything, although I must admit that I was not as put out as I should have been. We phoned Dad at least once a day and my uncle-in-law, Charlie Mc Hugh, had brought Mam, Valerie and Christopher up to see him, as Micheál and I were working. We decided to have our Christmas dinner on the Sunday, Christmas Eve, and surprise Dad by going to Dublin to visit him

on Christmas day, which we duly did, with Micheál driving us up. He was in great form and so delighted to see us.
On 27 December, Dermot Prior and I went for two days to the Holy Ghost Fathers in Kimmage. Fr. Seán Casey, a Holy Ghost Missionary priest, had given a retreat in St. Pat's the previous term. He was lively, interesting and entertaining. He had cuttings from newspapers to show the ills in society and presented the Christian message in a modern manner. He talked about sex in a very open and refreshing manner. I remember him saying that while he thought girls were very attractive, he did not necessarily want to see their St. Bernard underwear every time he passed them in Dublin, due to their skimpy short skirts. I doubt if it was his intention, but for years afterwards, anytime I passed Dunnes Stores, his words came back to me. He invited anyone who was interested in the missions to attend a two day induction course in their head house in Kimmage. I had no intention of being a priest but Dermot Prior suggested going, and as it meant heading to Dublin for a few days, I readily agreed.
On a very cold, snowy Wednesday morning, I walked down to meet Dermot and get the 8.30 bus to Dromod for the train. As it hadn't arrived by 8.50 we realised we would have to get a lift quickly in order to made the train. We raced up through a deserted Ballinamore and woke Dermot's father Tom, a publican, who was getting a well-deserved lie in after the busiest day in the year, St. Stephen's. As we waited for him, we noticed Mrs. Farrelly, the doctor's wife, and her daughter trying to start their car. A quick glance between Dermot and I established that if we were to be good Samaritans we might be late for the train, so we studiously avoided seeing them. Nothing was said between us, although I think we both felt a little guilty. Tom, a thorough gentleman, never complained and dropped us to Dromod. Who pulls up right behind us at the train station, but Mrs. Farrelly and her daughter. Had we been good Samaritans we could have gotten a lift with them (Karma). C.I.E. was running a promotion, 'The Great Train Robbery'. It included anyone under fourteen travelling for £1 return to Dublin, an incredibly cheap fare. I was fifteen and a half and Dermot was seventeen. We decided that I would purchase the tickets. At the hatch the man demanded, 'Where's the other fellow?' I beckoned to Dermot. The route he took to the hatch ensured that the man did not see him. As Dermot was quite tall, he appeared at the side of the hatch, with his knees bent to seem smaller and only his head visible. The man took one look at him and said in the most sarcastic tone possible, He's fourteen!' However he gave us the cheap tickets. 'Great Train Robbery' had a whole new meaning. The irony of the dishonesty did not strike either of us and we going to a seminary for two days about

working as priests with the poor in the Third World. We spent the day in Dublin and visited my father in hospital. He was very pleased and thankful and Dermot of course left us to talk. Then Dermot and I went to get our tea, where else but Wynnes's Hotel, the Mecca for all nuns and priests up from the country. The waiter was ever so friendly but incredibly patronising, obviously we did not pass for sophisticated young men. Consequently on my suggestion, we left a derisory tip of 3 pence. (Not one of my finer moments).

We spent two days in Kimmage, with other young lads. It was informative and enjoyable although neither of us had any intention of becoming missionary priests. We left on Friday and again I visited Dad in hospital. He was very shocked by what had happened in Belturbet the day before. A car bomb, planted by loyalists, had exploded killing local girl Geraldine O' Reilly, 15 and Paddy Stanley, 16, from Clara Co. Offaly, a helper on a bottle gas lorry, who happened to be making a phone call home from the local public kiosk[17]. It very much brought the 'Northern Troubles' home to us once again. Inspector Samuel Donegan had been killed by an IRA booby-trap near Newtownbutler on the Cavan-Fermanagh border on the 8 June the previous year[18]. As a result his son, Michael, who was doing his Leaving the week of his father's death, returned the following September, 1972, to repeat. Every time I saw him it reminded me of the reality of the North. That year, 1972, was the worst ever in the history of the North with 476 being killed[19]. On 1 December two people had been killed and 127 injured when two car bombs exploded in the centre of Dublin[20]. Amazingly I never worried, nor did my parents, about the possible danger when deciding to go to the capital for a few days. Later on 20 January 1973 another car bomb exploded in Dublin killing one young man[21].

Being young, Dermot and I had no sense of danger and after our stay with the Holy Ghost Fathers in Kimmage, as planned we stayed another day in Dublin, shopping and looking around. We didn't chance returning to Wynnes, but got burgers and chips in a take-away restaurant. We stayed with relatives of Dermot in Blanchardstown who it turned out knew my family well. On Saturday we got the train home. However we got our 'comeuppance', Karma, whatever you want to call it. Dermot had not felt well the night we spent in Blanchardstown. I got violently sick very shortly after I arrived home. Lines from Brian Friel's play, Philadelphia, spring to mind:

Anchored by the ass, bound by the bowels, tethered by the toilet[22].

The insulting tip in Wynne's 'backfired', thanks to the beef burger in the take-away.

Micheál went up to Dublin on Friday afternoon to collect Dad and they

arrived home at 11.00 that night[23]. It was great to see him home. However I had been intent on pushing my freedom a little more now that I was at boarding school, and so had my nose up for accompanying Micheál that night to a dance in the Mayflower in Drumshanbo. I was also playing on the fact that Dad being home was a joyous occasion and this might help me to get permission to attend a dance that was not local. Mam was disappointed as Dad was barely in the door when we were going. Of course Dad would not hear of stopping us. Like election campaigns and Christmas, the dance promised much but delivered little. I came home with nothing but the number one hit single, 'Long Haired Lover from Liverpool', by Little Jimmy Osborne, playing over and over in my head.
We had a turkey Christmas dinner the next day, with numerous relatives and well-wishers coming to welcome Dad home throughout the day. Shortly afterwards the results of my Christmas exams arrived.

Christmas School Report 1972			
Subject	**Level**	**Grade/Mark**	**Comment**
English	Hons.	55%	Just made it
Irish	Pass	55%	Satisfactory
Maths	Pass	40%	Needs to improve
History	Hons.	56%	Good
Latin	Hons.	21%	Speaks for itself
Science	Hons.	N.G.	Should take Lower level
Geography	Pass	71%	Working well

I was happy as I expected that Science result and knew that I had not done well in Latin. The Geography was a pass exam so I knew my mark was a bit inflated. The president, Fr. Terry had commented that overall progress was good, but should I consider a grind in two subjects. I had to ask my mother what 'grind' meant. Mam in turn had to enquire of me as to what N.G. meant (no grade) in Science. Micheál, my ever helpful brother, quickly interjected that is stood for 'No bloody good'. Dad and Mam were pleased that I was pleased.
I had one term completed and was ready to start the next. It did not strike my young mind at the time but the St. Pat's I was attending in essence had not changed that much in its one hundred years of existence.

Mc Rory Team 1972-73

Back (L-R) Mr. Patsy Lee, Matt Rudden, Pat Bradley, Paddy Sexton, Ciarán Brady, Aidan Elliott, Fr. John Murphy, Hubert Smith, John Costello, Louis Blessing, Owen Martin, Francis Mc Nally and Fr. Mallon (college president).
Seated (L-R) Peter Callaghan, Martin Brady, Brian Brady, Matt Cahill, Cathal Maguire, Hubert Conaty, Liam Bouchier and Michael Brady.

Lights out
(courtesy of Cian Duffy)

Generations have trod
(courtesy of Eoghan Mc Connell)

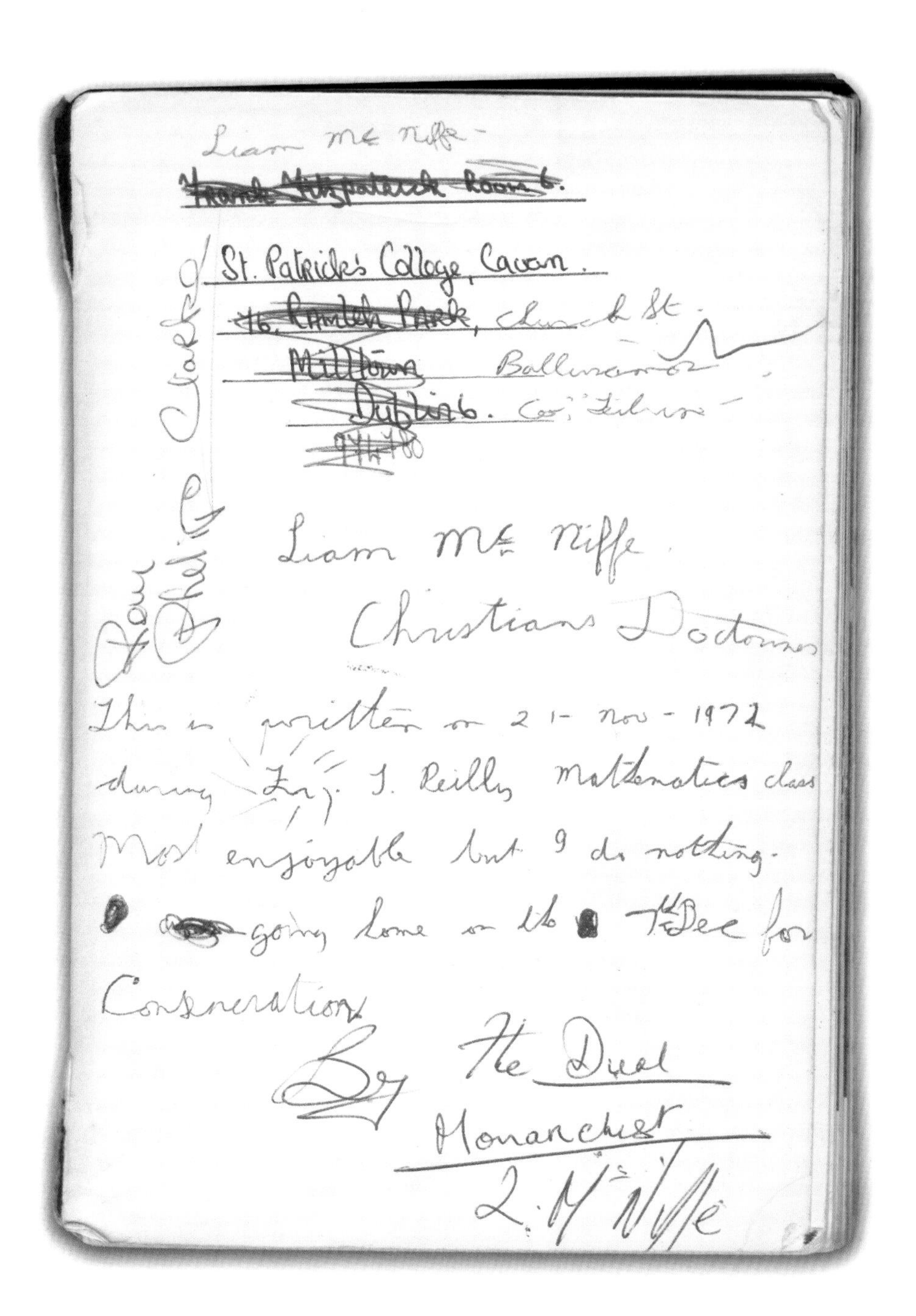

Author's Religion Textbook
Written on by author during Maths class. 'By the Dual Monarchist' refers to History class and was written by Dermot Prior to annoy author.

Chapter 4

History of St. Pat's

Type of school, Type of pupil

Before I describe what life was like after Christmas in the college, I will first look at what type of school St. Pat's was in 1972, what type of pupil went there and where they came from.

It is impossible to understand what kind of school it was like at that time unless its origins are understood. A number of questions arise: why significant numbers of pupils were drawn from distant parts of Leitrim and none from nearby Monaghan?, why daily routine was so rigidly organised for boarders with such an emphasis on religious observance?, why the very impressive late nineteenth century building was designed the way it was?

The geographical area served by the Diocesan College, St. Pat's, that I entered in September 1972 had its origins over eight hundred years earlier. The reorganisation of the Irish Church in the twelfth century brought the diocese to the forefront as the unit of church organisation.[1]. There were no county divisions in Ireland, the country being ruled by a number of over lords who in turn controlled local lords[2]. By and large the reorganised twenty six dioceses reflected these existing political realities[3]. The vast bulk of the lordship of O'Rourke of Breifne (excluding south west Leitrim) became Kilmore diocese[4]. It was from this same area in 1874, that St. Pat's, being a diocesan college, was to begin drawing its students, a tradition that lasted for almost one hundred and thirty years. Pupils from nearby County Monaghan (which was in Clogher Diocese), attended their own diocesan college, St. Macartan's in Monaghan town. In 1972 St. Pat's was just one of over twenty nationwide diocesan colleges, most of which had been built between the middle of the nineteenth and the early part of the twentieth century.

The rationale underlying the organisation of life for pupils, particularly boarders, in St. Pat's in the early 1970s, can also trace some of its origins back to the middle ages. A new wave of monastic orders, such as the Cistercians and Augustinians, arrived in Ireland in the twelfth/thirteenth centuries. The monks' day was organised around prayer, work and study.

They rose at 6 am. attended prayers in the church, followed by breakfast in the refectory, after which they walked and prayed in the cloisters. Then they dispersed, each according to his own task, either to work on the farm, teach students, copy manuscripts or prepare meals. Dinner was in the refectory, followed by prayers in the church, return to work, and supper in the refectory before final prayers in the church and retire to bed in the dormitory. Our daily routine as boarders in 1972 was not totally dissimilar to this. We rose at 7.10, attended Mass in the chapel at 7.30, followed by breakfast at 8.00 in the refectory. Morning study followed at 8.40 and the day's class began at 9.00. Dinner was in the refectory at 1.00. Class resumed at 2.00 and ended at 4.00. Afternoon tea was in the refectory at 4.00 followed by recreation until 5.30. Study was from 5.30 until tea at 7.00. Study resumed at 7.45 until 9.45, followed by night prayer in the chapel. Lights out at 10.30.

The template of the design of those medieval monasteries, as well as the terms used, was still very much in evidence in St. Patrick's College in 1972. The imposing front building housed a chapel and library at the eastern side, connected by an imposing corridor to the refectory at the western end. This joined another long green-tiled corridor running north-south. An infirmary as well as a number of dormitories and double bedrooms were located upstairs in these two blocks. While not enjoying the full four sided rectangle of the medieval monasteries, St. Pat's had two full sides of a rectangle with the college chapel making a half third side. The terms 'infirmary', 'refectory' and 'dormitory' were still in use and the corridors were cloisters in the sense that they looked out on to the semi-courtyard and the red-tiled one was used for prayer and recreational walks by the priests during inclement weather.

The physical design of St. Patrick's College and the daily routine of its boarders were also influenced by the general rise in institutionalisation in the eighteenth and nineteenth centuries. Throughout Europe prisons, barracks, poorhouses, hospitals, asylums and schools began to manage large numbers of people on an institutional basis[5]. The strict discipline, whereby the daily routines governed every waking moment, was strikingly similar in all these institutions. The twentieth century French philosopher, Foucault, identified this kind of institutionalisation as a key feature that only came to an end in the 1970's[6]. A feature of these buildings was the pointed arch windows, part of the Gothic revival[7]. William Hague (Jnr.), the architect for St. Patrick's College in the early 1870's was a member of the school of Gothic revivalist architecture[8]. Gothic features are in evidence in the college, especially in the double height Gothic window at the back of the building where two floors come together in a centrepiece[9].

The reorganisation of the Irish Church in the twelfth century explained why St. Pat's drew its pupils from most of Cavan and much of Leitrim over eight centuries later. The daily routine of the medieval orders, and the design of their monasteries, greatly influenced the life of a boarder in the early 1970's. The effect of institutionalisation on the building and on daily discipline has also been looked at. But how did the medieval influences migrate from the twelfth to the twentieth century? In other words why were diocesan colleges set up and why on the particular lines on which we came to know and expect them to be?

The Protestant Reformation of the sixteenth century split the church into Protestant and Catholic throughout most of Europe. Subsequently the Catholic (or Counter) Reformation began to reform the Catholic Church from within. Central to this was the Council of Trent. In 1562 it legislated for the establishment of diocesan seminaries to provide a pastorally competent priesthood with some knowledge of theology[10]. Each diocese was to set up its own seminary with a structured environment for the training of men for the priesthood. Ireland, although overwhelmingly Catholic, was subordinate to English power and so had a Protestant establishment in Church and State. Consequently Protestant opposition and lack of resources meant that Irish ecclesiastical students had to travel abroad to study for the priesthood[11]. The new seminaries followed what was essentially a monastic type of daily routine and in many instances copied the rectangular style building. Eventually Irish seminaries were established towards the end of the eighteenth century; Kilkenny in 1782, Carlow in 1793 and Maynooth in 1795[12]. The number of priests in Kilmore Diocese increased rapidly in the period after 1800[13]. Church building in the diocese accelerated with the construction of thirty six new churches from 1820 to 1840[14]. Elsewhere in Ireland a number of diocesan seminaries had been set up by this stage[15].

St. Patrick's College had its origins in St. Augustine's Seminary, opened by

Bishop James Browne in Cavan town on 28 August 1839[16]. It was primarily a minor seminary to prepare boys to go to Maynooth and other major seminaries. However Browne also wanted to provide an education to prepare young men for the professions and for business life, so it also fulfilled the role of intermediate school[17]. As a result St. Augustine's, (more commonly known as the Kilmore Academy), provided second level education for the sons of well-off Catholics, with nineteen boarders and nineteen day-boys in that first year[18]. Rev. Bernard Finegan, who took over as president in 1865, sought to bring it more into line with the contemporary thinking of both the Vatican and Archbishop Cullen of Dublin on minor seminaries. He oversaw the provision of a purpose built chapel, the introduction of ecclesiastical dress (soutane and surplice) for formal occasions, ensured that the Academy was called the seminary, and by 1866 the staff was made up entirely of priests[19]. By 1867 the Vatican was still not convinced that St. Augustine's could be called a seminary, citing the fact that theology was not taught there and there were too many day pupils to allow the proper environment for the education of young seminarians[20]. Nicholas Conaty, Bishop of Kilmore also had reservations about St. Augustine's, with students, as he put it, 'living in the whiskey shops of Cavan town'[21]. It was at this stage that a decision was made to build a new college that would be more in line with the views of the Vatican and of Archbishop Cullen (now Cardinal). In 1868 Fr. Finegan left on a two year fund raising trip of the USA to secure finance for the new college[22].

On 12 March 1874 St. Augustine's ceased to exist and the staff and most pupils transferred to the new purpose built college in Cullies just outside Cavan town[23]. There was little ambiguity as to the function of the new St. Patrick's College. It had no day pupils and all but ten who entered the minor seminary intended studying for the priesthood[24]. It was also a major seminary, educating young men up to ordination[25]. In effect it was both a second and third level educational institution in the one college. It was run on the same lines as Maynooth, with the rules aimed at cultivating in the student a spirit of prayer, self- discipline and obedience to authority[26]. In 1878 St. Patrick's College started a day school in the building of the old Academy, run by a priest and a lay man attached to the new college. It was opened in response to a local demand for further education for boys from Cavan town who could not afford the St. Pat's boarding fee and also to provide additional income for the college[27]. In 1886 St. Patrick's College ceased to be a major seminary, while remaining a minor seminary. The St. Patrick's day-school was closed and its pupils were admitted to the college at an annual fee of five pounds[28].

St. Augustine's had begun in 1839 as a minor seminary and accepted day-boys. It was fairly radically restructured in 1874 as the new St. Patrick's College, not only a minor seminary now closed to day-boys, but also a major seminary. In 1886 it underwent another radical transformation when it ceased to be a major seminary, but remained a minor one, and opened its doors once again to day-boys. This new role was one it was to maintain for the next one hundred and fourteen years, until boarding ceased in the year 2000[29].

Another major change in the role of St. Pat's in education came five years before I went there. In September 1966 the Minister for Education, Donogh O' Malley, made a dramatic announcement that was to revolutionise second level education in Ireland. The president of St. Pat's, Fr. Bob Mc Cabe, went into a Leaving Cert class the next day to relay this dramatic news that there would be free post primary education from the following September. He was really excited about the free bussing of school-pupils[30]. Prior to this all pupils (whether day or boarders), had to pay for tuition, about £20 per year for secondary school (one week's pay for my father in 1965). Tuition fees for Vocational schools were nominal, about £1 for Ballinamore Vocational in the mid-1960s. As a result those from better off families tended to attend secondary schools and those from less well-off families went to 'the Tech' (short for Technical school). The former offered an academic education up to Leaving Cert while the latter offered a more practical education, with the Group Cert exam after two years. There was no school transport system. Pupils had to walk, cycle or be driven to school. Many families had no car. With no easy transport available for those living far from a secondary school, boarding was the only option. Again, while it was at a very reasonable cost, it was prohibitive for many people. All this meant that the cohort of pupils in St. Pat's, especially the boarders, tended in general to come from better off families. This did not mean they were all well-off by any stretch of the imagination, but they were able to get the requisite money to give their son an academic education. At this stage in Ireland it was possible to gain entry to some levels in the Civil Service without even a pass in the Inter Cert and to gain entry to some university courses with little more than a pass Leaving

Cert. As a result some pupils, even in the academic setting of St. Pat's, did not finish the five years[31]. The following table illustrates this[32]:

Retention Rates of Pupils Entering St. Pat's 1962-66 (incl.)

Year	No. entered College	% Completed Inter Cert	% Completed L. Cert
1962	96	80	62
1963	82	74	52
1964	90	86	56
1965	83	81	59
1966	80	79	69
Total: 1962-66	431	80	60

In the five years before the introduction of free second level education, four in five pupils in St. Pat's completed the Inter Cert and three out of five completed the Leaving Cert.

The numbers attending second level schools dramatically increased in the years following free second level education. Between 1967 and 1974 there was a 61% increase nationally, with St. Pat's recording a 57% rise[33]. However increased numbers were not the only change. Schools now had to cope with pupils of a wider range of ability and social background[34]. St. Pat's now found itself not only having to build extra classrooms and an assembly hall to facilitate a massive rise in numbers, but it had also to expand the curriculum it offered. Many of the pupils now availing of free education and free school transport would not otherwise have had the opportunity of attending St. Pat's. Many were very bright and prospered in the academic environment. A new cohort of pupil however now arrived in the college, the less academic, and their needs had to be addressed.

In January 1973, the president Terry Mc Manus, referred to some of these changes[35]. The classics had been downgraded somewhat with the dropping of Greek from the curriculum. Latin was retained however. Fr. Mc Manus stated that new subjects had been introduced, 'catering for students of average ability', such as Commerce, Arts and Crafts, Agricultural Science and Biology, all up to Leaving Cert level. Woodwork was introduced up to Inter Cert level. (The dean, Fr. Paddy Brady, had begun this subject and

Finian Callaghan, former principal of the recently closed Kilnaleck Vocational School and now teaching in Cavan Vocational, began teaching the subject in St. Pat's). He was also very happy that General Musicianship was on offer to Leaving Cert level. By today's political correctness standards, the President's reference to 'average abilities' appears condescending (Special Needs were not even acknowledged by most people at this time). However the college, like most secondary schools in Ireland, was adapting to meet the changing needs of its pupils.

A total of 522 boys entered as new pupils (not all were First Years) between 1968 and 1972. The following table shows the distribution by county of these 522[36]:

County of Origin of All Pupils Who Entered St. Pat's 1968-72 (incl.)		
County	No. of pupils	% of total pupil population
Cavan	428	82
Leitrim	42	8
Dublin	16	3
Meath	9	2
Longford	5	1
Donegal	5	1
Westmeath	5	1
Louth	5	1

One pupil came from each of the following counties: Monaghan, Carlow, Tipperary, Cork, Sligo and Mayo. One pupil, Val Tierney, was from Northamptonshire in England.

The number of boarders in the college peaked at 241 in 1964[37]. A policy decision to reduce this number to 185 was taken in 1966. This decision, coupled with free transport meant that less pupils boarded. In the early seventies this had dropped to 166. By September 1972 there was a total of 430 pupils in the college, 58% day-boys and 42% boarders[38]. Although the number of boarders had risen to 190 in 1973, the trend of day-boys constituting the majority of pupils continued. While half of the boarders (51%) came from County Cavan, the next largest cohort came from neighbouring Leitrim (21%), followed by Dublin (9%)[39].

This next table shows the parish/town of origin of all pupils who entered the college in the years 1968-72 (incl.)[40].

Parish/Town of New Entrants 1968 -72 (incl.)		
Parish/town	**Number of pupils**	**% of Total pupils**
Cavan town	147	28
Ballinagh	36	7
Killeshandra	25	5
Belturbet	21	4
Ballyhaise	20	4
Laragh	19	4
Dublin (city and county)	16	3
Butlersbridge	15	3
Kilnaleck	14	3
Ballinamore (Leitrim)	11	2
Lavey	9	2
Ballyjamesduff	8	1.5
Redhills	8	1.5
Corlismore	7	1.5
Ballyconnell	7	1.5
Manorhamilton (Leitrim)	7	1.5
Kiltyclogher (Leitrim)	6	1
Carrigallen (Leitrim)	6	1
Crosserlough	5	1
Templeport	5	1
Mullagh	5	1
Dowra	5	1
Arva	5	1
Moynehall	5	1
Bailieborough	4	0.8
Carrickaboy	4	0.8
Virginia	4	0.8
Kingscourt	3	0.6

Parish/Town of New Entrants 1968 -72 (incl.) *(contd.)*		
Parish/town	**Number of pupils**	**% of Total pupils**
Drung	3	0.6
Killinkere	3	0.6
Glangevlin (Glan)	3	0.6
Crossdoney	3	0.6
Drumshanbo (Leitrim)	3	0.6
Bawnboy (Bawn)	2	0.4
Milltown	2	0.4
Crosskeys	2	0.4
Blacklion	2	0.4
Cornafean	2	0.4
Mountainlodge	2	0.4
Shercock	2	0.4
Swanlinbar	2	0.4
Cootehill	2	0.4
Tullymongan	2	0.4
Mountnugent	2	0.4
Knockbride	2	0.4
Glenfarne (Leitrim)	2	0.4
Rossinver (Leitrim)	2	0.4
Kilmainhamwood (Meath)	2	0.4
Oldcastle (Meath)	2	0.4
Kells (Meath)	2	0.4
Ardee (Louth)	2	0.4
Drogheda (Louth)	2	0.4
Castlepollard (Westmeath)	2	0.4
Finea (Westmeath)	2	0.4
Lanesboro (Longford)	2	0.4

The following areas each had one pupil who entered the college in the 1968-72 period:

Cavan: Corlislea, Cloverhill, Tullyvin, Loughduff, Munterconnaught, Killydoon, Mullahoran, Derrylane, Castlerahan, Castletara, and Lisduff.
Leitrim: Glenfarne, Ballinagleara, Drumreilly, Spencer Harbour and Drumkeerin.
Donegal: Donegal town, Ballybofey, Ballyshannon, Buncrana and Tullygullion.
Longford: Ballinalee, Granard and Lisryan.
Meath: Navan, Kilmessan and Dunshaughlin.
Louth: Dundalk.
Offaly: Tullamore.
Westmeath: Streets.
Sligo: Strandhill.
Monaghan: Monaghan town.
Carlow: Carlow town.
Mayo: Killala.
Tipperary: Borrisokane.
Cork: Mitchelstown.

There was often 'slagging' (mocking) between pupils from different counties and even within counties. In the early years of the twentieth century it was political and very serious. The 1908 Leitrim by-election was between the Sinn Féin candidate Charles Dolan (former pupil of St. Pat's) and Francis Meehan of the Irish Parliamentary Party. It caused a split between the pupils of Leitrim and west Cavan who supported Sinn Féin, and those of east Cavan who were strongly Hibernian/ Irish Parliamentary Party[41]. In 1921, during the War of Independence this split had become vicious and flowed over into violence and gang warfare. As a result the football and hurling leagues had to be called off for a number of years[42]. In the early 1970s there were no political divisions in the college. However there was always banter and sometimes a little more between Cavan and Leitrim, with those from Cavan suffering from superiority complex and those of us from Leitrim not prepared to suffer anything. In 'Spectrum', the college student magazine in June 1971, one very well written satirical article refers to a Leitrim student in an upcoming election expecting, 'to poll well in backward areas. As he looked out over the Aughavas hills from his home in Tintown Rd., ... he hoped to have a large number of carts out on election day'[43]. I may be wrong but I always sensed a slight superiority the more easterly you travelled. East Cavan towards Meath and its environs looked down on the rest of Cavan. They had better land and regarded themselves as more sophisticated. Cavan town of course, being the only large town, had to regard themselves as above everyone else. Those from west Cavan, Templeport, Bawn, and Ballyconnell were looked down on by the rest of Cavan, except Dowra and Glan who were regarded as backward by most. Leitrim was also regarded as backward, which was somewhat new for me. I came from Ballinamore, a vibrant and proud small town, with possibly the best organised and most enjoyable annual small-town festival in Ireland at that time. In addition we had a great football team. In fact most of the good teams in Leitrim at that time (I stress 'that time') were in a cluster of small towns in South Leitrim. So of course we tended to look down on North Leitrim, it was more rural and rural was equated with backward in our perverted snobbery. The reality is that most fellows from all areas were fine, but there was the underlying snobbery with regard to our place of origin. The irony of it all is that the lads from North Leitrim in general were honest, hardworking, decent, what you saw is what you got, and I think most of them saw through the stupidity of the geographical superiority.

The student magazine 'Spectrum', was produced for a number of years around the 1970s. It had reviews of music, films, college football as well as short stories, satirical pieces and poetry. It was of a very high quality and very humorous. The following is the table of contents of 'Spectrum', June 1972, Vol. V11, with its student authors included:

Charybdis' Revenge	Martin Cosgrove
Is this how it should be?	George Mc Keon
Films 1971-72	Liam Tuite
An Unusual Faith-Healer	Peter O'Callaghan
Monday Morning	Paddy and Gerry Quinn
The Night they raided Minsky's	Seamus Gallagher
Top Ten- Class 7	Brian Rahill
Debating 1971-73	John Jackson
Senior Diary	P. Mooney, C. Dunne, N. Brennan, M. Donegan, A. Kelly.
South Pacific	Tom Flynn
Hogan Cup Winners, 1972 - A Tribute	Francis Mc Nally
A Hairy Tale	Michael Gaynor
A Ghost's Story	Rory Caslin
Behind the Scenes	Liam Tuite

The Ten Commandments for Safe Driving	Niall Murray
Boarding School	Frank Fitzpatrick
A-I-S-L-I-N-G	George Cartwright
The Year of the Hogan	Matthew Cahill
Rannafast Cup 1971-2	Gerard O'Brien
Hard to Swallow	Liam Bouchier
Red Cross	Gerry O' Brien
Pioneer Activities	Fran Treanor
Junior Scrapbook	Cathal Maguire & Dermot Prior
Childhood	Michael Donegan
Top Twenty	Ciaran Brady
Corn na nÓg	Donald Brady

In one way the St. Pat's I entered in 1972 was substantially the same as it had been for the previous eighty six years. It was a secondary school for boys, boarding and day pupils, offering a mainly liberal academic/ classical education, with sport being a major part of its extra-curricular activity. However it had undergone significant change in the previous five years. Its numbers increased dramatically, there were now more day pupils than boarders, bussing was an integral part of school life and a wider social and economic cohort of pupil had to be catered for by the curriculum. While the numbers entering the school had risen, what about retention rates after the introduction of free education?

Retention Rates of Pupils Entering St. Pat's 1968-72 (incl.) [44]

Year	No. entered College	% Completed Inter Cert	% Completed Leaving Cert
1968	97	76	60
1969	104	72	51
1970	118	76	66
1971	107	79	67
1972	121	88	67
Total	547	79	62

The average percentage of students completing the Inter Cert and Leaving Cert remained almost identical for the 1962-66 and 1968-72 periods. However this masks a major underlying change that was beginning to take place in education. Far more students were coming to the college, far more students were completing the Inter Cert, far more students were completing the Leaving Cert and far more students were going on to university[45]. The educational revolution was well on its way.

How well did St. Pat's cater for the needs of its now more diverse student intake, the traditional academic pupil and the less academic? From 1970, an average of 35% of those sitting the Leaving got at least two honours, the minimum required since the previous year, for entrance to university[46]. The college president, Fr. Mc Manus, speaking in January 1973 referred to the Leaving Cert result of the previous year[47]. It was the largest group to date that ever sat the exam in the college. The 7% failure rate (passing less than five subjects) was way below the national average of 23% for boys[48]. Virtually all the Leaving Cert class satisfied conditions of entry for the Regional Technical Colleges, but every one of them was barred from qualifying for a scholarship by the manner in which the scheme was designed. Seven students had been called for interview to St. Patrick's Teacher Training College in Drumcondra. Ten students got the requisite four honours for a university grant (followed by a means test). St. Pat's was catering for its less academic pupils while not neglecting its traditional type, the sign of a good school.

In early January 1973 I returned to this college with its long and distinguished history, for what was to be a year I would never, ever, forget.

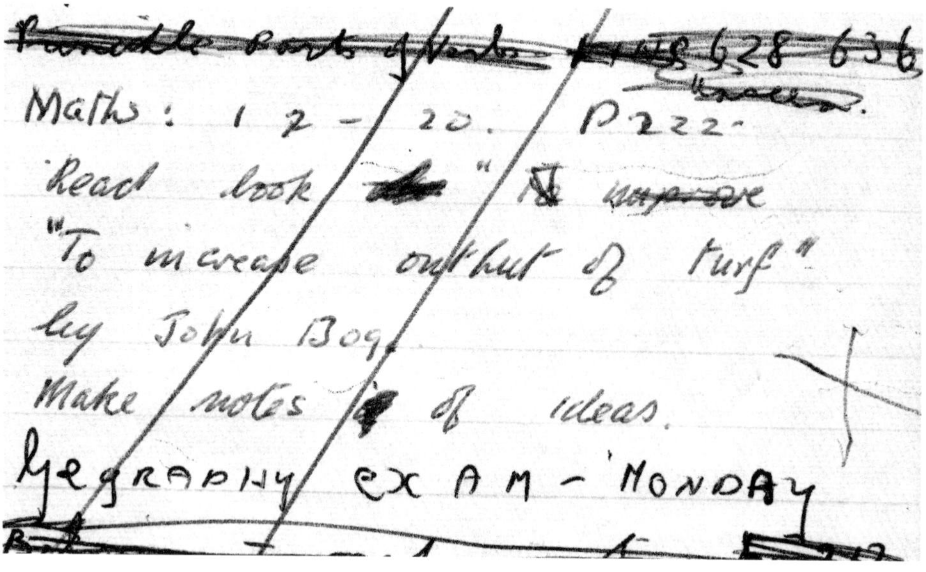

Slagging Leitrim

Unknown classmate pens spurious homework about bogs in author's journal

The bell tolls for all pupils
Seamus Callaghan ringing bell on green-tiled corridor, 1974

Chapter 5

Snow

January - February 1973

I returned to St. Pat's with a new year's resolution, a brain wave as I saw it, but in retrospect a hare-brained idea if ever there was one. I had gotten up early the previous spring at home to study for my Inter Cert. I intended to do likewise now in Fourth Year in my new school. However the scene was drastically different. While the evenings were beginning to lengthen, the January mornings remained stubbornly dark. My big red alarm clock, with its two silver bells on top went off at 5.40. I did not enjoy a good night's sleep as I was afraid the clock might waken my roommate, Gerry Mc Govern. I need not have worried, Gerry could sleep through an earthquake. I crept down to the library in an unlit and unheated building, listening to every creak and afraid that the dean might hear me. I studied for one and a half hours and then had to surreptitiously slink out of the library, and try to blend in with the half-asleep lads as everyone trudged into morning Mass at 7.30. I also had to sneak back, unseen, after Mass and return my books to the study hall. God forbid that you were found out doing extra study, it would certainly not add to your 'street cred'. For some unknown reason I was very tired at evening study and after a week or so, common sense prevailed and I abandoned my master plan.

The president Fr. Terry was not a fan of long hair. Samson-like, many of us pupils felt our strength (of personality at least) was in our hair and jealously guarded its length. Dan was another Delilah, a constant threat to our flowing locks. Many of us had locks, not real facial hair as many of us wished we had, but long, long strands of hair that covered our ears and substituted as terrible looking locks. Before Dan's Irish class in particular, dandruff-laden greasy combs were borrowed and long hair was tucked behind ears, in reality drawing more attention to the length of the mane. If Dan was in a 'smare' (bad temper) and you did not know your grammar, you could be told not to return to class without getting 'that hair cut'. Occasionally Terry organised a general haircut, in that a local barber came out to the college and cut pupils' hair in what was called the barber shop, a short corridor that led out from the study hall towards the assembly hall. In preparation Terry visited the study hall, checked length of hair and noted names of those who had to attend. The cost was added to your bill for laundry and other miscellaneous items at the end of the year. One day-boy from Cavan town, who was not in Dan's class, had very stylish and incredibly long hair. He used go to Peter Mark's in Dublin to get his hair cut. That was the first I had ever heard of Peter Mark.

Senior boarding pupils were allowed smoke if they had written permission from their parents. Approximately twenty lads had such permission. The designated area was the end of the ambulatory near the ball alleys. They could smoke there after night study, around 10.00 pm. for about fifteen minutes. From my curtain-less bedroom, I could see the vermilion glow of the cigarettes, come rain, hail or snow. Smoking inside was strictly forbidden. However when study ended for tea at 7pm. a number of lads lit up in the study hall, for a quick drag. Unfortunately Terry arrived down one evening and caught one fellow who had not extinguished his cigarette in time. He was suspended for a week. Terry left him home by car, a distance of twenty five miles, late at night so as not to be seen by the neighbours and so cause embarrassment to the family. I often wondered what conversation, if any, took place in the yellow Escort car on the road home.

On Saturday mornings we Fourth Years had to attend a one hour class on classical music. We regarded it as a chore, although it was actually providing a free, very liberal education. Fr. Gerry Kearns gave up his free time to about thirty lads who were not particularly interested. However I remember him explaining Tchaikovsky's 1812 Overture, and how the music reflected the initial invasion by Napoleon's Grand Armeé in 1812 and the subsequent successful defence by Russia of the motherland. It opened up a window for me to classical music that has allowed me to enjoy it (albeit at a simple level) ever since.

I loved swimming from the time I taught myself in Pol on Easa, a natural pool in a river in Aughnasheelin outside Ballinamore when I was ten or eleven years old. Cavan had no swimming pool, but the college arranged for boarders who were interested to travel, for a small price, by bus on some Sunday afternoons to Longford town pool. It was great but I always felt a bit lonely or dispirited when returning on the bus, somewhat cold and hungry, to the college, and so I did not avail of every opportunity to travel.

The year, March 1972-March 1973 was probably the most successful twelve months ever in football for St. Pat's College. Not only did we win the Mc Rory Senior cup for the first time in ten years, but went on to capture the All Ireland Hogan cup for the first (and only) time ever. In addition we won the Ulster Rannafast cup for the first time in twenty seven years. In November 1972 we started very well in the only other Gaelic football college competition, the Corn na nÓg (under 15), in our first outing of the year. The tabloid-type heading of the Celt reporting on the game against St. Michael's of Enniskillen said it all: 'St. Pat's Juveniles run riot'[1]. In a feast of goals we won 9.2 to 4.1 at Clones. A week later we routed a mismatched Omagh side at Irvinestown by 7.4 to 2.2, to reach the quarter finals[2]. Although the competition did not restart until February, team trainer, Fr. Leo O' Reilly, arranged challenge games against C.B.S Roscommon, and twice against the Franciscan College in Gormanstown. The quarter final had to be postponed for one week due to terrible weather, and took place on Saturday 24 February in Knockbridge, Co. Louth against St. Colman's Newry. We won once again, but this time by the slenderest of margins, 2.8 to 2.7[3]. The Celt reported that St. Pat's superior size and stamina saw them through[4]. The semi-final saw us drawn against the other Newry school, Abbey C.B.S., played on 3 March in Carrickmacross. Despite being behind at half time, we won 4.3 to 1.8 to reach the final[5]. That was played on 11 March in Dungannon against St. Mary's Belfast. It was a walk over, with St. Pat's scoring 7.7 to St. Mary's 1.8. Our college had not won the Corn na nÓg competition since 1955. The panel included: Gerry. Strong, Francis. Maguire, Paul Myers, Seán Quigley, Torlac Smith, Ray. Cullivan, Frank Mc Kiernan, Felim Costello, Pauric Martin, Donal Donohoe, Paddy Mc Govern, Jim Reilly, Cyril O' Keeffe, Kevin Mc Donagh, and Paul Murphy[6]. The success of the college teams was the headlines for the Celt in its review of the year 1972[7]. Many of the college staff were also involved in the administration of the G.A.A. at county level. Having led the college senior team to All-Ireland victory, Fr. Benny Maguire, was appointed manager of the Cavan senior team[8]. The county Minor Board had the following St. Pat's staff as officers: Rev. Seán Brady, Treasurer, Mr. Patsy Lee, Secretary, and Rev. Paddy Mallon, Registrar[9].

Sr. Rosarii Haughton arrived to St. Pat's around this time and the college was never quite the same. Whatever she lacked in stature, she compensated for by sheer force of personality and persistence[10]. I knew Rosarii from Ballinamore as she was a Mercy nun in the school there. We lads from Ballinamore were caught between being courteous to a teacher from our former school, and yet fearful that we might be seen as 'sucks' (sucking up to, pets). While there were two religious sisters in the school already, Sr. Kathleen Lynch in charge of the kitchen and Sr. Margaret Mary Gilfinnan, the nurse and in-charge of the infirmary, Sr. Rosarii was a teaching nun in what was essentially an all-male preserve. I admired her pluckiness. She was greeted with whistles from the top corridor, which she sensibly ignored. In early January she supervised us for a class, where she distributed sheets on which we had to write down our names and native parish. The fact that some lads from Cavan town did not know that they were in the parish of Urney did not impress her. As a result lads started to pass smart comments, in the vein of 'who does she think she is'. We thought nothing of it until our next class was interrupted by the entrance of Sr. Rosarii accompanied by the college president, Fr. Terry. It was not a social call. He was angry with how we had treated Sr. Rosarii and she pointed out a number of lads whom she thought had misbehaved. They were slapped by Terry there and then. I felt really sorry for Noel Barrett, an absolute gentleman who never misbehaved and who incidentally was one of the few who knew the name of his own parish. True to character he took the punishment philosophically and I really admired his maturity. It would not have been my reaction had I found myself in his shoes.

In English class one day the term 'castrati' emerged in our study of Shakespeare's play, Coriolanus. Fr. Ray Brady explained that it was a type of classical male singing voice, produced by castration of the singer before puberty. Like all good teachers he demonstrated what he was explaining with an impromptu high pitched note, to which Noel Barrett, in a dead pan voice asked, 'Father, how can you reach such high notes?'. Everyone, including Ray, burst out laughing.

We had Fr. Paddy Mallon for C.D. (Christian Doctrine/ Religion) class. He was an incredibly learned man, who was reputed to be able to speak nine or ten languages. He spoke in a very low and at times somewhat indistinct voice, and the unchristian joke among us was that he could speak ten languages but not English. He was a gentleman and in many ways was too nice to be a teacher. It was not actual bedlam in his class but at times we acted the eejit. We had a number of elastic bands, and when he was writing on the board, we would try to hit each other before he turned around. Unfortunately Dermot Prior tried to prevent my shot at another pupil, and as a result it was totally misdirected and hit the blackboard a resounding crash, right beside where Fr. Mallon was writing. The class fell silent, Fr. Mallon, uncharacteristically spun around to face us and asked 'Who did that?' I was mortified as I thought he was such a nice man, so I immediately owned up. I think he was surprised by the prompt admission and simply stated, 'Don't do it again'. He had a droll sense of humour which in many ways I loved. He gave us an essay once, 'Is Christianity worth living?'. To set the context he related to us the story concerning one hundred Roman soldiers who refused to give up their Christian faith and were forced to stand barefooted on a frozen lake until they recanted. After a number of hours one soldier gave up his religion. Fr. Mallon's comment: 'He got cold feet', to which we gave a universal groan. Another famous one was about the thief who was always stealing from his neighbour. The neighbour heated the handle of a wrench in the fire for hours and left the implement on their dividing wall. True to form the thief lifted the wrench and was severely burned. Fr. Mallon's comment, 'He was caught red handed'. Another groan. On the few occasions when he was angry, he would point not one but two fingers, the index and little finger at you, while his intervening three fingers faced the ground and state: 'Either you go or I go, and I'm not going'.

In History class, Dan was hammering home to us the importance of 'The Dreikaiserbund' (League of the Three Emperors) and that its aim was to preserve the status quo. As usual he 'slagged' the suave John Rahill (Cavan town) with the quip, 'If Status Quo was the name of a band you'd know it Rahill'. We were ripping that John did not give the riposte that in fact it was the name of a famous band. Major opportunity missed.

In ways, Fr. Torlac O' Reilly reminds me of Dr. Emmett Brown, the genius and eccentric professor in the 1985 comic science-fiction film, 'Back to the Future'. Torlac was a genius and thought outside the box. He and Bill Henry (father of Liam in my class) scripted and produced what had become an annual pantomime in the town hall in Cavan. Some smart ass in our class remarked what was all the fuss about, that our Maths class was a pantomime every day of the week. On Tuesday night, 30 January, about one hundred of us were allowed walk out to the town hall for the production. Admission was 30p (£4 in today's terms), but we got concessionary rate at 10p (€1.30). It was called 'The Three Mugateers' and was hilarious[11]. At a time when special effects were a thing of the future, Torlac was amazing. There were some actors in black, with white skeletons painted on them in psychedelic luminous colours, the effect with UV lighting was that we 'saw' skeletons moving on the stage. I had attended a number of pantomimes in Cavan over the previous years as we used attend as a family before I came to St. Pat's. My mother was there that night with friends, Paddy and Rosaleen Joyce from Ballinamore. Dad was tired and did not come. Returning to the college was somewhat surreal. All of us pupils walked along a very quiet and deserted Farnham Street. It was a lovely crisp and clear moonlit night as we walked up the college avenue. It was almost exhilarating, with that extra sense of energy and wellbeing that we sometimes feel at night when our senses seem more alert. And yet I felt a little lonely. It was only when I was out of the college and out of routine that I realised what I was missing in some ways by being in boarding school. Our next break was not until St. Patrick's Day, almost another seven weeks. It was like coming back down to reality after the escapism of the pantomime and realising that I still had to be up at 7.10 the following morning.

A few days later I met a boarder in my own year on his way to see the president Terry. He explained to me that someone had gone into his room, taken his pillow case and 'shit in it', leaving it back in his room for him to find. He was going to report it to the president. I listened sympathetically, although at fifteen years of age and in a boys' boarding school, anything is a diversion and bodily functions tend to get a laugh rather than natural revulsion. I must admit I was intrigued as to how he would explain what actually happened to Terry. I stayed out of sight, just off the red tiled corridor as the pupil met the president who was walking on the corridor near the pros'(professors, what the teachers were called) refectory. The lad tried to tell the incident as clinically as possible but Terry did not get the import. Eventually in exasperation Terry said, 'Young man, spit it out, what was left in your pillowcase?' to which the pupil, probably equally frustrated at this juncture, stammered, 'Shit, father, shit'. I almost burst out laughing and raced off to tell my friends. Young lads can be very cruel and I was no exception.
Fr. Patrick Mc Niffe (no relation), former president of St. Pat's (1937-53) died on Saturday 3 February. He had been P.P. in Ballinamore since 1964. The college was sending pupils to form a guard of honour for his funeral, and we pupils from Ballinamore were chosen. The Mass was at 11.00 on Monday. We were to go there and back by minibus. We wanted to be able to spend some time in our homes and Dermot Prior suggested I approach Terry to 'humbly' ask could we just call up to our families for a very short (unspecified) time. Terry replied in his crisp and clear Fermanagh accent, that we were representing (which he repeated) the college and that it was not a 'social visit'. I could only concur with his conclusion and left with my tail between my legs. At least we had tried. About a dozen of us left on Monday morning, including Paddy Sexton, a Leaving Cert boarder from Killeshandra. Paddy obviously got a severe bout of homesickness as we passed through his home town and got out, checking what time we would be returning and asked the driver not to forget to pick him up. A few of the college priests also attended the Mass, including Fr. Fintan Mc Kiernan from Templeport. After Mass he suggested to a few of us that we could call up to our houses for an hour and a half. He would then collect and bring us back to the college. We were delighted and made an unexpected visit home. Dad and Mam were there and I wolfed down some food. Fintan called a while later and spoke briefly to my parents who knew him well. I remember getting a dozen stamps from Mam, carefully folding them and then stuffing them into my modern trousers, hipsters with very small pockets on the inside of the waist. Not a good idea. When I returned to the college the stamps had all stuck to each other and I could only salvage two of them.

In the second week of February there was an incredibly heavy and prolonged fall of snow[12]. It was that lovely soft, light snow that had no intention of disappearing overnight, so loved by young people with no responsibilities. We were in heaven. Most school buses could not run, so the vast majority of day-boys were not in. Some lads from Cavan town, like the soldier in Fr. Mallon's story, got cold feet and did not turn up either. A number of pupils from way out the country hitched and arrived to class only to be sent home at lunchtime. The authorities were afraid the day-boys would not be able to get home after 4 pm. As a result we had about three half-days, free from 1 pm. until study at 5.30. The dean, Fr. Brady, very sensibly worked out that we were going to have snowball fights irrespective of whether it was forbidden or not. As a result he stipulated that anyone enjoying the snow had to first wear football togs, socks and jersey over their ordinary clothes. A brilliant idea. The priests, usually walked up and down the front avenue after dinner. A number of fellows crept up, down the side avenues, and got behind the priests and started pelting them with snow. To be fair to 'the pros', who were out at that time, (most of whom were in their late twenties, early thirties), they retaliated and gave as good as they got. However they were soon seriously outnumbered as lads appeared from all sides. Naturally they started running for the front door and the safety of the 'old wing'. The pupils had anticipated this, and had left the door visibly open, as was normal. However just as the priests arrived, the door was unceremoniously shut in their faces and locked by a few strategically placed pupils inside who had been waiting. Meanwhile the hordes of ecstatic and almost frenzied pupils closed in for the kill. Unfortunately one pupil from Virginia opened the door and allowed the priests refuge.

Some lads procured plastic bags, used for artificial manure, from the farmyard. The very steep 'ramp' between the Inter pitch and the much lower Senior pitch, made a natural tobogganing slope. Of course fellows were not satisfied with simply sliding down the ramp. No, a few constructed a little bridge at the bottom from the perfect snow. As a result the lads coming down the steep incline, hit the bridge and then were airborne for a time before landing on the pitch. Another level to the fast developing sport was that the snow slope soon became a gauntlet, with numerous pupils vying with each other to inflict the maximum discomfort by throwing well-formed snowballs at the intrepid tobogganists. The Fourth Years and Fifth Years had a major snow fight, with one group on top of the snow-laden ambulatory roof and the other on the ground. Testosterone, perfectly malleable snow, over four hours of freedom, no class, less homework and almost two hundred fellows, made these few days idyllic. Ray Dunne's description of 'football socks and

togs dried stiff on radiators' was perfectly apt[13].
I missed the Fourth v Fifth year snowball fight as well as the ambush of the 'pros'. My next door neighbour from Ballinamore, Mrs. Josie Mc Govern, was in Lisdarn Hospital having given birth to a son, Frank, the previous Friday[14]. I got permission to visit her on the Wednesday afternoon of the 'snow week'. Walking through Cavan town was unreal and beautiful. There was that fantastic exhilaration felt when it has snowed, the air seems pure and fresh and our energy level seems unlimited. There was very little driven dirty snow. Far fewer vehicles were in Ireland at that time and many of those that were, did not venture out during those days. I distinctly remember walking in the middle of the street as I came into Main Street with Whelan's shop on the left and the Surgical Hospital on the right. I paid my mandatory visit to the chipper beside the relatively new Post Office building in the centre of the town. I then visited the Post Office to see if they would redeem my compacted and useless stamps. The assistant behind the counter was none other than the scribe from my days in Ballinamore who wrote, 'Class Two', on my stomach. We greeted each other with the somewhat awkward 'Oh', type salutation, which was an acknowledgement that we knew each other but were not friends. He was professional but pointed out I could not get an exchange, but to try steaming the glued stamps apart. As I left I remember thinking he does not even remember that he wrote on my stomach. I had a great chat with Mrs. Mc Govern and of course loved being treated like an adult, a trend that I would get used to very soon. I returned to the college that evening to detailed accounts of the snow fights I had unfortunately missed.
My younger brother Christopher was in Crumlin Children's Hospital since mid-January. He had a rare condition, galactosemia, which meant he could not break down lactose, found in milk and some other foods. Despite my mother's best efforts, this was not discovered until he was three months old and as a result had damaged his eyesight. He was having cataracts removed. My brother Micheál arrived to collect me one Sunday in February to go to Dublin to visit Christopher. Micheál had brought a suit for me. He had discarded it and I had brought it to a tailor, James Murphy in Ballinamore, to insert a different and darker material at the seams from the knee down. It made the trousers more flared and was very chic, at least in my eyes. An argument ensued in the car in front of the college, as I wanted to change into the 'new suit', but Micheál pointed out that the president Terry was walking with other priests on the front avenue and it was supposed to be Dad who was collecting me. I just grabbed the trousers and raced like hell up to my room, changed and reappeared, jumping into the car. Christopher was only

seven years old but was very much at home in Crumlin Hospital. It was funny to see the youngest act as host to his two much older brothers as he showed us his surroundings. The following Sunday Micheál and my sister Valerie, who had a weekend off from boarding school, collected me and we again visited Christopher. It was a new experience, the three siblings heading off to Dublin driven by Micheál. Valerie had brought lovely sandwiches and two flasks of soup. When we returned she insisted I bring what was left of the soup.

I didn't feel right that night, although I certainly enjoyed the soup. The next day I felt sick, but in fact it was homesickness. (I had only really experienced it once before in my life, for one day in the Loch an Iúir Gaeltacht in Donegal in the summer of 1970). After tea that evening I walked the graph, alone and in darkness to try to see what was wrong with me. I really did not know what was wrong, except that my stomach felt empty, but I did not feel sick. I was fine the next day.

On Thursday I got an unexpected visit from Micheál who was on his way home having collected Christopher from hospital. We sat in the car at the back of the Old Wing near the steps down to the study hall and talked briefly. Christopher looked small and vulnerable, with a blanked wrapped around him as he had just left the warm hospital and come out to a cold February day.

Unexpectedly I was to see them again the next day under very different circumstances.

For drying football socks
(courtesy of David Wilson)

Overflowing with cups: Corn na nÓg Champions 1972-73, holding the following cups: Hogan, Mc Rory, Rannafast and Mc Niffe cups

Back (L-R) Kevin Mc Donagh, Francis Maguire, Francis Mc Kiernan, Fr. Patrick Mallon, Paul Meyers, Padraic Martin, Paul Murphy, Seán Quigley, Declan Young, Ray Cullivan and Damien Mc Goldrick.

Front (L-R) Felim Costello, Dermot Flaherty, Denis Connerton, Gerry Strong, Paddy Mc Govern, Turlough Smith, Cyril O' Keeffe, Jim Reilly, Donal Donohoe and Jarlath Mc Dermott.

Chapter 6

Mid-Term Break

February - March 1973

'*Was the president not talking to you?*' my mother exclaimed on the phone, in answer as to how Dad was. *'No, about what?'* I replied somewhat perplexed. Mam explained that my brother Micheál was on his way up to the college to bring me home and that she had gotten permission from the president, Fr. Mc Manus, earlier that afternoon. It was Friday evening, 23 February 1973. For the previous few weeks Dad had been working away as usual as far as I knew. He had driven a number of times with Mam to Dublin to see Christopher in hospital. In the last ten days he had been sick and from Monday it had developed into pneumonia[1]. I had phoned nearly every day since that. Two days previously, I had talked to him and he seemed to be improving so I was not worried. However Mam now told me that he was not well and that my sister Valerie and I were coming home for the weekend. I left down the phone in shock, not knowing what to think. I ran to tell my best friend, Dermot Prior, who was sympathetic and very understanding. I told the dean and then packed my big, red suitcase, not sure should I bring books or not. I grabbed a few and also a book on Kevin O'Higgins, that Fr. Dan had given me to read. I never read it.

Seamus Heaney's beautiful and poignant poem, Mid Term Break is biographical[2]. Heaney recalls being brought home from boarding school in mid-term, because his four year old brother, Christopher, had been killed by a car. The poem evokes powerful emotions in me, and expresses very accurately my thoughts at that time. The title 'Mid Term Break', would have sounded alarm bells years ago, as we did not get mid-term breaks. Halloween break, yes, but no break between Christmas and St. Patrick's Day, no February break. Heaney starts with:

> I sat all morning in the college sick bay
> Counting bells knelling classes to a close.

I spent forty five very long minutes until 8.30 pm. waiting for Micheál to collect me. I hovered on the deserted top corridor in the New Wing, at the top of the stairwell, listening to all the lads racing around below. Then the bell for study rang, and for the first time since September I did not obey its command. An eerie silence followed. Fr. Dan Gallogly came across me, and good humouredly accused me of mitching study, (which he knew I wouldn't). When he realised the real reason he was very sympathetic. Being from

Ballinamore he knew my parents well and offered to pray for Dad. I was growing up by the minute. Mam was a nurse and this coupled with being a mother often left us children with the belief that she was over cautious regarding health. So I was hoping that things might not be as serious as she had sounded on the phone. However my hopes were soon dashed. Micheál arrived and I immediately asked how Dad was, to which he replied, 'He's not good'. I was in no doubt now but that Dad was very seriously sick. We drove home, already a new type of relationship developing, not much said, apart from establishing facts as to what exactly had recently happened. On approaching our house I was struck by there being lights on everywhere, and numerous cars outside. Unlike Heaney I did not meet 'my father crying', instead I met my mother who embraced me and was clearly much shaken and nothing needed to be said. There were neighbours and friends everywhere in the house, with women 'bessying' around with dishcloths, sandwiches and tea. When I came in, like Heaney:

> I was embarrassed
> By … men standing up to shake my hand.

I had celebrity status, often dreamed about but not in these circumstances. It was unreal, our house was public property, people coming, going and staying. Sometimes I could overhear people talking about me, again Heaney so accurately conveys the atmosphere with:

> Whispers informed strangers I was…
> Away at school.

Valerie overheard a close relative declare that she 'never knew orphans not to do well'. We felt offended by this, as Dad was not dead and we did not like being talked about as if he were.

I went in to see Dad who was conscious and I lied to him that we had a weekend off so as not to unduly worry him. It did strike me that he detested lies but I knew it was the best option. I kissed him as we always did, saying good night.

The next day continued much as the night before, except that we had a procession of callers, some to enquire how Dad was, and others to leave in food to help feed the callers. I vividly recall a neighbour Hugh Mc Tague calling and I explaining how serious the situation was. Many, like Michael Mc Glynn, called having enrolled Dad with the contemplative order of nuns in the convent in Drumbshanbo. One man, who lived nearby, owed over two pounds to us for an unpaid shop bill (our small grocery and light hardware shop had closed in 1960). He arrived on Saturday afternoon and insisted on paying it. Ominous. While Dad was very seriously ill, I did not expect him to die. I always prayed each day, and I prayed so fervently that afternoon, standing alone in the basement under the noise of feet and speech in the sitting room above. I beseeched heaven if ever anyone did. I promised not just the sun, moon and stars, but an entire galaxy of good intentions if Dad were to get better. I had heard about the upcoming Kilmore Diocesan pilgrimage to Lourdes and I promised God I would go if Dad got better. Dad, who was not keen on flying, had likewise promised in 1965 to go to Lourdes if Christopher, who was a very sick child, survived. Thank God Christopher survived and Dad kept his promise. That night Dad improved. The local doctor, Ned Farrelly had been calling with increased frequency the previous week or so. About midnight he was talking with Dad and Mam in the room and we four children, all went in. We all talked, including Dad who was sitting up and fully conscious and just seemed weak.

At Mass the next day, I was trying to avoid people who were asking how Dad was. Word had obviously spread all around Ballinamore. Leo Plunkett, who had gone with me from Ballinamore the previous September to Pat's raced over to enquire had we a week end off. Tommy (Spike) Mc Cormack, a very good Ballinamore forward, had broken his leg training at football in January. He worked for Leo's father and so Leo had been brought home a few weeks earlier to help and was going to return in September to repeat Fourth Year. I explained the situation to Leo.

Dad's seventy seven year old mother was still alive and she and Dad's brother, Thomas Patrick, and sister, Mary Brigid, who were each married locally, were there all day. At one stage during the day Dad turned to Grandma as we called her and said, 'Mother, this is no place for you'. We had two crises that Sunday. Mrs. Logan, a neighbour and owner of the supermarket where I worked, had just arrived with two roast chickens. At 3.15 the electric bell above Dad's bed (which he had installed himself in all our bedrooms when we moved into the new house a year earlier) alerted us that there was something wrong. We raced up, but after about twenty minutes Dad's laboured breathing subsided and we relaxed. Fr. Micheál had brought oxygen cylinders from Cavan Surgical Hospital that afternoon. Molly Dolan, a friend and nurse was there and she had offered to stay up and look after Dad that night.

There was another crisis before nine that night. Again we all raced up. Dad's brother and sister were there. Grandma, a lovely woman of incredible faith, with full belief and trust in 'God's will', sat in a chair at the side of Mam and Dad's bed and watched as the life drained out of her forty six year old son. Dad was lying on his side and all of us, Mam and we four children, Micheál, Valerie, Christopher and myself, were right beside him. We were holding him, touching him and saying the Rosary. Auntie Kathleen kept wiping Christopher's tears with a towel as he cried. He was only seven years old and was on his hands and knees, in his pyjamas and blue dressing gown, on the bed. In fact he had already gone to bed when Mam called him to come to Dad's bedside. We were accompanied in the Rosary by a room full of twenty or more people, my uncle Fr. Micheál Kelly, first cousin Willie Mc Niffe, uncle Thomas Kelly, neighbours and friends, Seddie Mc Govern, Josie Martin and Paddy Joyce.

The term 'slipped quietly away' probably best describes Dad's death. There was nothing laboured about it, no rasping of breath, no discomfort, just an almost imperceptible cessation of breathing. I looked at Mam and knew by her that Dad was dead. Dad died at 9.05. Her life was irrevocably changed.

In an era before mobile phones or indeed landlines in many cases, neighbours, relatives and friends quickly departed to tell families. As it was a Sunday night, a number of nieces and nephews were already on the road back to Dublin for work. When they reached their flats in Phibsboro and Ballsbridge they received the news that 'Uncle Willie had passed away'. Arrangements had to be made to return to Ballinamore. Our phone was used by close family to give the news that 'Willie Mc Niffe', or 'Willie Michael' as he was known by many, was dead. In the early 1970s, an undertaker, did not 'undertake' to do everything concerning a death as is common today. Instead Joe Smith, the funeral undertaker, was contacted and his task was principally concerned, with the coffin and a burial plot in Oughteragh, the local graveyard. There was no local radio so the all-important death notice for the next morning's Irish Independent was a priority. We had to arrange that by going to Murphy's, a local newsagent with the details. Mam and one or two other ladies 'laid out' Dad. Mam had performed this good deed many times before, for neighbours, friends and close family, but it must have been heart rending for her to wash and dress Dad for his final journey. At that time a dead person was not dressed in their normal clothes and laid in a coffin, but dressed in a 'habit', usually either white or brown (Dad's was white) and laid out in a bed. Later that night, to quote Heaney again:

> '... I went up into the room...
> And candles soothed the bedside. I saw him
> ....paler now'.

A little paler perhaps, but Dad actually looked very well. He did not have cancer, it was his heart that gave up. He had only been very seriously sick for a short time, so looked just to be asleep. It had not been a fight. He was forty six, with not a grey hair on his head. Mam actually discussed with us, getting someone in Kieran's chemist to take a good photo of Dad, but we decided against it. A pity! We did however take a lock of his hair, which each of us has kept. A bedside vigil was maintained from that moment until Dad's body left the house the following evening. I went out the front door about midnight to deposit something in the rubbish bin and met three neighbours, Gerry Mahon, Paddy Holland and Aidan Mc Goldrick, who shook my hand and told me that 'they were sorry for my trouble', the hackneyed but genuinely felt form of words used universally to sympathise. It was a real moment of insight for me as I realised Dad was indeed dead, and I was now being treated like an adult by grown men who had previously seen me at most as 'young Mc Niffe'.

Micheál, Michael Mc Glynn who was a very good friend of Dad, and John Milton, stayed up with Dad's body that Sunday night. Mam and the rest of us were persuaded to try to get a good night's sleep. I awoke to a very active but quiet house. Women I knew like Eileen Prior and Mary Holland, but had never seen before in our home, were in our kitchen and offering to make breakfast for me. People were already calling to sympathise. They went up the stairs to Mam and Dad's room where Dad lay. Grandma was beside the bed as was Mam for much of the day. Micheál, Valerie and I were up and down continually. Christopher was only seven at the time and his slightly older cousin, Michael Kelly, introduced him to his first and last attempt at smoking on this day. (Christopher related this to us years later). My grandfather's wake (Dad's father) in 1965 in the countryside, was a real old fashioned Irish one, in the sense that there were cartons of cigarettes available and plenty of drink for sympathisers. In addition there was a sit down meal for many, many people. We lived in the town and this was a little over seven years later, so while there were cigarettes available, there was little in the way of drink. Neighbouring women and relatives made tea and sandwiches all day long for the ever increasing stream of visitors. Neighbours brought sandwiches, cakes and home baking. It is a fairly universal custom, recalled in that brilliant novel, '*To Kill a Mockingbird*', which states

'Neighbours bring food with death, flowers with sickness and little things in between'[3].

The grave was dug by my father's first cousin, Thomas Joseph Mc Niffe and cousin Seán Mc Niffe and Micheál Gilheaney. As was customary there was no mechanical digger, no professional diggers, just friends and relatives who regarded it as an honour, tough and all as it was. Sandwiches and tea were ferried out to 'the men in the graveyard', digging deep in the unforgiving, wet, dauby soil of Leitrim, on a cold February day.

'The Removal', was that evening, arriving at 6.00 in our local Ballinamore St. Patrick's Church. By 5.00 the house was packed and my uncle, Fr. Micheál led the prayers. The rosary was said, with each of us saying a decade. Christopher was well used to saying the rosary but the occasion may have distracted him, and Micheál had to quietly remind him to say the 'glory be to the Father', when he was on his thirteenth Hail Mary. The room was cleared and the reality began to hit home. I was privileged to help Micheál and the undertaker to lift Dad out from the bed and turn him slightly so as to lay him in his bright coloured coffin. It struck me at how relatively light he seemed. It was a very intimate, emotional and special few minutes as we fixed Dad in his final bed. I always was very childish in wanting either to be first or last in everything, so long as it carried boasting rights. I don't know was that the reason for my next surreptitious action, or was it a memory to treasure for ever, but I quietly stroked Dad's hair just as the lid was being lowered, the last to touch him in this life. We carried him down the stairs and were met by an incredibly large crowd outside. It was a dry evening and the coffin was carried the entire way to the Church, with relays of men taking turns. Micheál and I helped shoulder it as we left our house at the start of that journey. We again took over with two other men as we approached the Church. It was, and has remained, the proudest moment of my life, surpassed only by the birth of my children. It was bright when we entered the Church at 6.00 and dark when we exited at 6.30. (All my life I know that by the end of February it gets dark around 6.20). People didn't come up in the Church and sympathise as they do nowadays. Outside I was surprised and pleased to meet three of my teachers from St. Pat's, Fr.Dan Gallogly, Fr. Seán Brady and Fr. John Murphy.

When we returned to the house, it was awful. Dad's absence was like a terrible presence. Somehow while Dad was there, even if he were dead, it was not so final. Now it was final, we were home without him and he would never again be in our lovely new house, of which he was so proud. Relatives and some neighbours were there already. Mam sat on the sofa and cried. The image will forever remain in my mind. A little while later the doorbell rang and I went out to see Dermot Prior, Leo Plunkett and Peter Mc Caffrey. Dermot and Peter talked excitedly about how they managed to get home. I could just imagine how they were nervous as to what to say and took refuge in the details of getting permission. I did appreciate them personally calling to see me, on what must have been a fairly daunting visit from their point of view. However it struck me that we were talking about everything but what really mattered.

Mass the next day was at 11.00 said by my uncle Fr. Micheál. I was doing one reading and Valerie another. Before Mass, I met Fr. Mallon from St. Pat's in the sacristy, who sympathised with me and conveyed apologies from the president, Fr. Mc Manus. I was somewhat taken aback that the president felt it necessary to send his apologies. The Church was thronged. At that time many people attended the funeral Mass, as Ireland was a rural society, with many women not working outside the home and people more free to take time off. Offerings were part of a funeral Mass. People put money in an envelope with their name and the amount on the cover. After Mass the priest paused, while close relatives of the deceased stood behind a table and mourners filed up and deposited their offerings. There were no priests' dues, so this was the main source of income for the clergy. A person's status in the local community was determined by how much the offerings amounted to. It was a major source of conversation. 'What was the offerings?' was a common question asked by those who didn't get to the funeral Mass. People who could not attend sent their offerings with someone else. The usual was 15 pence (decimalisation currency) (€2.05 in today's terms). A few gave just 5p (€0.68). Close friends might give 25p (€3.30) while relatives gave 50p (€6.60) and siblings etc. gave one pound (€13.20). The family of the deceased received the empty envelopes and knew what people gave. Until a few years before Dad's death, the priest in each parish actually read out what each person contributed, to low murmurs of disapproval if it was below the expected contribution. He also read out the total amount contributed, the litmus test of one's popularity. By 1973 both of these practices had been discontinued. I remember serving Mass for an old woman who had no family and the total offerings had amounted to £5 (€ 66 in today's terms). The undertaker informed us later that afternoon that Dad's offerings amounted to £196, (€ 2,713), a colossal amount. In fact that evening more offerings were dropped into the house for us to give to the priest. In effect it passed the two hundred pounds mark, a source of great pride to me. Not a very Christian response perhaps, but it lessened the pain to think that Dad was very well known and very well liked, which he was. It was only years later that I realised that Dad' death cast a dark cloud over the town at the time. He was very young, had a young family, and was known by everyone and universally liked.

When we emerged from the Church we were greeted by a guard of honour, not very usual at that time to my knowledge. St. Pat's had class mates of mine there, which was very nice, but what really impressed me was that St. Felim's College, the school I had 'abandoned' the previous September, also had a guard of honour made up with my former classmates. I was surprised and very pleased. Some girls from Valerie's school, Ard Lughaidh in Bundoran were also there as part of the guard of honour.

The funeral cortege drove down Main Street and up our own Church Street, pausing briefly at both our old and new house as a mark of respect, then on out the mile to the cemetery in Oughteragh. As we were lifting Dad's coffin from the hearse on to our shoulders, the undertaker Joe Smith, shouts, 'easy, easy now, he's only a young lad', in reference to me. Micheál was five years older than I was, and while we got on well we were not into showing affection or emotion. However I remember Micheál slightly squeezing my shoulder, and I returned the affirmation, as we linked arms carrying our father the thirty yards to his grave. Dad's was laid beside Elizabeth, his baby daughter who had died nine years earlier, when only one week old. There was no effort to soften the reality of death as happens nowadays. The inside walls of the grave were just earth, not lined with greenery, there was no cloth put on top of the coffin to lessen the harsh sound of the first clods as they struck the timber. The mourners waited while the grave diggers filled in the grave, no artificial verdant cover to protect the family from the harsh reality of what was happening. As we drove away from the graveyard, Mam remarked that she could be like Mrs. Reynolds, waiting forty years to join her husband in death. Mary Reynolds, T.D. for Leitrim from 1931-61 (except 1933-7) had just died a short time before Dad and was buried nearby. Mary's husband, Paddy, a T.D. was shot dead while out canvassing in 1931, and his wife was a widow for forty two years[4]. We returned to a dinner cooked by neighbours in our own house, with Dad's immediate family there. The custom of an extended family, neighbours and friends going to a local hotel after a funeral had not commenced at this time.

The minute details of those few days, replayed themselves over and over in my mind for weeks, months and indeed years to come. The presence and support of, as well as sympathy from, a local community has an enormous effect in lessening, or at least softening, the loss of a loved one. I had a different appreciation of every funeral I attended after Dad's.

There was a general election the next day, 28 February 1973. Taoiseach Jack Lynch, had gone to the country although his Fianna Fail Government had eighteen months to run. The Troubles in the North, including the sacking of two Ministers and the resignation of another over the Arms Crisis, coupled with the deteriorating economic situation, set the context for the contest. Our family were quietly Fine Gael, supporters of Pat Joe Reynolds (Mary Reynold's son), but we were never to tell anyone our allegiance. My parents felt it was personal information, like your mother's age, known but not to be disclosed. Mam and Dad always brought some of us to vote with them. I remember accompanying them into the actual pooling booth for every election from the general election of 1965. We all accompanied Mam to vote that day and afterwards drove up to visit Dad's grave.

I returned to St. Pat's the following Monday evening. While I was away, Fr. Terry Mc Manus had been moved as parish priest to my home town Ballinamore, and Fr. Paddy Mallon was our new college president. Terry was great for dramatic entrances to the study hall to make some important announcement to the assembled boarders. We loved anything that broke the monotony of evening study. It seems that Terry announced to the boarders a few days before I returned that he was leaving and being replaced by Fr. Mallon. The lads burst into applause, as that was how many of Terry's announcements were greeted. He took no offence, seeing it as appreciation of his service to the college. However as he was leaving the study hall, one pupil, from the Ballinagh direction, 'booed', which led to an investigation as to who was the culprit.

Terry had taught in the college from 1939 until he was made president in 1967. He was a very pious, devout and in many ways an innocent man. When we were pupils, there was a story going the rounds regarding Terry and a prank played by another priest, Torlac O' Reilly. It may have been apocryphal but as young lads we never let truth get in the way of a good story. Terry was almost obsessed with the threat of Communist Russia and its anti-religion philosophy. The Cold War was at its height and tension was palpable during the Hungarian uprising of 1956. Torlac rigged up Terry's radio which he religiously turned on every morning to hear the news. What Terry heard was a fabricated news informing listeners that the Russians had invaded Western Europe and were coming towards England. Terry ran to the Church and implored God's help in a very public and loud plea. For someone who taught boys for over thirty years Terry was sometimes easily fooled. On one occasion he raced after two boys whom he saw misbehaving. One took refuge in the Church, followed by Terry, who found a pious pupil standing at the seventh Station of the Cross. Terry withdrew, assuming he had mistook the flight path of the miscreant. In fact he had the culprit, who astutely positioned himself half way through the Stations, knowing Terry would only suspect someone at the First Station[5].

Preparations for the annual school musical, were in full swing when I returned. Fr.Ray Brady was producer, Fr. Gerry Kearns musical director and set design, Frances Sullivan choreographer, Ray Dunne stage manager and lighting, Patsy Lee set design, Fr. Paddy Brady set construction, and Fr. Leo O' Reilly, lighting. I could not sing, but had auditioned singing the National Anthem in as low a voice as I could muster and got in. Frances O' Sullivan had eight of us as dancers, as well as being in the general cast. While I was away another lad had taken my place, but upon my return I was absorbed back into the dance group that now had nine of us. The atmosphere was fantastic leading up to the week of the musical. It was mainly lads from non-exam classes, boarders and day-boys who were involved, in total numbering over seventy of a cast[6]. For the evenings immediately preceding the show, many of us were out in the hall awaiting our call to go on stage. When I returned that Monday evening I went to the practise in the assembly hall. It was somewhat awkward as lads at that time were not good at showing emotion. I was trying to act as if all was normal. In order to cover up my embarrassment I took a good few sips from Ms. O'Sullivan's Cavan Cola mineral sitting on top of the piano. When she discovered someone had been drinking it, I volunteered to get her a new one, without explaining that I was the culprit. I duly got Fran Treanor, shop boy, out of study as 'Ms. O'Sullivan wanted a mineral'. I paid.

Some lads did actually sympathise with me, others didn't know what to say, but most were quiet and considerate around me for the first day or two. One lad from Cavan town had thoughtfully gotten a Mass card for Dad which he gave me as he sympathised. One friend talked to me about Dad's death, and referred to the fact that his father had insisted on the radio (no TV in house) remaining silent for one month, after their grandfather died. I agreed it didn't make sense, assuming he thought it was ludicrous. Instead he replied that a fortnight would be sufficient in his eyes. There was no ban on listening to radio or watching television at home since Dad's death, it was just we had very little interest in doing so.

Dad's death was not nearly as real to me in St. Pat's, as it would have been had I been living at home and noticing his absence daily. I still woke up happy. For a few seconds I would forget what had happened, followed very soon by a sense of something being wrong and then the realisation that Dad had died. It was the same for weeks. At that time, people were less critical of life and what it meted out to them. We didn't feel we were owed a good time and that God was to blame if it didn't happen that way. I was lucky, I did not feel angry. I did not criticise God, I was obviously heartbroken, shocked and sad but not angry. I felt closer to God and now felt I had an advocate in heaven, Dad, who would always be there for me. I suppose in ways it made my religion very personal. Of course I did not analyse this at the time but I did pray continually to Dad. However this did not answer the incredible emptiness in my stomach that came and went for months. At times when I was totally immersed in some activity in the college I used feel guilty, echoing Worthsworth's lines in reference to his recently deceased daughter Catherine aged four:

But how could I forget thee?
... As to be blind to my most grievous loss[7].

On a number of nights I woke up around 3 am., upset. I called in next door to Dermot Prior who never complained, just listened for over an hour and added a few words of wisdom. His roommate Michael Martin (Ballyjamesduff) had a much interrupted nights' sleep on those occasions. I phoned Mam every evening, a habit that continued until I finished the Leaving Cert the following year.

The major impact Dad's death had on me was that I grew up almost overnight. I was fairly mature in some ways to begin with, in the sense that our parents always told us what was going on, and there were no secrets. In fact my Dad, who left school at fourteen and came from a small farm with a country shop, did not have us believe in the man from the North Pole. He saw it as somewhat dishonest. Of course we were severely warned not to ruin it on any child. We all spoke at the kitchen table, irrespective of age, and there was no hierarchy as existed in most of my friend's families growing up in Ballinamore. Dad and Mam's belief in honesty was incredible in retrospect. There was a red circular tin (originally Cow and Gate baby food) that acted as a money box in the kitchen. When we wanted money we just went and got it. I definitely abused the trust while I was in primary school as I usually waited until Mam was not looking, and I went and got lots of money for chocolate at lunch time. The trust paid off however. As I started working in Logan's shop I got much more responsible with money, (my own and my parents) and had saved a considerable sum already. Dad had instilled in us that a man was expected to look after his sister or mother. As I result I felt it incumbent on me to look after Mam, or at least lessen her worries. In effect I took full control of my own life. It was not totally altruistic, as I had never liked been a child, could not wait to grow up, and hated being told what to do. This way I was my own boss and the collateral benefit was that Mam did not have to worry about me.

'Calamity Jane' was the fourth annual musical in the college in recent years. Matt Cahill (Dublin) played Wild Bill Hickok and Jim Gallagher (Drumkeerin) played Henry Miller. Jackie Mc Laughlin (Butlersbridge) did a fantastic impersonation of Frances Fryer. The Celt afforded us advance publicity with an accompanying photo of rehearsals[8]. The class hall nearest the back door to the stage became the 'green room', and was a hive of activity, with Betty Hickey, Bill Henry and Fr. Pete Casey doing the make up on every member of the cast. The all-pervasive smell of Pond's cream has remained with me always. It had to be explained to us that if we did not wear foundation cream we would have great difficulty in removing our make-up. We were receiving a well-rounded education. It was an all-male cast. Consequently it was somewhat surreal to meet other pupils, resplendent in flowing gowns and made up as cowgirls, covered in well applied rouge on the corridor between the stage door and the study hall. It was crucial that the beautiful Soprano voice of Peter O'Sullivan (Dublin), playing the female and central role as Calamity, did 'not break' before the show, as had happened the lead singer in a previous musical. His voice held and the show was not only a great success, with large attendances on four nights, but what it gave, even those of us in minor roles, was experience and memories for life. When I now hear the song, 'Take Me Back to the Black Hills', I am transposed immediately to the low blue atmospheric lighting of the assembly hall stage, the hills of Dakota painted on the backdrop, we the cast walking in quiet procession off the stage, down the centre aisle of a darkened hall, each carrying a candle singing the haunting melody of:

> Lost my heart in the Black Hills
> The Black Hills of Dakota
> Where the pines are so high
> That they reach the sky above.

It was magic. On a more prosaic level, we the dancers had various routines, such as accompanying Calamity into town on the stagecoach. We, in effect, were the horses! We had a few changes of costume, which had been hired out for the show. One such outfit consisted of bright red velvety-type trousers, held up by straps that went over the cowboy shirt and over the shoulders to be fastened at the back. The 'fork' at the front was not shy, it consisted of about six large buttons that were fastened, with no covering flap as was normal in gents' trousers at the time. When we were finished that particular dance one night, some of the lads noticed that Owen Martin (Templeport) had forgotten to close his buttons, much to the immense merriment of the rest of us.

The show finished on Thursday night, 15 March. The college was closed the next day for St. Patrick's weekend. Nobody was allowed home until Friday morning, as otherwise there would have been a mass exodus on Thursday afternoon, and that would have been unfair to the cast who would in effect be penalised for their involvement. All of my family were at this final night's show and I had asked the president, Fr. Mallon for special permission to go home with them directly after the show. He readily acquiesced and I kept news of the concession as quiet as I could.

I was not averse to using natural sympathy for me because of Dad's death to me own advantage. Fr. Larry Kearney, my Physics and Chemistry teacher who knew Dad, spoke of his shock and surprise to hear of Dad's untimely death. I used the occasion to ask him could I give up Physics and Chemistry as I was totally lost and wanted to concentrate on just six Leaving Cert subjects. He had no objections, so long as I got the president's approval. I explained the situation to Fr. Mallon who agreed but shrewdly remembered that I had done Commerce for my Inter Cert. He suggested that he would check the timetable and see if I could join a Fourth Year class that was doing business at the same time. I demurred and left. At that time although I didn't know the Jesuit maxim, 'It is easier to get forgiveness afterwards than permission beforehand', I went ahead and abandoned the Physics and Chemistry class. It was the best move I made in second level school. I now had five free classes per week. Anyone who had a free class was expected to go to the study hall and work. However it was impossible to get any study done, as there was no supervision and everyone talked. Instead I knew that the recep. room near the front door in the Old Wing was usually free and I commandeered it for each of my free classes. I had to unobtrusively get to and from it, and hope I was not found there as I would ironically be sent 'to study', in the study hall. I lived on my nerves for the first few weeks but then relaxed. I devoted these free classes to learning the English translation of all 901 lines of Virgil's Aeneid, worth almost 25% of the marks for Latin in the Leaving Cert. Before Dad's death, I had hoped to get a university grant by achieving four honours. That would save my parents the expense, although I was not sure if I would qualify under the means test. Now I would certainly qualify but I had to get the four honours. There was now no safety net, as Mam could certainly not fund my further education. Her widow's pension was approximately eleven pounds per week, considerably less than Dad's pay of twenty eight pounds per week. Four honours or repeat the year added some extra pressure, but it was totally self-imposed and I did not see it as a terrible burden.

Once home for the St. Patrick's Day break, my new found maturity was soon seen to be sown on stony ground. While I had only been back in St. Pat's for ten days since Dad's death, I had been back in routine, away from home, and it seemed much longer to me since Dad had died. Mam was under a tsunami of paper work and forms, as not only had she to contend with the normal bureaucracy that attends the death of a spouse, but had also to replace Dad as one of the three who owned the garage, that had only recently been set up. Micheál was still salesman in it. Not only was there the usual high with coming home, but I was also elated after the musical. However I was beginning to realise the reality of life for Mam, but obviously not soon enough. I met a few friends who intended going to a local dance in a few days' time. I nonchalantly mentioned to Mam in my new found self-confident mature voice that, 'I might go to the dance'. I was riveted by Mam's when she replied, 'Dad is not three week's dead', not in anger, but in disbelief and sadness. I felt so sorry and so selfish.

I returned to St. Pat's the following Tuesday. The musical and St. Patrick's Day break were now over. Dad's death was gradually sinking in more. A harsh return to boarding life, although it was to be softened by a trip to Lourdes and my first kiss.

Author's parents, Willie and Elizabeth Mc Niffe, 1970

Playing: Cast of Calamity Jane 1973

No play-acting, this is serious: Rehearsals for Calamity Jane 1973

(L-R) Fr. Ray Brady (producer), Seamus O'Callaghan, Seamus Mc Enroe, Peter O'Sullivan, Eamon O' Gorman, Con Linehan, Frank Fitzpatrick, Liam Bouchier, Gerry Skelly and at the back, Ciarán Brady.

In the Wings: Calamity Jane 1973
Peter O'Sullivan and Matt Cahill, with Michael Martin (back-stage team) in the wings

Chapter 7

First Kiss

April - May 1973

'*He didn't come down the drainpipe, did he?*' shouted one pupil while another retorted, '*Well you tell me then how else did he get into the chapel unseen?*' The pupil in question was a seemingly quiet Second Year from Crosserlough, with the nickname 'Spear'[1]. He had an uncanny ability to circumvent any of the college rules that he wanted to, without apparently being caught. The recent episode concerned being on time for morning Mass. The dean noticed his absence, and went to check his room. There were two iron gates, one on each stairs that led to the bedrooms in the Old Wing. Occasionally these were locked during the day to prevent any pilfering from pupils' rooms. That morning the dean locked these, to prevent any stragglers getting to the chapel unnoticed, as they would now be forced to come down the president's forbidden stairs. The dean went up the president's stairs, but found no 'Spear', who meanwhile had appeared somewhat miraculously in the chapel, and was innocently sitting in his seat when the dean returned. We all knew who the dean had been looking for, and we were gleeful that Spear had avoided capture. We felt like cheering but dare not. He quietly claimed that he had climbed down the drainpipe that ended beside the outside door at the chapel. Many of us checked the possibility of such an explanation and it was possible, the drainpipe was very sturdy and ran from the upstairs window. Spear stuck to his story.

On another occasion Spear was out on the middle corridor in the Old Wing, away from his own room, after lights out. The dean heard the steps and shone his flashlight, whose beam did not quite reach the elusive pimpernel. Spear stopped, quickly removed his shoes, opened the door of a room, threw his shoes in, told them to say nothing, banged the door closed and continued to run, quietly now, in his stocking feet. The dean went to the room at which the footsteps stopped, interviewed the two official occupants and having checked under the bed, found nothing amiss. Another one up for Spear, who naturally went on to become a detective in the Garda Síochána. Despite Spear's achievements, the dean was not at all easy to outwit. Earlier in the year a stomach bug had spread very rapidly, with over fifty lads in bed. Their meals had to be carried up from the kitchen. After one such day, the dean announced that as they had a stomach ailment, their recovery would be better aided with just bread and tea for meals. He was proven correct, as an almost

miraculous recovery took place, with over forty lads cured overnight.
Shortly after I returned from the St. Patrick's Day break, Mam, Micheál and Christopher unexpectedly visited me at recreation time one afternoon. I was togged out on Inter pitch playing a friendly game of Gaelic that we had organised among ourselves. When I saw the car nearby, I excused myself and met them. Mam insisted I finish the game as there was not much time left. After missing five minutes I went to resume, when I was shouted at by one of the players, 'you can't play as someone else joined while you were away and your place is gone'. I was a bit taken aback, but that was more than compensated for by the fact that Christopher was able to recognise me at a distance for the first time in his life, the result of his recent eye surgery. In the course of conversation, Micheál alluded to 'The Claudia'. I didn't know what he was talking about. The Claudia was a vessel loaded with weapons for the I.R.A. from General Gaddafi's Libya that was captured by the Irish Naval Service on 28 March 1973. It was major national news at the time. In boarding school we lived in a news vacuum, we did not see newspapers, we did not hear news on radio or see it on television. To be fair, about a decade earlier the president, Fr. Bob Mc Cabe, had introduced a newspaper for pupils to read. He heralded its advent with a short speech on the value of current affairs and led one class down to the basement, to see where it was kept. And there it was 'gone'. End of experiment[2].
I went home for Dad's month's mind Mass on Friday 30 March. Fr. Micheál collected me on his way from Bailieboro. I stayed at home for the weekend, ate good food, got good sleep and still did all my homework. Every visit to Ballinamore brought Dad's death home more to me.
At a national and indeed local level many changes were happening in education. The distinction between Secondary Schools, such as St. Pat's providing an academic education and the Vocational schools providing a much more technical and practical education, was beginning to change. Cavan Vocational School already provided the Leaving Certificate cycle. It now had a new state-of-the-art school, just completed on land previously owned by and adjacent to St.Pat's. It was ready to open the following September[3]. Virginia Vocational school was permitted by the Department of Education to provide the Leaving Cert cycle, albeit only on a temporary basis, until a proposed Community School for Ballyjamesduff- Virginia was to be established[4].
The subject Irish had to be passed to obtain the Leaving Cert. James Mc Cann, a very hardworking Leaving Cert pupil from Blacklion, had received most of his primary education in England, before coming to St. Pat's and hence had no proficiency in Irish. Yet he had to pass it in the Leaving Cert.

He was very bright and poised to get honours in everything, but was under pressure to get a pass in Irish. The Minister for Education in the new Fine Gael-Labour Government, Richard Burke, announced that it was no longer compulsory to pass Irish to pass either the Inter or Leaving Cert. In addition, an honour in Leaving Cert Irish now counted as two of the requisite four honours for a student grant for third level[5]. It was still compulsory to study however. The latter stipulation did not worry the usually quiet James who, upon hearing the news, went screaming down the green-tiled corridor with delight. His teacher Fr. Dan was less happy as he had spent years ensuring that James would pass Irish, whereas now James did not care.

The renowned Cavan County footballer and member of the St.Pat's teaching staff, Jim Mc Donnell, was appointed the first Vice Principal of the college in late March. An advertisement appeared in the Celt in April and again in May, for enrolment of new students for the coming September for St.Pat's. Woodwork and Music were included in the subjects offered, with 'tuition ...also available in Italian, German and Greek'[6]. At the same time, Loreto College's advertisement for enrolment included the following statement:

> Rumours to the effect that this college will shortly cater for boarders only or that the day school will be fee paying are unfounded.
> No vacancies in the Boarding school[7].

The De Salle Brothers, who had run the boys primary school in Cavan town from 1943, announced in April, that due to falling numbers in vocations, they were forced to withdraw from St. Felim's school[8].

Top of the Pops continued to attract its faithful followers to the assembly hall each Thursday night, with such hits as Get Down (Gilbert O'Sullivan), (accompanied by Pans People and numerous dogs on stage), Cum on Feel the Noize (Slade), Killing me Softly with his Song (Roberta Flack), and See my Baby Jive (Wizzard). The Eurovision Song Contest was a major event at this time and the entire school was allowed to watch the final on Saturday evening 7 April. The majority of pupils packed into the hall. Subsequently it was discovered that the college shop had been raided while the song contest was on. There was no money in it, but sweets and chocolates were taken. A subsequent inquiry saw two pupils brought before the Council about ten days later. The Council was a disciplinary body composed we assumed of the president and some of the priests. What had happened was innocent enough in its origins. Acting the eejit the two lads managed to kick/push/shove the half door of the shop open. Seeing their opportunity they got pillowcases, packed them with goodies and hid them in the woods. One of the fellows was well-connected and we saw a close family member arrive, we assumed to see the president. In any event the two pupils were expelled. We were shocked. We knew the theft was wrong, but these were not bad lads, in fact they were very likeable lads who had never done anybody any harm. Secretly I was impressed that what I assumed was natural intercession by a well-connected family member did not influence the Council's decision. However we all felt awful that night. The lads sat in study as they were not being collected until the next day. I was in a moral quandary. One of them had a fantastic atlas that he won as a prize the previous year. I used get the loan of it each evening at some time during study to do my geography. On asking him would he sell, he very generously offered it for nothing, (not untypical of him). I refused but offered 60p (€8.20 in today's terms) which he accepted. I felt uncomfortable, but not uncomfortable enough not to buy it. The next morning, word spread that this lad had run away. The college authorities were naturally worried. That evening he was located, none the worse for it, in a nearby field. His close friend Gerry Mc Govern who roomed with me was quite upset. The mother of the other expelled lad, who was only in her mid fifties, died a few months later from cancer.

We got Easter holidays on Spy Wednesday. I did not work in Logan's shop as I valued my free time from boarding school. I had decided to go on the Lourdes pilgrimage, which was to take place in early May. As I would be missing almost a week of school, I brought home books with me, and while I did not kill myself studying, I did a reasonable amount. Fr. Dan had devised a brilliant method of getting us to revise for summer and Christmas exams. He would give us the titles of eight essay type History questions a few weeks before the exam. We prepared them, knowing that four of these would be on the paper, with no choice. With some prompting from Dermot Prior, I quietly asked Dan would he give me the questions over the Easter holidays so I could start work on them. Dan dropped a brown envelope with the questions, in my letter box at the start of the holidays, with Mr. Liam Mc Niffe, Jnr. B.A., on the front. I was chuffed. Of course I felt obliged to share the advance information with Dermot, which I duly did.

Mam was very busy with trying to get Dad's affairs and matters regarding her widow's pension in order. I remember the local Social Welfare Officer, Frank Mc Govern being in our house on numerous occasions with forms for Mam. I celebrated my sixteenth birthday while I was at home. Birthdays had always been special in our house, not a universal custom in every house at that time. We always had a simple party with Dad and Mam and all of us there, with a cake and candles and a present. Mine was the first birthday since Dad's death, and its celebration only accentuated Dad's absence. To add to

the poignancy, my present, very fashionable at the time, a flowery paisley shirt with matching tie, had been bought by Mam in February when she and Dad were up in Dublin seeing Christopher. It was Dad's last present to me.
Boarders usually went back the night before class commenced. However on this occasion we were not due back until 11.00 on Tuesday morning after the Easter break. Fr. Dan Gallogly and his green Volkswagen kindly carried a number of us Ballinamore lads back that morning. What seemed an extra night at home actually left me with an awful feeling. We arrived to the college, raced up to our rooms, flung the cases in and down to the study hall to get our books and were in class at 11.15. A cold shower-type return to boarding life.
During History class the following morning, Dermot nudged me and whispered, 'Oh my God'. I had quietly returned the sheet with the exam questions to Dan the previous evening. He was now calling out the questions for the class to write down. Unfortunately he was using the sheet he had given me, which included a short note, 'Dear Liam, Enclosed...', which was very visible to Dermot and to me. Fortunately everyone was so busy jotting down the all-important questions, nobody noticed the incriminating evidence. Being regarded as a 'suck', (preferential treatment) was inexcusable.
With two hundred teenage lads in close proximity, it was inevitable that scuffles would break out. Frequently they were just friendly wrestling matches that were over as soon as they started. Occasionally they were a bit more serious, but left to themselves, the two pupils would stop before it got really serious. The problem was that sometimes they were not left to themselves. Boredom and a base instinct for bloody entertainment, meant that two lads who were squaring up to each other, frequently found themselves surrounded by up to fifty fellows all screaming,' row, row, row', thereby attracting more and more to the anticipated row. If it became really serious, it was re-scheduled for the back alley during some suitable recreation time. I remember one such fight that year. Word spread like wildfire that a big Second Year was going to fight a Fourth Year at the back alley immediately after study at 7.00 pm. About forty of us raced up to the venue. It didn't last long, the Second Year was winning when it was stopped by friends of the Fourth Year. I doubt if the fight would have been stopped if the Fourth Year had been winning. We all raced back to the refectory for tea, about ten minutes late but there was no trouble.
A drama group came to put on a production of Macbeth in the assembly hall. It was on the course for the Fifth Years, but Fr. Ray strongly advised us to attend. I have since seen at least ten productions of 'The Play', including one in Stratford itself, and another in Christ's Church in Dublin. However I have

never witnessed as good a portrayal of the famous witches as on that bare stage in St. Pat's. With a white backdrop, the play opened with an apparently empty stage. Then these three evil fiends began to emerge as if from the ground at the back of the stage. In fact they had a white sheet that blended in perfectly with the backdrop. As they lowered the sheet, it appeared as if they were miraculously appearing from out of nowhere. It was magical.

The Leaving Cert was fast approaching for the pupils a year ahead of us. It was obvious it was serious business. The top class included a quiet, hardworking fellow Elio Malocco from Dundalk. (Later he was to reach national headlines as the high flying solicitor, married into the De Valera family, who was jailed for fraud. He subsequently became a film maker). John O'Reilly, a quiet, studious lad from Ballyconnell was a mad Leeds United supporter. The F.A. Cup final was contested between Leeds, the previous season's winners and one of the dominant teams in English football at the time, and Sunderland, then playing in the Second Division. It was a David and Goliath contest. However in one of the biggest shocks of the competition, Sunderland won 1-0, the first time a Second Division team had won the competition in over forty years[9]. On that lovely sunny Saturday afternoon, John was hoisted by his ever helpful classmates and carried shoulder high around the study hall, with two hundred lads roaring and shouting 'Sunderland, Sunderland. So much for sympathy!.

After class on Tuesday 8 May, Fr. Micheál, who was also going on the Kilmore Diocesan Pilgrimage to Lourdes, collected me and I stayed in his house in Bailieborough that night as we had a fairly early flight the next day. I had promised to go to Lourdes if Dad got better, which he obviously hadn't. However the idea had been planted in my mind and I was always very keen on foreign travel. As a family, we had gone on holidays. Like most Irish families however it was not abroad and I had never been outside Ireland. I paid for the trip from my savings from working in the shop. It cost £55 (€750 in today's terms), about eight weeks work in Logan's. People were very generous giving me money. Mrs Josie Mc Govern, my next door neighbour, gave me an envelope, which I assumed to be just petitions for the grotto in Lourdes. After I came home, I discovered that she had included £5 (€69) for me, a very considerable sum. We convinced ourselves that the authorities would be well used to this and would have extracted the money before burning the petitions. Mrs. Logan and Sister Rosarii each gave me £1. Many did likewise. Bishop Frank Mc Kiernan, whom I knew as president of my previous school in Ballinamore, was leading the pilgrimage for the first time. When we arrived at the French customs there appeared to be no one on duty.

I was beside the bishop, and being forward suggested he go ahead. He did so only to be followed by a security guard shouting something in French, which I didn't understand but it was not welcoming our bishop. A distressed courier ran after the guard, shouting something else in French. I blended back into the general body of Kilmore pilgrims.
France appeared exotic to me as I had never studied French and few locals had much English. Furthermore, unlike today when European cuisine is commonplace in Ireland, there was only French food and it was very different. However it all added to my enjoyment of the five days. There was a bidet in each room, and while I didn't know its name, I did know its function. Not everyone was so knowledgeable, and some of the hotel staff asked my uncle, Fr. Micheál, to explain to some of our group that it was not a toilet. While there was daily Mass in different Churches, Fr. Micheál told me the first day not to bother going and instead get a good sleep. It was in Lourdes that I first witnessed lay people being allowed receive communion in the hand. Although I was probably the youngest travelling, (apart from children who were sick) there was a great sense of comradery amongst us pilgrims from the Kilmore Diocese consisting of mainly Cavan and Leitrim. Fr. Colm Hurley and Fr. Seán Brady, both teachers of French in St. Pat's were also with us. Lying in the foothills of the Pyrenees, the weather was characterised by numerous heavy showers, and some intermittent bright spells. While the very fast flowing local Gave de Pau river was a torrent after such showers, there was a lovely fresh, peaceful and vibrant air when the skies cleared, captured in Wordsworth's lines[10]:

> Loud is the Vale! the voice is up
> With which she speaks when storms are gone
> A mighty unison of streams…
> In peace is roaring like the Sea

What struck me most about Lourdes was the peace. There was silence around the grotto, with numerous old-fashioned and more modern-type crutches hanging there from pilgrims who were cured. You did not really need to pray, you just had to be present there to experience the peace. The sight of so many disabled people, young and old had a salutary effect on me. The mode of conveyance for most disabled people was not unlike a rickshaw, but with three wheels, pulled from the front by someone, using the long handle. I pulled such contraptions on a few occasions, bringing people to and from the grotto. One day I witnessed two young lads from another country race each other while pulling invalids in the rickshaws. One turned over and shot the poor person out on to the pavement. Fortunately they did not seem badly injured.

The famous baths were an experience. Two muscular rustic-type local men held each of my arms while I was immersed in what to me was not much removed from a cattle trough. It was like a conveyor belt. I got out, wrapped in a very dirty looking blanket and without drying (it was part of the process) put back on my clothes. Nobody got sick from not drying themselves and no one got infection from the same blanket. It was all part of the miracle that was Lourdes. If I felt that the men's baths were rough and ready, I saw one of the women attendants emerge from the women's baths and I was thankful that I was a man. I had never thought of bringing the family box-camera, so I got the loan of a camera from another guest, purchased a film and took over thirty photos one evening. Subsequently not one of them was capable of being developed.

We were assigned one waiter for our entire five days in our hotel, who spoke no English and did not seem to understand or want to understand our needs. All he ever said was 'voila' as he deposited the food on our table. I was somewhat taken aback when our courier announced that we were taking up a collection for him, and advised us to each contribute 50p (€6.80), which we all duly did. This was given to our 'voila' that night. Either he used it for an all-night linguaphone crash-course in English or the Holy Spirit had descended on him, but the next morning his vocabulary was greatly enlarged, his demeanour greatly improved and his good wishes to us as we departed emotional. It was a miracle.

I returned home on Monday evening and dispensed the few gifts I had bought for my family. I also had Lourdes holy water in a hot water bottle, as it was much cheaper than purchasing a small and expensive holy water container. I decided not to return to St. Pat's until Wednesday morning. Micheál was to leave me back. Micheál was not exactly a morning person, so I told him I had to be back at 9.00 for class on Wednesday. In fact I had a Physics and Chemistry double at that time, so in effect I had no class until 10.30. As we were going up the front avenue at 9.30 Micheál apologised for having me late, I explained that in fact I had the first class free and was still on time. I did not bother him with the full truth that in fact I also had the second class free. I phoned Fr. Micheál that evening to thank him for lifts and general help. He advised me not to be talking too much about the serenity and peace of Lourdes as lads might be laughing at me. He need not have worried, I was back down to earth in more ways than one. A few days later my post card to Dermot Prior arrived, with my phonetic spelling 'ouveraugh' for au revoir, I got lots of slagging about my competency in French.

The Cavan Post-Primary Schools Field and Track Championships were held on the college grounds, in glorious weather on Saturday 19 May. There was a very festive atmosphere. The grounds were thronged with over three hundred competitors from nine schools. In addition there were numerous supporters and almost two hundred boarders[11]. While St. Aidan's Cootehill won a great number of events, some of St. Pat's athletes did well, such as Jimmy Fox (Cavan) who won first place in the boys' intermediate 100 metres race, Pat Bradley (Virginia) and Hubert Smith (Ballinagh)[12]. Some St. Pat's pupils scored very well that day although they were not entered in any competition. One Fourth Year pupil, whose nickname was 'The Pope', 'went with' (kissed) at least two girls. I witnessed one of his amorous encounters as I walked between two buses parked side by side near the senior pitch. This Fourth Year had come a long way from the very quiet and pious First Year who spent much of his early days in the college chapel (hence the nickname). He managed to chat up, find a secluded spot in a much thronged area, and go off with, not one but two girls. Rumour had it that he had actually gone with three girls, but I could only vouch for two I saw him with. He should have been rechristened Casanova, but his ecclesiastical title stuck.

The college's own sports day was on the last Sunday before the summer holidays. It was much less exciting, with very poor weather, and not a girl in sight. The pope was nowhere to be seen. The events however were very hotly contested with the following among the winners, Declan Murray (Cavan) senior shot, Owen Denneny (Killeshandra) road race, Jimmy Fox (Cavan) sprints, Aiden Cornyn (Dowra) long jump, Michael Martin (Ballyjamesduff) 1500 metres, Luke Smith (Ballyjamesduff) and James Reilly (Tierworker)[13]. The Leaving Cert top class won the much coveted basketball final, with John Boyd (Belturbet) named player of the match.

More excitement followed the next week. A Presidential election was in full swing, between Erskine Childers and Tom O'Higgins. Liam Cosgrave as Taoiseach paid a flying visit to Cavan town to drum up support for the Fine Gael candidate, O'Higgins[14]. In the days before mobile phones, every pupil and all staff were outside the main door of the Old Wing waiting for his arrival. After thirty minutes we were sent back to class. Just as we were arriving to our classrooms, the shout went up 'he's here'. Everyone stampeded back to the front. The president, Fr. Mallon welcomed him, while four hundred lads swarmed round them both. It was all very brief. As the Taoiseach made his way up towards the adjoining Bishop Mc Kiernan's house, we all started chanting, 'half day, half day', which Fr. Mallon granted. There was one blemish on the day. We discovered that afternoon, that Sister Margaret Mary who was the infirmary nun, had secured a vantage point to view the proceedings, on a stool looking out the library window. Unfortunately the perfectly polished library floor caused the stool to slip and she broke her wrist.

It was announced that a disco was to be held in the assembly hall for senior pupils from Loreto and St. Pat's. I don't remember any requests from us pupils for such an event but we were quite pleased. The official teenage response had to be fairly muted of course, as you had to feign disinterest in almost everything. I had noticed a distinct difference between many of the boarders and my classmates in my previous school. It concerned their attitude towards the opposite sex. Ballinamore was a mixed day school. We boarders in St. Pat's lived in an almost exclusively male world, only getting home for five weeks between early September and early June. I distinctly remember Loreto girls arriving to the assembly hall at night for some event, and the whistles, hoots and shouts from the corridors above, (albeit from mostly Junior pupils), startled me. It was like what you would expect had it been a prison. It was not that my Ballinamore classmates and I had been totally comfortable talking to girls, but we at least tried to appear normal in such encounters. I remember seeing a few of the boarders who were a year older than me, at a dance during the previous Christmas holidays. From what I knew of them, big lads, good footballers, exuding confidence, I assumed they would be out dancing all night, if not already hooked up with a girlfriend. In fact I saw them hanging around the back of the hall, rarely if ever even asking a girl to dance. At least in Ballinamore we had progressed to the stage of being refused. The disco was arranged for a Sunday evening in late May, from 7.30 to 9.30. It was a very tame affair. That afternoon my hair was washed, combed fastidiously, but flicked when finished to give an air of nonchalance. I got the loan of a jumper from Dermot Prior and then covered myself in Old Spice (how exotic). We walked at a forced leisurely pace to the hall and attempted to appear uninterested. Of course the day-boys from Cavan town were way ahead of us. They knew many of the Loreto girls and passed comment on them quietly to us as each arrived. According to our self-appointed critics, we were advised not to go with one girl as she had the pox. I had never heard the expression before but had a fair idea what it meant. The essential modus operandi was to 'play cool', although we did not know the term at that stage. There was very little atmosphere but it was still enjoyable. Of course a number of apparently quiet lads were getting 'fixed up'. I danced a number of girls. Towards the end of the night as I was dancing this nice girl from North-West Cavan, a friend who had scored and was dancing beside me with his new girlfriend, stated in front of my partner in a nice way, 'Well Liam are you going to ask .... to stay on. I calmly replied that while I had not done so, I hoped she would'. The die was cast.

Both of us were nervous while trying to appear in control of, and well used to, a situation like this. In the Donegal Gaeltacht as a thirteen year old, I had somewhat reluctantly spent one afternoon walking, holding hands, with a wee girl from Cookstown, when I would have preferred playing football. As a fourteen year old I had again walked on the local old railway line one night, holding hands with a girl a year or so younger. Now I was again holding hands. We walked slowly down towards the basements. A number of couples headed off to the shower area and my new found friend and I did likewise. It was somewhat embarrassing trying to find an empty cubicle. As we walked from cubicle to cubicle we invariably discovered yet another couple in an embrace, and we seemed like peeping toms. Eventually we left and walked further down the back avenue, my mind desperately trying to think of a suitable venue. The day-boys bicycle shed! Oh the romance of it, corrugated iron, debris, smell of (don't ask), and litter. At least it was private and empty. We attempted to kiss. There was much nervous laughter on both sides, teeth jarring off each other at times, pauses for breath and not sure when it was officially to end. The kiss was platonic, clumsily close and affectionate but not sexual. We emerged from the shed to walk the steep avenue back up to where the Loreto bus was parked between the assembly hall and the Senior pitch. We joked with each other as the bus load of girls starting shouting my friend's name and teasing her. Of course I was secretly chuffed. My self-esteem had been given a great boost. Later I realised that many of the so called 'tough men', had not gone with girls that evening.

The next day a dramatic story did the rounds. Phelim Plunkett (Ballyhaise) was saying good night to a girl in a classroom on the green-tiled corridor when he heard the adjoining doors being opened and the rooms checked by the dean. As it happened the dean had witnessed me walking with 'my girl' back towards the bus and there was nothing said and no repercussions. However Phelim was not aware of this, and sensibly decided that he should not be found in this situation. So he climbed out the window, one storey up, and held on to the window sill, while supporting himself by his footing on the raised stone of the outside wall. The dean found a girl on her own, innocently combing her hair. Phelim then pulled himself back up and in through the window again. We never knew if this was true. However having checked the stone on the outside wall and knowing Phelim, it was not just possible, but probable.

A day or two later, a few of us who had 'been with' Loreto girls, sent short letters to them, couriered by a trusted go-between, in case the nuns might check the post. I never met the girl again, but at least I had the long summer holidays and football to look forward to.

All Eyes: Basketball 1973
(L-R) Philip Brady, Frank Fitzpatrick, Gerard O' Brien, Peter O' Callaghan (referee), Seamus Mc Enroe, Francis Maguire, Francis Mc Goldrick, Jimmy Fox and Pat Bradley.

Keeping an eye on those to his left, Fr. Pete Casey and College staff, 1973
(L-R) Fr. Charles Heerey, Fergus O'Connor, Fr. Raymond Brady, Raymond Dunne,
Fr. Seán Brady, Fr. Colm Hurley, Fr. Larry Kearney, Michael Collins, Fr. Peter Casey, Fr. Leo O' Reilly, Tom Caslin, Fr. Fintan Mc Kiernan,
Gerry Mc Allister, Patsy Lee and Fr. Dan Gallogly.
Seated (L-R) Fr. John Murphy, Jim Hannon, Fr. Benny Maguire, Sr. Kathleen Lynch, Jim Mc Donnell, Fr. Patrick Mallon (president),
Fr. Seán O' Reilly, Sr. Margaret Mary Gilfinnan, Sr. Rosarii Haughton, Fr. Patrick Brady, Fr. Torlac O' Reilly and Fr. Gerry Kearns.

'Are we going to shake hands?': Taoiseach visits college, May 1973

(L-R) First pupil recognisable from left, Philip Clarke, Fr. Mallon partly hidden, Taoiseach Liam Cosgrave shaking hands with John Rahill. *Boys standing in window:* Liam Henry, Francis Goodman, Michael Gaynor. *Directly in front of them:* Michael Dolan. *Behind pupil with blazer:* Jimmy Nugent, Gerry O'Brien. *In window behind:* Mel Bouchier.

Chapter 8

Summer work, football and ... pure thoughts

Summer 1973

'*I suppose you'll be heading off to West Cavan every weekend now,*' laughed Marie Glancy who was one of my workmates in Logan's supermarket. I was only home from St. Pat's about two hours and had called down to the shop where I worked to see my friends. Of course I was secretly very chuffed that news of my romantic encounter had reached Ballinamore, although I was mystified as to how Marie had been informed. Later I discovered that Dermot Prior had already called to the shop and gave Marie the gossip with which to slag me. I feigned annoyance as was the expected teenage reaction.

I started work the next morning for the entire summer in Logan's, working five and a half days a week. It struck me that the last time I had worked here was before Christmas and that Dad was alive at the time. In fact Dad's death gradually sank in with me as the summer progressed. I suppose the shock had registered with me when Dad died, but now I realised what life was like without him around. The atmosphere at home was different. Mam was naturally very lonely. Coupled with this was the actual absence of Dad.

I was working with Seamus Farrelly, a little older than myself who knew every phrase from every Western film I had ever heard of. We had great craic. I got a raise to £8 (€110) per week. Among numerous items, the supermarket stocked such popular brands as Findus beef burgers, Birds Eye chips, Galtee rashers, Little Chip marmalade, HB Vanilla ice-cream, Cross and Blackwell salad cream, Goodall's YR sauce, Goldenvale cheese, Cookeen cooking fat, Yoplait yogurts, Jacob's biscuits, Gateaux Swiss roll, Campbell's soup, Lyons tea, Kellogg's cereals, and Maxwell House coffee[1]. Popular confectionery included the famous Curly Wurly bar, Twirl, Rolo, Tofo, Crunchie, as well as bars of Honeycrisp, Tiffin and Dairymilk chocolate.

Most evenings I raced home at 7.30, ate and cycled down to 'the park' for G.A.A. training. It was totally unlike the sophisticated and professional training enjoyed and or endured by young footballers today. Anything up to twenty of us young lads, aged thirteen to seventeen, started playing with a small number occupying the goal mouth, the rest sending in balls (usually 3-4 on the go at one time). Of course the greatest laugh erupted when one lad rising to collect an incoming ball, was walloped from the blind side with another ball that he never saw coming. A little later the senior players arrived and we all did some training, a few laps around the pitch, followed by sprints followed by press ups etc. Then we got down to the real business of the evening, football. We formed two teams. Every ball was as keenly contested as if it were a county final, and the slagging was phenomenal. It was exciting and exhilarating. We frequently did not finish until it was dark, one night togging in at 10.55. Official training was each Tuesday and Thursday night, but with nothing good on television and nothing else to do, we young lads often went down on our own and kicked around at least one extra night per week. I was playing Under Sixteen and Minor. The captaincy rotated among three of the Under Sixteen team, Michael Reynolds, Thomas Mc Tague and myself. We had a fairly good team, bolstered by an incredibly talented bunch of lads who were two years younger. We had reasonably high hopes of doing well in this competition. The fact that the seniors were doing very well meant that we had great training sessions at least twice a week. It was a fairly full schedule between attending senior matches and playing in Under Sixteen and Minor games. I lived for football. Each Wednesday night, when returning from the park, we would see if the local paper, the Leitrim Observer, had arrived into Kavanagh's shop. We would then scrutinise it carefully, hoping to see our own names mentioned as having played particularly well. At least the journalist had started to get my name correct. Previously it had appeared as Liam Mc Conboy, a mistranslation of my name as it appeared in Irish on the G.A.A. watermarked notepaper, Liam Mac Conduibh.

The results of my summer exams arrived in mid-summer. I was very happy. I had gotten 66% in Latin, with the comment from Fr. Seán Brady, 'has made good progress'. I also had got the honour in English, History and Geography, with a good mark in pass Irish and a mid-forties mark in pass Maths.

In July I went to Cavan one Wednesday afternoon (the weekly half-day) to buy some clothes. I purchased a pair of black, bellbottomed trousers with a turn up. However my real joy was buying a white polka-dotted shirt on a black background. I bumped into a classmate and friend from Cavan town, Declan Mc Donald who persuaded me to stay for the night and go with him to the Paul Goldin show. I phoned Mam to let her know I would not be home until the morning. It was a beautiful sunny afternoon as Declan and I walked around Cavan. In day school, your friends are near you all summer and more than likely playing football with you. Boarding school was very different. You rarely met any of your classmates. I was surprised when Declan showed me his bedroom, in the lovely Georgian house opposite the Surgical Hospital. The wall was adorned with two lovely pictures of nude females. I remember remarking to him what my mother's response would be if I attempted to similarly brighten up my room. Paul Goldin was an internationally renowned hypnotist, and his appearance in Cavan was a big event. The Celt advertised his shows with the caution, *'Nervous people and those under eighteen while welcome, are asked not to volunteer'*[2]. Those who volunteered to be hypnotised, missed the entire show, but provided the entertainment for the rest of us, who burst our sides laughing at their antics. One lad lay on the floor and kept one of his legs raised about one foot off the floor for over twenty minutes, under hypnosis. As we left a number of the volunteers had been sent out to the street looking for leprechauns under cars parked outside. The next morning I got the 9.00 bus back to Ballinamore and went straight to work.

I had been getting dizzy spells and my blood pressure was a bit raised. My mother was concerned. Having visited the local G.P. a number of times, it was decided I would be sent for investigation to hospital. I was not worried. Unfortunately Jervis Street hospital in Dublin phoned that a bed was ready for me on Friday, 3 August. Big problem! We were playing our arch rivals, Aughawillan, that evening in the Under Sixteen quarter final. It broke my heart to have to miss it[3]. Micheál, Mam and Christopher accompanied me to Dublin. We won the match, but the irony was that it was a bank holiday weekend, and no tests were done until the following Tuesday. I had a great time in hospital as I was not sick. I read novels, looked out to the public park directly opposite my window, talked to other patients and had great fun with some of the nurses who were only a few years older than me. Liz Mountain, was one such nurse on whom I used play pranks. She got her own back, as I woke up one morning to discover she was plastering my face with a thick, gooey-like gel that was not easily removed. Valerie visited me a few days later. I got home having spent ten days there. Nothing appeared abnormal. The local G.P. believed it was my mother being over cautious after Dad's death. (However a few years later, I was delayed entering the teachers' pension scheme, due to high blood pressure, and a heart problem was discovered. Mothers tend to be right).

I returned to work in Logans and more importantly I had only missed two days of the Festival, the highlight of the summer. The marquee dances included Evelyn and the Envoys, Jack Ruane, Hi-Lows and Wells Fargo. The Sahara show band was a regular feature for the night of the Agricultural 'Show Dance' when farming couples of all ages appeared. I went to The Hillbillies, one of the best bands at that time on the closing Tuesday night. Songs such as 'Tie a Yellow Ribbon Round the Old Oak Tree' by Dawn, 'Power to all our Friends' by Cliff Richard, and 'Monster Mash' by Bobby Pickett and the Crypt-Kickers, as well as Olivia Newton- John singing 'Take Me Home Country Roads', reverberated in my head for days afterwards.

Now that the Festival was over there was only the football left. We were easily beaten in the Minor grade as we had an exceptionally young team. We had an unbeaten and impressive run in the Under Sixteens. However, in fairly dramatic fashion we squandered our chance to reach the final, relinquishing a five point lead with ten minutes to go. We also missed a penalty. The result was mainly due to inexperience, as we were relying on a very good Under Fourteen panel, helped by a few solid but not spectacular older players like myself. The recriminations began as we started togging in, with one self-appointed mentor, pointing out to us in no-uncertain terms how we lost the game. I intervened, to tell him, in fairly unparliamentarily language, that we knew we had lost and did not need a lecture from him. A few days later he approached me to see if I would go on a GAA quiz team in the local hotel. I readily agreed and all was well. Fr. Dan was the quizmaster, and each participant was brought out to the front of the very high stage, and asked questions individually before a packed Slieve an Iarainn hotel ballroom. Dan tried to put me at my ease, by publicly telling me to take it easy, that I had often answered questions from him, under more trying circumstances. It was very daunting however with lights on my face, and half the town below me, including peers, the latter ready to celebrate if I missed an easy question. I did. Dan asked me, for two marks to finish the saying, 'One swallow does not' ... (make a summer). I was stumped. Later that night my mother was incredulous that I could not finish it. I did however manage to answer correctly, Samuel Taylor Coleridge for six marks, as the author of 'The Rhyme (Rime) of the Ancient Mariner'.

On Sunday 26 August I was in Carrick-On-Shannon to see our seniors draw with Allen Gaels (Drumshanbo, Drumkeerin and Ballinaglera) in the county final. That night I got a lift to Dublin with a few who were returning after the game. I had taken the last week off from work, in order to give myself a holiday in Dublin. I stayed with my first cousin, Margaret Kelly, in her flat in Ballsbridge. I spent the week shopping, going to films and I visited the zoo. I bought a black tank top and a pair of glossy brown, very high platform shoes. At that time Ireland was in the throes of change. Over half the population was under twenty six years of age[4]. Dublin was at the vanguard of this modernisation, as the historian Diarmaid Ferriter states:

> 'Girls working in shops were jingling with golden chains and bangles ...elephant flares, platform-heeled boots and floral shirts were in vogue, ...cheesecloth, bell bottoms, tank tops and four inch platforms, ... satin hot pants ... girls strolled down Grafton Street in the skimpiest of skirts ... the bishops objected but the harm had gone out of their clout'[5].

'The Sunday World' newspaper was launched that year under the provocative advertisement headline, 'Are you getting it every Sunday?'[6]. For us young lads in Ballinamore, Sunday meant Mass. The teenage girls in the choir feigned shyness as they drew up the rear of the procession to communion, from the gallery at the back of the church, up to the altar rails. With heads bowed, eyes cast down and hands joined in saintly fashion, they relished the opportunity to show themselves off in all their finery[7]. All of Ireland was in the turmoil of a sexual revolution and I was a testosterone teenager. The summer of '73 consisted of work, football, and impure thoughts. The latter never appeared when I was in the all-male environment of St. Pat's, but they sure made up for lost time when it was the summer holidays. Ballinamore was fertile enough ground but Dublin in good weather was a veritable hot-house.

I headed home on Saturday, a lovely bright warm sunny day. Instead of getting a bus to Blanchardstown and hitching home from there, my knowledge of Dublin was so limited that I got a bus just as far as the city-side gates of Phoenix Park. As a result I had to walk all through the park and almost all the way to Blanchardstown before I got a lift. New tight fitting platforms may have been very stylish but not very practical when thumbing one hundred miles. I got home a few hours later with a big blister on each foot, but much wiser.

A few days later I was due to return to St. Pat's. On the day I was going back, Micheál returned from being down the town, with news that changed my final year in St. Pat's and had a big influence on me as a person.

Leaving Cert Class 1973-74

Back standing (L-R) A. Mc Breen, L. Flynn, P. Seagrave, T. Fitzpatrick, J. King, S. Kilkenny, D. Kennedy, D. Prior, M. Gaynor, G. Comiskey, P. Mc Caffrey, O. Martin, P. Mc Gee, G. Skelly, M. Coogan, T. Smith, B. Rahill, G. Cartwright, B. Donohoe, G. Mc Keown, R. Harwood, M. Mc Entee, T. Conaty, N. Reilly, J. Mullery and R. Slowey.

Middle standing (L-R) J. Conlon, N. Barrett, P. Clarke, E. Sheridan, D. Rawle, T. Mc Kiernan, J. Phair, E. Donohoe, B. Farrell, M. Ryan, C. Mc Cabe, M. Maguire, V. Coyle, L. Mc Niffe, M. Cosgrove, B. Flood, J. Mc Laughlin, G. Reilly, S. Mc Enroe, G. Mc Govern and P. Connolly.

Front seated (L-R) B. Flood, J. Rahill, L Flood, J. Mc Govern, C. Maguire, C. Brady, S. Callaghan, J. Clarke, M. Martin, P. Bradley, E. Mc Govern, B. Smith, F. Goodman, L. Henry, D. Mc Donald, T. Caffrey, T. Finlay and P.J. Fitzpatrick.

Front, on ground P. Plunkett and J. Denneny.

Soundings
Classmates writing on author's English poetry book.

Leaving Cert Class 1974-75

Back standing (L-R) J. Fox, C. Halton, J.J. Beirne, J. Mc Morrow, G. Brady, P. Quinn, L. Mc Cabe, P. Gaffney, T. Moore, M. Mc Clarey, M. Leddy, P. Clarke, E. Ferguson, M. Whyms, F. Maguire, C. Lenehan, A. Vesey, N. Conaty, D. Connerton, F.O' Sullivan, E. Gaffney and F. Costello. *Second row standing (L-R)* P. Myers, O. Brady, M. Brady, W. Brady, M. Young, T. Keegan, L. Slacke, H. Cafferty, P.J. Denning, G. Clarke, O. Monaghan, T. O' Connor, N. Mc Hugh, P. Cusack, P. Fay, B. Murray, M. Mc Kiernan, G. Strong, G. Quinn, P. Gargan, F. Cusack, D. Mc Entee, T. Mc Tague, L. Plunkett and C. O' Keeffe. *Third row seated.* M. Wilson, P. Mc Gowan, M. Goldrick, G. Tierney, J.O' Donnell, C. Fay, C. Reilly, P. Mc Grath, M. Donohoe, F. Mc Gauran, B. Smyth, J. Sheerin, F. Duffy, G. Brady, G. Murphy, P. Gaffney, J. Murphy, P. Mc Govern and F. Mc Kiernan. *Front row (L-R)* R. Mc Dermott, A. Cornyn, S. Gallagher, F. Smyth, S. Farrelly, O. Mc Inerney, P. Kelly, M. Reilly, J. Mc Gurk, K. Colton, E. Kennedy, P.J. Mc Guire, L. Fitzpatrick, P. Farrell, G. Mc Cabe and M. Mc Loughlin.

Chapter 9

Prefect

September - December 1973

'*You're going to be a prefect, that's what I heard up the town'*, Micheál said[1]. I was gobsmacked on two counts. How did someone in Ballinamore know anything about who was going to be a prefect in St. Pat's? Secondly, I had never any expectation that I would be a prefect. I didn't dare believe it. Micheál dropped me and all my belongings back to the college.

A number of new First Years were from Ballinamore, Declan Dolan, Oliver Honeyman, Barry Reilly and Gerard Lynch. Also two lads I knew from Ballinamore school now joined St. Pat's as Fourth Years, Peter Quinn (Garadice) and Frank Smith (Drumreilly). Leo Plunkett also returned to start Fourth Year again. We had a new dean, Fr. Charlie Heerey, who had previously been college bursar. Bursar was no longer a full-time position, with a number of the priests on the teaching staff now becoming responsible for various aspects of the job. He exclaimed to me that he was feeling very old as he had just met Paddy Dolan, a former classmate from his time in St. Pat's. Paddy was leaving off his son, Declan, who was entering as a First Year. Some of us Leaving Certs witnessed numerous mothers helping young sons make their beds. We passed snide remarks and smiled smugly to ourselves at what we regarded as fussing, knowing that next year, these same lads would not let their mothers within an ass's roar of their rooms.

The bell went for evening prayer and we all trooped off to the chapel. It was there that we would hear who were prefects and in what order. Prefects played a fairly important role in helping the dean look after pupils, especially the First Years. Being a prefect meant setting an example by acting responsibly and having set duties to carry out. In return, prefects enjoyed privileges and a certain status. Just as the bell called us to the chapel, one wit from West Cavan, who had a somewhat chequered discipline history, very loudly told friends that as he was too busy to attend evening prayer, would they come back and tell him which prefect position he had secured. We all had a great yahoo at his self-depreciation.

Prefects sat at the very back of the chapel, in order of importance. Cathal Maguire (Bawnboy) was head prefect, Brian Smith (Ballyjamesduff) was second, I was third, John Clarke (Ardee) was sacristan and Joey Mc Govern (Ballyconnell) was fourth prefect. I was genuinely very surprised and incredibly delighted. Of course nobody believed me when I stated that I was surprised as that was what you were expected to say in any event. I was only one year in the college. Granted, the previous September, Charlie O' Gorman who likewise joined as a Fourth Year, had been made a prefect after just one year. But Charlie was a talented musician, played the chapel organ and to me was a model pupil. I didn't see myself in that light. In addition to the prefects there were four shop boys: Book shop, Cathal Mc Cabe (Crosserlough) with whom I was friendly and Pat Bradley (Maghera); Tuck shop, Michael Martin and Philip Magee (both Ballyjamesduff)[2]. In addition Dermot Prior was sixth prefect and had responsibility for the assembly hall. He was like St. Peter with all the keys he held.

While the daily routine of class remained the same as the previous year, being one of the prefects did influence the rest of the day in many ways. Not only did we sit apart from our classmates in the chapel, but also in the refectory. Each prefect sat at a table with junior pupils for all meals in order to help maintain order. I was seated with a group of Second Years. Prefects were usually in bedrooms beside the First Year dormitory. I was in a room next door, sharing with Peter Mc Caffrey, from Ballinamore. The head prefect was allocated a room on his own and also allowed sit with his own class at meal time. At lunch time, before I got to dinner I had to get junior pupils out of a prefab. classroom that was located on the basketball court near the chapel, as well as a classroom beside the shop. I also had to reopen these on time. On rotation, each of the four prefects collected and gave out the letters at four o'clock break. There were privileges also to be enjoyed. At four o'clock break in addition to the standard bread and butter, there was cheese, crackers, sandwich-spread and jam for the all prefects and shop boys who sat at a table apart.

As was the norm each year, the third prefect was also the substitute sacristan. The sacristan's role was to prepare the vestments each afternoon for the priests saying Mass the following morning. While one priest was on duty to say public Mass for us pupils, each priest said Mass daily, usually on one of the side altars. The sacristan had a fair amount of work to do each evening. In order to give him a break a sub-sacristan was supposed to do the work at least one evening for him. John Clarke was a very reliable pupil, and as sacristan meticulously showed me how to layout the vestments and check that everything was in order. In fact I had almost nothing to do as John often accompanied me to the sacristy on my evening and did most of the work, as I was much slower than him. The big pay-off for being sacristan (and sub-sacristan) was access to the infirmary and its small kitchen.

The college infirmary was also home to the three nuns who lived in the college. St. Margaret Mary Gilfinnan, a retired nurse tended to pupils who were sick. There was an actual sick bay there, hence the term infirmary. In fact very few lads stayed in the infirmary unless they were quite sick. Usually they remained in their own rooms. Twice daily, at appointed times, pupils were allowed attend the infirmary if feeling unwell. Emergencies could be seen anytime. A famous white tablet (name unknown) was dispensed on numerous occasions. Years later when a cupboard was being removed from the area, loads of these tablets were discovered discarded behind it. At least we were not pill-pushing pupils. Sr. Margaret Mary was pious, serious and genuine. Her job was not easy, as some lads got sick just as an exam was looming and she had to have all her wits about her. Sr. Kathleen Lynch was in charge of the kitchen. She was kind, motherly and had a sense of humour. At that time lads revelled in the pungency of their flatulence. On one very smelly occasion, in the refectory as we were collecting food, she remarked with a smile. 'Who has been eating beans?' Sr. Rosarii, as already mentioned was on the teaching staff. One day in November, I arrived to the infirmary to see all three sisters glued to the television watching the royal wedding of Princess Anne and Mark Phillips. Sr. Margaret Mary remarked to me that the Anglican ceremony was very similar to our Catholic practice. Looking back on it, the three women were three very different personalities, carrying out their different vocations in the one school.

Every night after study John, as sacristan, accompanied by me as sub-sacristan, went up to the infirmary for food. It was an old tradition and I was certainly not going to question the hand that fed me. On occasional evenings there was some surplus food from the nuns' own supper or from the priests' refectory. What was available every night however was the facility to make tea and more importantly, toast. Every night I made two slices of toast, and tea, with no sugar. It was heaven. Of all the privileges being a prefect bestowed, this to me was undoubtedly the greatest by far. What was unfair was that the other prefects did not have access to this kitchen, and I did, although I was only third prefect and had no great extra workload as sub-sacristan.

Fr. Charlie Heerey, as dean, ushered in a new era. He greatly humanised what was a fairly rigid system. By and large he replaced slapping with written exercises as punishments, a practice begun by his predecessor, but greatly expanded by Fr. Heerey. In general his philosophy was to try to get fellows to act responsibly and he treated us, especially seniors, as adults. He was not soft however and maintained a very orderly atmosphere. A number of changes were introduced. Morning study was abolished, so pupils had an extra twenty minutes in bed, with Mass at 7.50, not 7.30. Batch bread was available for all pupils for breakfast. It was fantastic, seemed much fresher and much more enjoyable than the traditional sliced pan. Of course we all stowed away extra batch slices in our lockers to be produced for tea that evening. Night prayer was changed from after study at 9. 45 to before study at 7.45. This meant that when study finished at 10.00 you did not have this feeling that now we have to go to the chapel. I thought it was a better arrangement. Each evening, the dean gave out the rosary and we, prefects, said a decade each. One Sunday evening however, disaster struck. The dean must have been away, and Fr. John Murphy who taught Irish, was on duty in the chapel for night prayers. He gave out the rosary in Irish. I still remember the absolute dread I felt in my stomach at the prospect of having to say my decade in Irish in front of all the boarders. It would be public humiliation. Some of the prefects were doing honours Irish, I wasn't. They managed fine. I knew I would be reasonably ok for the Holy Mary, but not the Hail Mary. Drawing on my memories of one stint in the Donegal Gaeltacht, and with the help of Dermot Prior who prompted me for the Hail Mary, I falteringly got through my decade. One of the prefects was not so lucky, and Fr. Murphy interjected early on and finished his decade for him.

One day as I was leaving the ref. a First Year, Kenneth Brennan (Corlismore), raced past me towards the heavy swing doors that led to the green-tiled corridor. They swung back and hit him full force, knocking him out. I rushed to him as did others. He came to, but was somewhat groggy. I carried him up to the infirmary and waited for about forty minutes until he was ok. A week later he gave me an envelope from his mother with 50p (€7). It was as unexpected as it was welcome.

Fr. Heerey gave us prefects a pep talk and explained what he expected of us and how he would rely on our being responsible. We had access to his small sitting room during the latter half of lunch time when he was having his own dinner. On hunkers, knees and standing, we all poured over *The Irish Independent* and it became a staple part of our daily diet. The unexpected Yom Kippur war, when Egypt and Syria launched a joint surprise attack on Israel to regain territories lost in the 1967 war, broke out on 6 October 1973. We were in Fr. Heerey's room every day at lunch time, following the news coverage of the dramatic developments. Of course as teenage boys we did not do subtleties and so were totally on the side of Israel. We tried to outdo each other, shouting out dramatic titbits of the conflict, as we devoured the war news, for the three weeks until a ceasefire was announced. Of course other lads joined us, and Fr. Heerey returned unexpectedly one lunch time to find about a dozen lads in his room. He ran everyone, except us prefects.

As prefects we were allowed to have one sleep-in per week, i.e. we did not have to attend morning Mass. It was a lovely feeling, both the night before and as the bell rang in the morning. The big hand bell dominated the day. Tommy Dawson, a young lad my age who worked in the college always rang the first bell[3]. At 7.30 he started on the middle corridor in the New Wing, walked all along it, then on to the top corridor and then likewise for the two corridors in the Old Wing. He left the bell in an appointed place for the Fourth Year who was on bell duty for that week to collect it. By the time Tommy had finished ringing the first bell, the pupil had to be ready to immediately start the second bell, and by the time this was finished, the same pupil immediately went and rang what was the third and final bell. Most pupils got up at the second bell. I had done my week on bell duty in Fourth Year. Pyjama clad fellows frequently stuck their head out their room door with the question, 'what bell?'. If the answer was 'the final one', it was usually greeted with an expletive. When on bell duty, your entire week was dominated by it. You rang it approximately twenty three times daily, between 7.40 am. and 10 pm., a total of approximately one hundred and forty six times in the seven days you were on duty. Rarely did fellows forget to ring it.

The first Sunday back in September saw the county finals in Cavan and Leitrim take place. Although Ballinamore were in a replay I did not even think of getting out to see it in Carrick-on- Shannon. We snatched a dramatic win over Allen Gaels, by getting two goals and one point in the last eleven minutes to win our thirteenth senior title by one point[4]. I was thrilled. The Crosserlough lads had not made it to the county final, but still retained the boasting rights of 'seven in a row'. That final was won by Annagh (Belturbet/Redhills) who beat Ramor United (Virginia/Maghera) by 4.11 to 3.8[5]. There was one first year boarder whose father was a key player on one of the county final teams. He was waiting from midday at the front of the college to be collected for the game, as had been promised. I was expecting visitors from home that afternoon in the recept. room, while he waited for his lift. My family came, we talked for a few hours and no one came to collect him. He was heartbroken and cried all evening. I felt so sorry for him.

Football within the college got into full swing fairly soon. Two of our three football teams were defending champions going into the 1973/4 season. The Rannafast team got off to a good start in September in Ballybay with a win over neighbouring St. Macartan's, Monaghan, 5.7 to 5.2[6]. As I was only sixteen the previous April, I was eligible for the panel. However, as I was doing the Leaving Cert I was not interested. Anyway I was not good enough to make the team. In the next game, we were down eight points at half time, against St. Michael's Enniskillen. We fought back well but still lost by two points, 4.7 to 3.8. St. Michael's eventually reached the final, only to be beaten by St. Columb's Derry. Our team included Thomas Mc Tague, Pauric Martin, Frank Smith, Cyril O' Keeffe, Ollie Brady, T.P. Martin, Ciarán Halton, Donal Donohoe, Martin Brady, Philip Magee, Robbie Mc Dermott, Gerry Strong, Eamonn Gaffney, Francis Maguire, Ray Cullivan and Francis Mc Kiernan[7].

The departing Leaving Cert class of the previous June was considerably smaller than the intake of new First Years in September. Consequently the number of boarders increased by twenty or so, making a total of almost two hundred. As a result the study hall was not able to cope with the extra numbers. A classroom, nearest to the back of the stage was used as an extra study hall. During the day it was used as a normal classroom, but in evening time it was study hall to twenty or so first year pupils. One First Year class had been reserved for pupils who wished to follow a course mid-way between the new Primary Curriculum and the Secondary Programme. These were usually lads who were quite young for ordinary First Year. Such boys would take four years to complete the Inter Cert. The new small study hall had a mixture of some who were doing this four year Inter Cert and others who were traditional First Years. In the main study hall the four prefects, on a weekly rotation, sat at the top, facing the pupils and keeping an eye on the First Years. This year I was asked to supervise the group of twenty plus First Years on my own. I was delighted. I had extra responsibility. I was supposed to have one week off and study in the normal study hall, being replaced by another prefect, Joey Mc Govern. However, very soon, we both realised that it was far less disruptive if I remained supervising my First Years all the time.

My study hall included the four lads from Ballinamore, in retrospect not a great idea as there was the temptation that some of them might be too familiar with me, unintentionally making it difficult to maintain discipline. I was doing my Leaving Cert which remained my main focus. I had up to two dozen, twelve/thirteen year olds in front of me for twenty two hours study each week. They included Charles Bermingham, (Dublin) and Simon Mc Evoy (Ballyjamesduff), both of whom were doing the four year Inter Cert. In fact Simon had been in a fairly serious car crash during the summer and my family had come across it on their return journey to home having left me off at Jervis Street Hospital. Both lads were a breath of fresh air to the college, even if they made life a little more complicated for me. First Years were called, 'Conors'. While the origin of the title is unknown, it is thought that it came from the Latin verb, 'conari', to 'strive' or 'try'. As new pupils they were

always trying to do the right or accepted thing. Simon and Charles had no such inferiority status. They were innocent in the very best sense of the word, afraid of nobody, prepared to ask questions that others no doubt wanted to, but dared not. There was a great spontaneity to the two lads. They had Fr. Dan, for some subject, and Simon would frequently relay to us, at the start of study, what had transpired that day in discussion between Dan and himself in class. It was hilarious as I knew that Dan's normal modus operandi in class was simply ineffective when teaching this new pre-first year group. Also included in my study group were Fergal Baxter (Mohill), Francis Corbally (Kilmainhamwood), Barry Fannon (Ballyshannon), Hugh Farrell (Templeport), Michael Faulkner (Kingscourt), Seán Mc Gahern (Gowna), Proinsias Mc Govern (Glangevlin), Terence Mc Govern (Glangevlin), Patrick Mc Hugh (Glenties), Terence Mc Manus (Glangevlin), Eugene Mc Partlan (Drumkeerin), Patrick Mc Partlan (Drumkeerin), Fintan Mc Teggart (Templeport) and Raymond Sheerin, (Rossinver)[8].
In general the First Years were perfectly behaved in study, not a word out of them and they and I got on with our work. I felt there was a nice atmosphere. One evening I noticed one lad, for whom homework would not have been a priority, engrossed in his atlas. After a while I silently walked down and discovered he had a comic inside the atlas. I quietly tried to embarrass him by stating, 'What would your parents say if they knew you were wasting your time reading childish comics?' Innocently and immediately he answered, 'But my father reads comics all the time'. I felt a right eejit, and told him he had to put it away anyway. On another occasion a lad was talking and I told him to stop. Despite a number of warnings he persisted. I then told him if he talked again I would throw him out of study. A fairly tall and robust pupil, he replied, 'Would you be able?' I felt my authority was being challenged and told him if he did not leave I would physically throw him out. He refused and I went to his seat and started dragging him towards the door, in front of all the other pupils. He then just let himself drop to the floor, a heavy deadweight. I told him to get out or I'd kick him, he didn't move. I kicked him on the behind with the side of my foot and then dragged him out and shut the door. By the end of First Year he was tall and strong enough to have taken me on, but he bore no ill will. He went on to be a great county footballer.
One other lad misbehaved in study, talking and distracting others. He was bright and usually difficult to actually catch doing something wrong. I felt he was a disruptive presence in what was otherwise a very nice group. Having warned him a few times about talking I caught him reading a comic. I asked

the dean could he be moved to the main study hall and there was no problem. But there was a problem. A few weeks later his mother, who knew my mother, was visiting her son. I met mother and son on the red-tiled corridor. We started talking, all friendly, when she turned to her son and 'innocently', asked, 'were you not in Liam's study'. I explained the incident about the comic. Of course the other pupil whom I had merely warned about reading comics was cited, all in a very ostensibly friendly manner. I replied 'but surely you are a lot more mature than...', and extricated myself as quickly as possible from a very awkward situation.

First Years finished study at 9.30 pm., a half hour before everyone else. Each week on rotation, one of us prefects, left study at that time and kept a check on them until ten o'clock when the dean was around. The First Years left their dorm at 7.50 in the morning for Mass and did not return until 9.30 at night. It was usually locked during the day to prevent stealing. Their dormitory had sixteen cubicles, each holding three beds. There were no doors on the cubicles, only three sided walls and no ceiling. Consequently any loud talk disrupted everyone in the entire dorm. One night Simon Mc Evoy was not in his bed and I found him hiding in a locker. How he managed to get into it remains a mystery. To be fair the lads usually settled down quite soon. One First Year was very homesick and could be heard crying on numerous nights. It was very tough on him and I am sure there were others, perhaps equally as homesick who did not let anyone know how upset they were. I remember a First Year, with an English accent, sitting on the steps leading up to the forbidden corridor (the kitchen female staff quarters) one night and crying. The big, tall and thin, Fr. Peter Casey, was sub-dean, on Tuesday duty when Fr. Heerey was on his partial day off. I was struck by the humane approach of Fr. Casey who just sat down on the steps beside the pupil in full view of everyone and quietly talked and listened.

In the eight weeks leading up to Halloween, I had visits from my family on seven occasions. This was the result of business and dental appointments in Cavan, as well as a desire to see me now that we had lost Dad. In early October I had a flying visit to the public clinic in Ballinamore to get my eyes tested. On the first weekend in October I wanted to go home and asked the president, Fr. Mallon, for permission. In general this was unheard of. However he immediately acquiesced. I left the college at 4.00, directly after class and thumbed home with all my weekend homework with me. Mam had no idea I was coming home and had anything happened me, no one might have known for a day or two. Carefree times!

Life went on as normal for the most part. There was a local school bus strike.

Pupils thumbed in to school for a short period until it was resolved[9]. In late September at a public lecture in Monaghan, a consultant psychiatrist posed the question, 'Should homework be abolished'? It was the main heading in the Celt, but nothing changed[10]. Each day as I was locking up the classrooms at lunch, a day-boy gave me a lovely slice of homemade currant bread covered with butter. I could not believe how lovely it was and each day he continued to do so. (I think I gave him a present at the end of the year, I certainly hope I did!). The bread meant that even if dinner was not that great, I still felt full. In fact the potatoes were much better than they had been the previous year. A number of boarders usually helped pick the college potato crop. Some fellows were mad to do this as it meant not only getting out of class for a few hours, but also receiving a really lovely tea. I was never asked to pick potatoes and was not really interested as I did not want to miss class.

The weekends were fairly uneventful. On Friday evening, if it was bright and the weather was half decent, we Leaving Cert boarders played soccer on the basketball court near the ambulatory. Sometimes I played as I loved soccer. However, I was somewhat on the fringes of the group, partly because I did not play every weekend. The once weekly showers were also available at this time. Sometimes I preferred to shower, change clothes and generally freshen up on a Friday afternoon. This marked off the week from the weekend and left me feeling energised. Joey Mc Govern was a gifted musician. One Saturday, a few of us spent an hour or two in the small, windowless room that held a piano, opposite Fr. Dan's room. Joey played whatever pop song we requested and we tried to outdo each other in shouting, (not really singing), the lyrics. We then turned our attention to songs from our recent musical, 'Calamity Jane'. Fr. Ray passed by and jokingly commented that he had heard us 'kill' a number of the songs.

If a pupil was somewhat different or unusual he could be teased, taunted or bullied. There was no anti-bullying policy in those days. What is viewed as bullying today was seen as part and parcel of boarding school at that time. Invariably this took place out of hearing and sight of the teachers or dean. One lad had a major hygiene problem, in that he appeared to never wash his hair or change his clothes. A few fellows tried to push him into the shower with his clothes on. One day I saw his parents visiting him and was astonished to see that they were not just normal but in fact well off, with a very good car, the main status symbol that we pupils knew or cared about. Some Leaving Cert lads used 'slag' this fellow as to what shampoo he used and could he recommend one to them. A much more serious issue was how one very quiet fellow, who kept to himself, was in effect bullied by a group of his own boarder class mates. A small group of them (four to five) imitated his slight speech peculiarity, and continually made fun of him in numerous ways. There was no physical abuse but there didn't need to be. They made this fellow's life hell. What really annoyed me was that one of his main tormentors had been at school with him before coming to St. Pat's. This bully, small in stature, appeared to feel important by hanging around this group of hard men and being to the forefront in bullying his classmate. On one occasion one of the hard men was sick in the infirmary. The victim of bullying challenged his main tormentor to a fight when the latter began to abuse him. Of course like all bullies he was basically a coward and refused the challenge. Most of us would have loved to see, as one fellow put it, the victim 'kick the shite out of the little shit'. The rest of us were uneasy that he was bullied, but to our eternal shame did nothing about it. We should have. At one stage the pupil went home sick for three weeks. The persecution eased somewhat after that.

On Wednesday 31 October we got home until the following Sunday for Halloween. On Friday Micheál and I went to a dance in Carrick-on-Shannon. The next day I went to confession, with unfortunately nothing of any significance to confess[11].

November was dark and dreary as usual. My reading glasses arrived by post the first week back. They were Council glasses, free but not very modern. I was embarrassed but reluctantly wore them. To be fair nobody slagged me but I was mortified. However I soon persuaded myself that they were not rectifying my eye problem and after a few weeks stopped wearing them. At the end of November we had an official weekend off, although I am not sure why. While at home I persuaded my mother that I needed a second opinion about glasses and got my eyes tested with the local optician. I got new lenses and picked very modern gold rimmed frames. I was thrilled but Mam was not as they cost £5 (€68), almost half of her weekly pension. I went to the local Slieve an Iarainn hotel dance on that Saturday night.

The Corn na nÓg team, trained by Fr. Colm Hurley, were scheduled to play St. Paul's Lurgan in St. Pat's on 10 November, but it had to be postponed due to heavy ground conditions[12]. However they got off to a good start in the defence of their title with a win over St. Mary's Belfast in Dundalk on 23 November by 3.6 to 3.2. They then played Colman's Newry on 1 December[13]. They were knocked out of the competition at a later stage. (Details not available as 6 Dec. issue of *The Anglo-Celt* not in Johnston Library).

My new glasses arrived a short time after I returned to the college. I wore

them with pride and they were helpful to my eyesight as well! December seemed to rain the entire time. I remember realising one day that apart from locking up and opening the pre fab. each day, I had not been outside the college buildings for ten days. Even I knew that was unhealthy and took steps to rectify it. Class went on as usual. I loved the short stories in *Scothscéalta* that we did in Fr. Murphy's Irish class. Beirt Bhan Misniúil, Neill, An Bhean a Ciapadh, Anam an Easpaig, Teatrarc na Gaililí and Nóra Mharcais Bhig. They were interesting, human and real. I loved the literature without having any great grá for the language. I'll always remember the word 'striapach' meaning prostitute. Before this I had thought there was no sex in Irish.
Cavan lads were always slagging us Leitrim lads as being backward. This was hard to take. Dermot Prior and I tried to appear sophisticated and urbane. In History one day, Fr.Dan was explaining how to pronounce the German term, 'Lebensraum' (Hitler's idea of living space for the Germans). He turned to Dermot and I who sat beside each other and stated: 'Mc Niffe and Prior, you'll have no problem pronouncing that, it's like how you say sthicks (sticks) and sthones (stones) around Ballinamore'. The class erupted and we saw months of our cosmopolitan outlook go down the drain. We had Fr. Gerry Kearns for one C.D. (Religion) class per week. He discussed social problems like alcoholism and other general drug abuse, although the latter was fortunately a relatively new and minor problem at that time. Fr. Heerey had us for the two other C.D. classes and we discussed the relevance of Mass and faith among other issues.
Boarding school allowed me the opportunity to study a great deal. From September we had three and a half hours study Monday to Thursday inclusive. On Friday we had three hours, on Saturday six and on Sunday just two and a half as there was a film that night. That was a total of over twenty five hours, with First Years having twenty two hours. In addition I had over three hours extra study as I did not do Physics and Chemistry, during which time I did most of my Latin. I also got the homework done for my two pass subjects, Irish and Maths, during recreation time each evening. Every night after I had my tea and toast in the infirmary, I returned to my own small study hall and did about forty five minutes more work. I often walked around the empty room reciting aloud to myself the main points to remember, especially in regional Geography. I went to bed around eleven, with the room lights centrally turned off, but the corridor light coming in through the fanlight over my room door. On Saturdays and Sundays I did about one hour each day during afternoon recreation. In total this meant I studied for thirty seven hours per week (twenty five compulsory and twelve extra on my own),

an average of over five per day. One Saturday afternoon I was working and Thomas Mc Tague, a friend from Ballinamore in Fourth Year came into the room. He was a very bright pupil and he had an English essay to write. He helped me with my Maths and while I was thinking of some ideas for his essay, he occupied himself by working out a Maths problem (from memory, from his honours Maths class) on the board. I was flabbergasted. Someone was enjoying themselves with Maths, it was a revelation to me.

It is possible that I did more study than any of the other Leaving Cert boarders. However St. Pat's, like most schools at that time, was not a place that you boasted about how much study you did. In fact you tried to keep it fairly secret. The other lads who were keen on doing well in June did study a great deal, maybe as much as me, but it did not appear so. However they were very bright, and may not have needed to study as much as I did. In any event it was noticed that I was 'pounding' very hard. The term was commonplace in many boarding schools to denote studying earnestly, like swotting in the English setting and later when I was in Maynooth College we referred to it as 'baking'. I assume the term pounding came from the idea of repeatedly beating information into your head, not exactly approved by modern pedagogy! One other Leaving Cert lad whom I knew fairly well, used call into my room before lights out at the weekend, when I was not doing the extra study. He was not very interested in studying, and smoked with the lads who did so in the ambulatory. He was always telling me that the 'lads in the ambulo' thought that I was overdoing it and would 'crack up' with all the pounding. I thought this was hilarious and it actually spurred me on to work harder. I told my friend Leo Plunkett about this and we had a great laugh. One night, before this pupil who was so solicitous about my welfare arrived, Leo hid under my roommate's bed. The lad arrived and with some prompting from me, duly proceeded to tell of the concerns of the 'lads in the ambulo' regarding my over work. Eventually Leo gave a massive roar and emerged from under the bed and calmly walked out the door. I feigned total surprise.

I worked very hard for a number of reasons. Obviously I wanted to do well in the Leaving. I had asked to go to St. Pat's in order to study well and go on to university. Now that Dad was dead, four honours, were the 'Sine qua non', (from my Latin 'without which there is nothing') of my Leaving Cert. In addition boarding school was boring in many ways. The routine could get you down if you let it. Looking on each day as an opportunity to get more study done, more of the course covered and more confident for June, was a great way of getting through what was inevitably a somewhat stressful year. In addition while I had always liked English, History and Geography, I was really enjoying them now. It did not mean that I was in ecstasy in every class and during every study period. I suppose what it did mean was that I was beginning to love knowledge for itself, not just as a means to an end, not just as a passport to university. The poem 'The Love Song of J. Alfred Prufrock' by that great American, T. S. Eliot, with its stream of consciousness, was brilliant. The idea of a private-self at variance with the public-persona was amazing. We got essays practically every weekend. The topics given (no choice) were, The Miser (prompted by the novel we were studying Silas Marner), Trees, Boredom, One Voice Cannot Make any Difference, Bureaucracy is Red Tape in Knots, The Value of a University Education, The Value of Tradition, Citizens of an Age of Transience, and Moral Cowardice. In History reading the newly published F.S.L. Lyons, '*Ireland since the Famine*', about W.T. Cosgrave and setting up the new Irish Free State was fascinating. In fact I remember one evening going ahead, forgetting all about time and reading pages on this period as I found it so interesting. I loved the regional Geography of the U.S. and Western Europe, despite it involving a lot of tough memory work to master for the exam. I was intrigued by the Roman History in Latin and got a great kick from being able to translate every one of the entire 901 lines of Virgil's Aeneid Book 6.

Despite my focus on work I still enjoyed myself. Fr. Dan used write the History notes on the board and talk at the same time, explaining them to us. Nobody dared misbehave in Dan's class, even though his back was turned. However one day Joey Mc Govern and I were exchanging 'skites' (friendly boxing) in order to put the other off writing down the notes. Keeping my eye fixed firmly on Dan's back, and without looking at Joey, I flailed out and hit him full whack on the chest, making a loud thumping sound. Dan swung around in a 'smear' (thick). Joey had been caught unawares as he thought our friendly sparring was over, hence he looked bewildered. I was studiously transcribing the notes. Dan, whose 'modh díreach' approach was to shoot first and ask questions later, shouted, 'Mc Govern get out'. 'But father, I did nothing'. Dan continued, 'Get out, get out'. Joey was on his way out when I interjected, 'Father it was me'. 'What? Alright, then you get out and Mc Govern you get back to your seat'. I left. What was interesting was that a few lads afterwards remarked to me as to why I owned up, instead of letting Joey take the consequences. I thought this summed up the difference between day school in Ballinamore and boarding in St. Pat's. In my old school people always owned up if someone else was being blamed in the wrong. I was allowed back to History class the next day. I was not so lucky the next time.

On Friday 14 December I had a visit from Mam, Micheál and Christopher, on their way back from Dublin from an eye appointment for Christopher. We boarders had our Christmas dinner and the Fourth Year concert sometime around that weekend. Christmas exams were starting the following Tuesday. The entire school, boarders and day pupils, had one full-day supervised study on the Monday. I felt that there was an extra air of work and seriousness about the exams as a result. The exams were organised very professionally. Different years sat beside each other, two to a desk in the study hall and in other areas of the school. All pupils were assigned a number and a corresponding seat. Vincent Coyle, a Leaving Cert pupil with a great sense of humour was sitting beside a Fourth Year, Anthony Vesey (Belturbet), who happened to be assigned the number 208. At that time, 208 meant one thing, Radio Luxembourg, as it was the waveband of this incredibly popular music station. Every time we met Anthony, a group of us would sing in chorus, 'Radio Luxembourg 208', the signature slogan and tune of the station. Anthony took it in good spirits.

On Thursday, the dean, Fr. Heerey, asked all of us five prefects to meet him in his room. He gave each of us a box of biscuits for Christmas. We never expected anything and were very pleased. He also alluded to the fact that we were sometimes taking more than the one sleep-in that we had agreed at the start of the year. Brian Smith interrupted to say that he did not remember making any agreement. Fr. Heerey asked us to please revert to just one sleep-in each per week. We agreed.

Friday 21 December was a half-day and start of the Christmas holidays[14]. I was in great form as the term had gone well, I loved being a prefect and was, in an innocent way, very proud of bringing home my box of biscuits. Fr. Dan was giving me a lift home. He was delayed in the college and I had to hang around the front door for an hour or two, seeing all the other lads quickly disperse. It was dispiriting to see the place desolate as the dark evening descended on the shortest day of the year. Dan apologised and his last errand was to go to Abbey Printers in the Old Church building to collect the Seán O'Heslin (my local G.A.A. club) annual magazine. We loaded all eight hundred copies of it into the back seat of his green Volkswagen. After about five minutes a sharp bend on the Crossdoney road ensured that they were now scattered all over the back seat and floor. Dan replied with 'Feck that'.

I was really looking forward to Christmas, feeling I had earned a good break and rest. When I came in to the sitting room, it was in darkness, lit only by the light from the adjoining kitchen. Mam's brother-in-law, Charlie Mc Hugh who had been very friendly with Dad was standing there, at a loss as to what to do. Mam was sitting on the sofa, weeping quietly but uncontrollably.

I came down to earth fairly quickly. Christmas was very lonesome without Dad. Again it took me being at home to realise the enormity of our loss. In fact the five of us sitting down to our Christmas dinner was awful, Dad's absence was so pronounced. We went through the usual exchange of gifts, but the fact that there was no Dad there to share any of it, made it all hollow. I went to a few dances over the Christmas period, in the Slieve an Iarainn and in the 'Mayflower' ballroom in Drumshanbo. Joe Prior and his wife Margaret were living opposite us at the time. They kindly invited Mam, Christopher and me to their house for New Year's Eve to play cards, Whist being the game that was my mother's forte. They were trying to lessen the pain of us being on our own for the New Year, especially as Valerie had just left the day before for Newtownards Hospital outside Belfast to begin training as a nurse[15]. Joe had been my very good English teacher for the Inter Cert in Ballinamore. He was now engaged in qualifying as a Guidance Counsellor. This period saw the beginning of the introduction of guidance teachers in Irish post-primary schools to help pupils, through counselling and vocational guidance[16]. We got talking about what I hoped to do after the Leaving and Joe offered to give me an aptitude test to see where my strengths and weaknesses lay. I spent a few hours the next day in his house completing the tests. A few days later Joe went through the trends that emerged from them. It showed that my expertise (such as it was) lay in verbal skills, language, and expression. This confirmed my belief that I wanted to study English and History for an arts degree in university.

The results of the Christmas exams arrived and I was quite pleased. I got low Cs in English, History and Latin and a high C in Geography (ordinary level class in which I was doing hons.) The pass Irish was fine with a good C, but the pass Maths was not great with a mark in the mid-forties. In the Leaving Cert I felt I could get three honours, English, History and Geography but was not sure about Latin. A pass in Maths was essential as six subjects had to be passed to get to University, irrespective of how many honours gained.

I felt I was ready for the next term, but I wasn't prepared for the conversation that was to take place in the car, on the journey back to the college.

Corn na nÓg team, 1973-74

Back (L-R) Fr. Colm Hurley, Seán Mc Gahern, Martin Flanagan, Seamus Lennon, Gerry Gallagher, Michael Dolan, Terence Brady, Seamus Henry, Fionan Mc Donagh, Jim Mc Weeney and Mel Bouchier.

Front (L-R) Hugh Quigley, Timothy Hurley, Ken Brennan, Martin Shankey- Smith, Seán Quigley, Hugh Brady, Brendan Murray, Michael Faulkner, Kevin Walshe and Michael Flanagan.

Rannafast team, 1973-74

Back (L-R) Fr. Colm Hurley, Jimmy Fox, Ray Slowey, Frank Smyth, Eamonn Gaffney, Paul Mc Evoy, Philip Mc Gee, Ray Cullivan, Oliver Brady and Pat Bradley.

Front (L-R) Seán Quigley, Ciarán Halton, Martin Brady, Donal Donohoe, Pauric Martin and Paddy Mc Govern.

Pounding
Study hall in more modern times

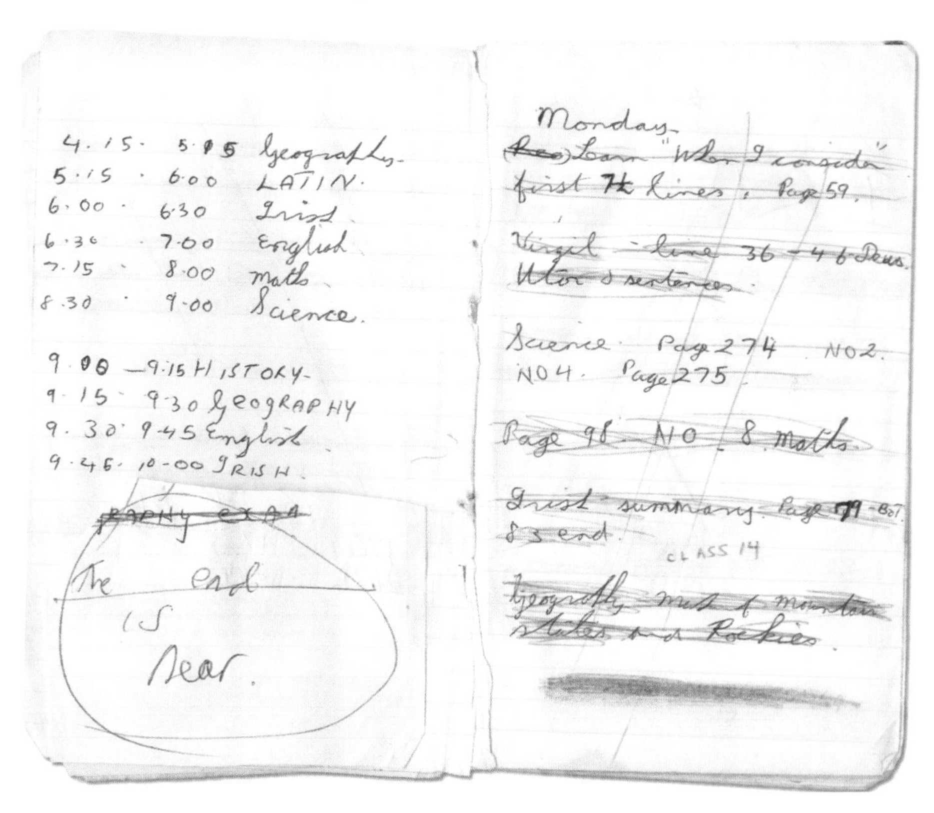

Homework schedule
Author's homework notebook, November 1972

Rem George McKeon
On a Friday during a C.D. Class
Fr Charles Harvey is taking class
and is now giving out notes which
you are taking down. "He could work
no miracle there".
We are going home for
Halloween next wendesday at
1.00 P.M. & Returning to the College
on Sunday at 9.00 P.M. Class
as usual on Monday.

Religion class
Note written by classmate George Mc Keon, October 1973 in author's homework journal

Red-tiled corridor, 1974

Gothic window and outside bell

Mc Rory team, 1973-74

Back (L-R) Fr. Seán Brady, Frank Smyth, Brian Rahill, Eamon Gaffney, Louis Blessing, Aidan Elliott, Jimmie Fox, Philip Mc Gee, Seán Kilkenny, Tom Fitzpatrick, Ray Cullivan, Bernard Donohoe and Cathal Maguire.

Front (L-R) Martin Brady, Ciarán Halton, Robbie Mc Dermott, Ciarán Brady, Owen Martin, Pat Bradley, Gerry Mc Govern, Pauric Martin, Paddy Mc Govern and Donal Donohoe.

Chapter 10

Centenary

January - Easter 1974

On 14 January, a dark Monday evening, I was returning to St. Pat's after three and a half weeks of holidays. This was not unusual at that time as there was no week-long February break and only seven school-days off at Easter. Micheál was supposed to bring me back to the college, but neighbours of ours had friends visiting and they offered to drop me off on their way back to Navan. As a result I found myself in the front seat of a car, driven by a mother, with her three children in the back seat. As the journey progressed she proceeded to tell me in barely coded language about her recent marital difficulties. I was both uncomfortable and excited. Here was an attractive woman, in her early to mid-thirties, whom I had never met in my life, confiding in me about her husband's infidelity. I remember thinking thank God it is dark as it would be even more awkward otherwise. I was uncomfortable as I knew she should not be confiding her problems in me, a sixteen year old lad, half her age. Of more pressing concern was my fear that her two sons or daughter might twig what was being discussed. Fortunately they were totally oblivious as they shouted and argued while I tried to think desperately of an appropriate response. However, overall, I must admit I found it somewhat exhilarating. Upon my return I dared not tell any other pupils.

When I arrived back, Fr. Heerey greeted me with, 'Liam, you look shook'. Being fair it had nothing to do with my recent conversation, but totally the result of a two day bug prior to that. Life got back to normal. It was cold and lots of fellows filled their empty big brown Cidona glass bottles from the hot taps, to use as hot water bottles. Occasionally during the middle of the night, I would be awoken with the sound of such a bottle falling, unbroken onto the floor of an adjoining room. I liked my comforts and so had brought back an actual hot water bottle from home.

The usual tuck shop melee continued. Occasionally the shop boys asked a friend to help them serve if one of the regulars was absent. It was taken for granted that the officially appointed shop boys were allowed recompense themselves with confectionery, as their work considerably shortened their recreation time. After a while of course numerous lads were only too willing to help out serving, including serving themselves. No money was taken but chocolate was taken as payment. On one occasion I was asked to help, and was only too delighted as I had worked in a shop for four summers at this time and regarded myself as a professional shop keeper by this stage. After helping for maybe twenty or thirty minutes the shop closed and like the others I rewarded myself, for me it was a bar of Tiffin chocolate. After a few weeks a solemn announcement was made that no one was allowed serve in the shop, except the designated official shop boys.

Cigarettes were not sold in the shop. Therefore the lads who had parental permission to smoke, usually brought back a supply of cigarettes after a school break, and then got day-boys to buy extra when that supply was exhausted. I remember hearing of one pupil from Laragh returning after Christmas with a very significant 'stash of fags'. He was doing nothing wrong as they were his own cigarettes and he had permission to smoke. Some of the lads who smoked noticed that there was someone stealing their cigarettes. One evening Fr. Peter Casey came into my small study hall and just casually walked around checking the hands of the First Years. It appears that the school authorities had put green dye on some packets that were subsequently stolen and were now following up to see if they had a culprit. I never knew if they got the guilty pupil or not.

I was sick in late January and missed one day of class, my only sickness in the two years. I didn't go to the infirmary but stayed in my own bed all day, getting my breakfast and dinner brought up. By late afternoon or so I was feeling better and got someone to bring up one of the prescribed modern novels on the Leaving Cert course, *The Great Gatsby*, by F. Scott Fitzgerald, so I could revise. I distinctly remember beginning to read it in bed and then moving my bed nearer the window as the natural light faded. The central switch for lights had not yet been turned on. Eventually I ended up standing at the window trying to read the novel with the weak January light disappearing. I found it a boring read at the time, while I loved some of the other modern novels on the course such as George Orwell's political allegory *Animal Farm*, which tied in perfectly with Stalin and the Russian history we were studying. I was also moved by the simplicity and pathos of another allegorical novel, Steinbeck's *The Pearl*.

My father had been in the Knights of Columbanus. It was an association of Catholic lay men, whose aim was to 'secure adequate recognition for Catholic doctrines and practices in all phases of life', as well as fundraising for charitable purposes[1]. It was secretive and had a certain social standing. When Dad died 'The Knights' as they were known, paid my boarding fees for my Leaving Cert year. On Wednesday 30 January they had a Mass in Ballinamore for Dad. I came home the night before and went back the next day after the Mass[2].

Nicknames were an integral part of school life, especially boys schools at this stage. I had gotten involved in a fight/scrap, involving probably a dozen lads, as an eight year old in the yard in primary school, during an afternoon break. In the subsequent investigation by the teacher, as to who was involved, it was discovered among numerous other things, that someone had been scraped on the neck. Another pupil blamed me and immediately someone shouted 'cat'. I had just received my nickname. I do not honestly know if I was responsible or not, I probably was as I would not accept defeat in any manner. But I do know that my 'punishment/sentence' of the name 'cat', blighted my entire childhood. Thereafter in school, every time I had a disagreement with anyone, they retaliated with 'cat', and I retaliated either with their nickname or a fight. Pupils in all classes knew the name and it ruined my life, both inside the school walls and especially on the way home from school. Some pupils had nicknames but not everyone. Only a few of us had nicknames that everyone knew, and that everyone was aware we would react to, if called by them. I was impetuous, strong-willed and consequently everyone knew that calling me 'cat' always got a reaction. I can honestly say it made my life hell. Despite my parents telling me to just ignore the jibe I could not, so my next four years in primary school were full of name calling, counter name calling, scraps and the occasional serious fight. I did not take it lying down, giving as good as I got, both verbally and physically. When we all progressed to secondary school, St. Felim's, our names travelled with us. Fortunately many of the lads from other primary schools who were now in my First Year class brought nicknames with them, so I did not feel as isolated. Of course I still reacted, usually verbally when called 'cat'. A few of us realised that four of the twenty eight pupils in our class did not have nicknames and we decided to find names for them. We announced this publicly during a free class, stating that we did not want the four individuals 'feeling left out'. We found suitable names and christened the four in one day. By Second Year 'cat' was still being thrown at me (albeit less frequently). However I suppose I had matured, I now had my part time job and felt much more secure in myself, had good friends in the class and it did not upset me as much. Its effect lessened somewhat more in Inter Cert Year.

Peter Mc Caffrey, Leo Plunkett and I agreed before going to St. Pat's that we would not let anyone know our nicknames. To be fair to the Ballinamore lads already in Pat's, they did not betray our names either. My brother Micheál, who had done his Leaving Cert in the college one year before I arrived, had been called 'sniff', a benign version of 'Mc Niffe'. I was desperately hoping that I would get this nickname as it was not vicious, and was no reflection of me as a person. Nobody was aware how delighted I was when after a few weeks a classmate, I think Noel Reilly from Cavan town, called me 'sniff'. I had to feign annoyance, to ensure that the name stuck. It did, but was not used that frequently and more as a slag, not as a humiliation. Was I happy!

Nicknames fell into three categories. A few were compliments as they were positive, for example 'the rinner' due to the speed of the person on the athletic track and his unusual pronunciation of 'runner'. Others were neutral, being a bastardisation of a surname, like my own 'sniff', 'sexy' for Sexton, or being the area one hailed from, like 'Ardee' or Dowra'. However most of the nicknames were less innocuous, ranging from the slightly mocking to the vicious. Boarding schools were not a place to display any difference, conformity was the unspoken rule among pupils. Fellows lived a very routine regulated life in close proximity to one another. We had little to do but observe the foibles of our fellow pupils. Some nicknames were brilliantly accurate, ingeniously conceived and incredibly perceptive. It was a harsh world. A few fellows no doubt looked on their nicknames as badges of honour, but I imagine for many others it was public humiliation.

One day in Torlac's Maths class we had a discussion about nicknames. Torlac told us about a new First Year, who had come to the college years previously. He had been warned by his brother, who had finished St. Pat's, as to older lads trying to make a fool of him. Unfortunately the new First Year had learned his lesson too well. On being asked his name by senior pupils, he replied 'Mick', his actual name. When pressed as to his surname, he decided enough was enough and replied, 'The Shite'. He was subsequently nicknamed, 'Mick the Shite' for his five years in the college. What was more, when his younger brother arrived a few years later, he too had his correct surname replaced with 'The Shite'. So much for being forewarned.

When I was a few weeks in St. Pat's we were going down to Mass one morning and one fellow called to another, 'hi dopey, what time is it?'. The lad helpfully replied with the correct time and was rewarded with the title, 'dopey' from that day forward. One lad who did not carry himself in a very coordinated manner, but appeared to be somewhat fluid was called 'watery', sometimes 'H_2O'. Animal names were the most common. If your Christian name was Mickey, you could get the appendage 'Mouse'. One pupil was called 'Frog'. He arrived back one September with a beautiful knitted 'yellow' jumper. Obviously his mother did not know his 'pet name'. A lad with a brown leather jacket (envied at that time) was called 'trout', by accident or design, I never knew. Teachers were not exempt. Fr. Seán Brady, like most of the priests, wore a soutane. But unlike the others his had no shoulder flaps or 'wings' (from his days in Rome?) hence his nickname, 'Wingless'. But of course in any teenage world, everything must be abbreviated, so he ironically was called 'Wing'. However most of the priests, if they had no nickname, were called their first names among pupils. This was obviously prefaced by 'Fr' as in Fr. Torlac, when referring to them in conversation with another teacher.

The following are other nicknames that either teachers or pupils had: Dog, rabbit, skippy, boar, butt, rooster, mow, bandy, tramp, killer, tiger, goofey, bawn, jumbo, madam, hawley, snake, lugs, mug, sherlock, blubber, bulldog, smigs, calf, spear, pope, sock, sweller, and chas. The kitchen staff had a very derogatory nickname, 'clatties'. The priests got incredibly angry if they heard this term being used.

In the early seventies, the term 'gay' was not used to denote someone who was homosexual. Every local town had at least one poor man who was locally known as being 'queer'. In the last number of years the term 'gay' has been used by students in schools as a derogatory term to annoy other students, irrespective of their sexual orientation. Fortunately such bullying is no longer acceptable. In my time in St. Pat's homosexuality was never referred to. It wasn't acknowledged by society, wasn't spoken about and was regarded as a perversion. It may have been below the radar but it had to be there. With over four hundred lads present, on the law of averages, a number of them must have been gay. Whether they knew it themselves at the time or not, I don't know. It was challenging enough for me growing up as heterosexual, I can't imagine what it was like for a contemporary who may have been gay in such a world. St. Pat's was no different from the rest of society. It expected conformity.

In late January Ray Brady gave us an essay entitled, 'Ireland in 1980'. As usual he spent the Friday class discussing the forthcoming topic, giving us ideas, and explained that as it was only six years ahead, we were not to be talking about driverless cars and other far-fetched inventions. The much heralded Sunningdale Agreement had been signed on 9 December 1973, setting up a power sharing executive in Northern Ireland[3]. In my essay I naively predicted that 'the people of Northern Ireland, exhausted by fear, tension and sorrow will begin the reconstruction of Northern Ireland both litteraly (misspelled by me) and politically'[4]. On the education front I forecast that, 'the extent of control enjoyed by the clergy and different religious orders will be more evenly shared by the people'. I continued in my self-confident vein when I grossly overstated the price I expected us to have to pay for an ordinary pair of shoes in 1980, £20 (273 in today's terms). I had not much hope for policy-driven local politics when I stated, 'our standard of local politics will not change to any extent, a policy typified by Shakespeare in his play Coriolanus (our Leaving Cert. play),

"I will practise the insinuating nod,
Tis a condition they account gentle".

I believed that the 'basis of the Irish social scene will change from the bar to the lounge bar in 1980'.

I went home for three weekends in a row, from mid-February to early March. The traditional long term from early January to St. Patrick's Day was changed with the introduction of a weekend off for all boarders in mid-February. It was a welcome interruption for pupils and I assume also for staff. The following weekend I went home for Dad's first anniversary Mass. My uncle, Fr. Micheál Kelly, C.C. in Bailieborough collected me from the college on the Friday evening. He drove the Hillman Hunter slowly as he explained he had to 'run it in' as it was new. Secretly I imagined my dead father laughing, as Fr. Micheál was not known for treating cars gently, he usually drove them very hard. It was great to get home for another weekend, the usual good food, sleep-in and still lots of time to do all my study. However this was all tempered by Dad's Mass on Friday evening attended by his mother, brother, sister and most of our relatives. Mam just went through the motions. Her soul mate was dead, and time, the famous 'healer', had not brought any lessening of the terrible, wrenching sense of loss for her. The rest of us missed Dad, but we had our own lives; Valerie was training to be a nurse in Newtownards in Northern Ireland, Micheál was starting to wind up the garage that Dad had set up and was beginning to look for a job in Dublin, I was away in boarding school and focussed on the upcoming Leaving Cert. Christopher, with the innocence and resilience of a seven year old, did not fully comprehend the enormity of losing his father at that stage in life. Mam's life was irrevocably changed and she was lost without her beloved 'Bill'.

In late February, the father of my class mate, Brian Rahill died. The fact that my own Dad had died at exactly the same time the previous February added to the poignancy. A number from our class attended the funeral on a wet and very windy day at St. Brigid's Church in Laragh.

I phoned Mam probably five times a week from Christmas as she was very lonely. On the Friday afternoon, five days after being home for Dad's anniversary Mass, I suddenly decided I wanted to go home to see her for the weekend. No doubt I also liked the idea of another weekend in Ballinamore. This was unheard of, as a boarder did not just decide he wanted to head home for the weekend. Dermot Prior told me I would be mad not to do so. I asked the president, Fr. Mallon, explaining that my mother was lonely. He immediately gave permission and I will never forget him for that. I quickly told the dean, Fr. Heerey, and got Joey Mc Govern to cover my First Year study group. I headed off at 4.30 on 1 March, hitching the twenty seven miles to Ballinamore. Fr. Pete Casey was heading to Dublin and he gave me a lift out to Tractamotors. I had my school books but no arm band, let alone a high visibility jacket. It would be dark at 6.30. My mother did not know I was coming home and the college just knew that I was gone home. So much for Health and Safety. I was home just before it got dark, much to my mother's surprise and delight.

It was now early March and the Mc Rory senior football was entering a critical phase. In the previous October St. Pat's had played three challenge matches. Our first three competitive games were all played in Dundalk. All of our games in the competition were played on Saturdays. We trounced St. Mary's Dundalk on 10 November, by 4.13 to a single point[5]. Aidan Elliott as goalkeeper was the only playing member of the victorious Hogan Cup team of 1972 to be on this team. Fr. Seán Brady was trainer[6]. The following week the team beat St. Mary's Belfast by 1.10 to 1.07[7]. The feeling before the campaign began was that the St. Pat's team was too young and inexperienced to succeed. However they were quite skilful with ten lads having played inter-county football[8]. Our third game was played in Dundalk against St. Colman's Newry on 1 December, which we won by a solitary point[9]. We were now through to the quarter final. During the break in the competition from early December until early February, the college won four challenge matches, including against St. Michael's Enniskillen and St. Macartan's Monaghan[10]. The latter two were still in the Mc Rory competition, so hopes in Cavan were rising somewhat. On 9 February 1974, in Lurgan St. Pat's had a convincing win over St. Mac Nissi, Garron Tower, Co. Antrim, beating them 2.10 to 0.5[11]. We were now in the semi- final of the Mc Rory, the Ulster Senior Colleges football championship. We were pitted against the previous year's beaten finalists, Omagh C.B.S. The game was played in Lisnaskea on 23 February. We were narrowly defeated, 0.8 to 0.7 in a very close struggle. Aidan Elliott had a superb game as indeed he had all season. Cathal Maguire was injured during the campaign and did not feature in the last few games. The St. Pat's team on that day was as follows: Aidan Elliott, Ray Cullivan, Frank Smith, Louis Blessing, Martin Brady, Bernard Donohoe, Owen Martin, Ciarán Brady, Pauric Martin, Pat Bradley, Jimmy Fox, Donal Donohoe, Philip Magee; sub. Paddy Mc Govern for Jimmy Fox[12].

The majority of day-boys entered and exited the school by the back avenue.

Consequently most of them came through the basements. This area held table tennis tables and some crude homemade skittles in the form of small chunks of wood. Occasionally some lads on their way home flung the 'skittles' at each other in good natured hi-jinks, but unfortunately one such incident resulted in a large window pane being shattered. No one owned up. The dean, Fr Heerey, went to one day-boy whom he suspected. The pupil denied it and Fr. Heerey asked him to sign a declaration that he was innocent, on the understanding that if it were subsequently proven that he was guilty, he would be suspended for three weeks. The lad signed the declaration, which we all heard about. A week later Fr. Heerey got evidence that proved his guilt, so the pupil was suspended. Some of us thought it was a very shrewd but fair move by the dean, but of course we could not say this publicly.

I had my own run-in with damage to school property around this time. One Saturday night, my friend Joey Mc Govern was in my room and we were talking. It was way past lights out and my roommate Peter Mc Caffrey was asleep. The craic was great and Joey, in a moment of exhilaration, opened the window and let an enormous roar out of him. He quickly closed the window, in the process knocking a glass Mi-wadi bottle into the sink, adding to the noise. We calmed down, but in five minutes, Fr. Murphy, whose rooms were on our corridor, appeared in his dark dressing gown, looking none too pleased. We apologised. The next morning he was on duty in the ref., so the dean must have been away. We apologised again. I felt I had let myself down but hoped it would blow over. However we soon realised there was a complication. The following Monday the hand basin in my room was leaking, as it had developed a crack. We were not sure that the Mi-wadi bottle's flight into the sink had caused the crack, but we could safely assume same. I reported just that it was leaking to the bursar, Fr. Leo. A few days later he approached me and pointed out that there had been hi-jinks a few nights previously in my room. I told Joey and to be fair to him he went straightaway to Fr. Leo and owned up. The sink was replaced quite soon and Joey got a bill that summer for £5 (€68).

St. Patrick's College had first opened its doors to pupils on 12 March 1874. Its centenary was planned for the week commencing 10 March 1974. Frank Mc Kiernan, Bishop of Kilmore, himself a past pupil and teacher of the college, heralded the forthcoming commemoration with an address to the St. Patrick's College Past Pupils Union. Its annual dinner was held the previous October in the Burlington Hotel and was attended by over 200 guests, made up of past pupils and their spouses[13]. Introduced by the president of the P.P.U., J.J. Smith, the bishop stated that it was hoped 'to celebrate the centenary with fitting solemnity next March'[14]. He also drew attention to the history of the college that was being written jointly by Dr. Terence Cunningham, a priest of Kilmore from Lavey who was Professor of Canon Law in St. Patrick's College Maynooth, and Fr. Dan Gallogly from the college staff. Bishop Mc Kiernan also pointed out that a great deal of development had taken place recently in St. Pat's and that he had set a target of £100,000 which would meet all these needs. In addition a letter from him was read out at all Masses throughout the diocese the following March, appealing for donations for the college.

An incredible amount of work and preparation must have gone into the planning of the week long celebrations. The college staff, both lay and clerical were young, with over eighty per cent of them under thirty five. In addition, the priests lived in the college and were on hand after class to help prepare and organise what was to be a major milestone in the life of St. Pats. It was decided that the annual musical, usually staged just before St. Patrick's Day, would go ahead as normal and be an integral part of the celebrations. The book on the history of the college would be finished in time to be launched during the week's festivities. In addition an impressive list of events attended by Church and State notables was to take place. All this was to happen during an ordinary school week with two hundred boarders on the school premises all the time and an additional two hundred-plus day-boys there from 9 am. until 4 pm. each weekday. As pupils we were more or less oblivious to all of this. We were aware that there were going to be celebrations but we had no idea just how big a deal it was going to be.

The Anglo-Celt gave unlimited coverage before, during and after the event. It publicised the programme of upcoming events. For three successive weeks in February, it ran a major feature on the college with articles by Fr. Dan Gallogly on the institution's history[15]. Advertisements for '*St. Patrick's College, Cavan, Centenary History*', at a special pre-publication price of £2 (€27) appeared in the *The Anglo-Celt*[16]. A hard-backed book with a beautiful picture of the Old Wing it was published by the college and printed in Monaghan. Dr. Cunningham dealt with the Kilmore Academy, 1839 -1974, the forerunner to St. Pat's, with Fr. Dan dealing with the hundred years of the college itself. While the book now looks dated due to the monochrome photographs and the old fashioned paper and printing, it is still an outstanding history of the college. Despite being written to mark an institution's centenary, by two authors who were priests and very closely associated with it, nevertheless it was an objective account of the school and the milieu in which it operated. It was very professional, very well researched with primary sources accessed and photographs from the nineteenth century unearthed and reproduced. With almost sixty illustrations, biographical notes on college presidents, lists of priests and lay people on the staff and details of parish collections for the college, it is still a very interesting and informative piece of work.

The musical being staged was Rogers and Hammerstein's, 'Carousel' with Fr. Ray Brady as producer, Fr. Gerry Kearns as musical director assisted by Fr. Fergus Clarke, Frances Galligan choreographer, Patsy Lee stage manager and Fr. Leo O' Reilly, lights[17]. The principal characters were played by Declan Dolan (Ballinamore), Brian O' Grady (Cavan), Peter O'Sullivan (Dublin), Con Linehan (Cavan), Tony Finlay (Cavan) and Jackie Mc Loughlin (Butlersbridge)[18]. Rehearsals went ahead as normal, although the musical did not feature much in my daily life as I was not involved. Generally speaking Inter Cert and Leaving Cert classes did not participate.

On Saturday evening, the eve of the week's celebrations there was definitely an air of expectation among us boarders. There had been painting and general tidying up around the college in the previous few weeks. A number of us Leaving Certs were walking along 'the half', mid-way between the Inter and the Senior pitch, when one of our group, Head Prefect Cathal Maguire, suggested we should help tidy up some of the branches that littered the narrow path. We duly obliged, our contribution to the college centenary.

Sunday was the start of the week's commemorations and featured the most significant ceremonies[19]. I think we boarders had a packed lunch instead of dinner, as the kitchen was preparing the luncheon for the guests. We all marched out to the cathedral for a three o' clock concelebrated Mass, with the principal celebrant being Bishop Mc Kiernan. The place was packed. Not only were the faithful from all over Kilmore Diocese in attendance, but everyone who was anyone in Church or State was there for the occasion[20]. On his arrival President Childers was greeted by the No.1 Army Band and inspected an F.C.A. guard of honour. Apart from the fellows from Cavan town, most of us had probably seen the now retired Kilmore Bishop, Austin Quinn, only once or twice in our lives, when he came to our local church every three years for Confirmation. While I knew the present bishop from I was a child, I was somewhat in awe of the spectacle, splendour and pomp of the assembled hierarchy at the Mass in the cathedral. Here was Cardinal Conway and Dr. Alibrandi, Apostolic Nuncio to Ireland. There were seven bishops present, including retired Bishop Quinn as well as four neighbouring prelates, Cathal Daly of Ardagh and Clonmacnoise, Patrick Mulligan of Clogher, Anthony Mc Feeley of Raphoe and John Mc Cormack of Meath. Joseph Gray, past pupil of the college and auxiliary bishop of Liverpool, was

also in attendance. The Rev. K.A. Smith, Lord Abbot of Kilnacrott, a past pupil was there. In addition there were over twenty priests on the altar from the diocese, including a number of priests from the college. Numerous other priests were in the congregation.
The opening hymn 'God is Love' resounded around the cathedral. The first reading was in Irish. The sermon preached by Dr. Peter Brady, a former pupil and priest from Sussex, was followed by the offertory hymn, 'Ag Críost an Síol'. In an age when politics had not yet followed the American presidential razzmatazz, your local T.D. was usually as much as you might have seen. Eamon de Valera had retired as president the previous year, a ninety one year old blind man who was rarely seen in public. Now in front of me up at the front of the cathedral was his successor, President Erskine Childers and his wife Rita. The Minister for Education Dick Burke was in attendance as was the local Minister for Lands, Tom Fitzpatrick. Local politicians included T.D.s, Paddy Smith, John Wilson, and P.J. Reynolds, as well as Senators Seamus Dolan, Andy O' Brien and Joe Mc Cartan. The presidents of neighbouring diocesan colleges who were all priests were also present. The Mass concluded with the recessional hymn:

'This day God gives me
Strength of High Heaven
Sun and Moon shining
Flame in my hearth'

After Mass we pupils returned to the college, where Cardinal Conway unveiled a plaque to the memory of the founder of St. Pat's, Bishop Nicholas Conaty. I had brought back my mother's box camera from home to record commemorations. I decided that the most strategic place to get a close-up photo of the dignitaries was with me on the steps of the college president's stairs, forbidden in ordinary times, but these were extraordinary times. From this vantage point I could view everything, without the dignitaries being necessarily aware of me. Perfect plan. I was all poised and ready as President Childers and his wife Rita arrived in the front door, surrounded by an entourage of other distinguished people, including Fr. Mallon, the college president. I naturally assumed that they were all going to proceed down the red-tiled corridor to the pupils' ref. that had been transformed to accommodate well over one hundred guests for dinner. Unfortunately suddenly Mrs. Childers begins to ascend the stairs, on which I was standing. I don't know whether I was more embarrassed if I were found to be in her way, or petrified that some of the priests would see me where I certainly should not have been on this, of all occasions. I beat a very hasty retreat, trying to soften the noise of my shoes when I left the carpeted stairs and hit the wooden floor boards of the corridor above. (Almost forty years later I discovered that I was not the only one who felt consternation when Mrs. Childers decided to ascend the stairs. In a practically all-male institution, nobody had foreseen that the president's wife might like to change her outfit before the meal. Her request to do so caused some small crisis, but nothing compared to the consternation when someone directed her to the nearest room at the top of the stairs, Fr. Mallon's. While the latter was renowned for his learning and gentleness, organisation and tidiness in his room were not some of his characteristics and the absence of a mirror did not help the situation[21]).

All the dignitaries, college staff, priests from the diocese and many others attended the refectory for dinner. They were joined by Church of Ireland Bishop of Kilmore, Elphin and Ardagh, Dr. E.F.B. Moore. The kitchen staff had been supplemented by a number of sisters drafted in from the Mercy Convent in Belturbet. A number of pupils, of all years, including me were also there helping in the kitchen and occasionally actually serving the tables, though obviously not the top table. As it happened I ended up at one stage serving the table at which Fr. Dan, my History teacher was sitting. In the circumstances this was somewhat problematic. In History class the previous Wednesday, we were revising the 1932 election, the time that de Valera and Fianna Fáil got into power, supported by the I.R.A. Dan, in full flight, described the conditional support by the I.R.A. for de Valera as a 'marriage of convenience' and posed the rhetorical question, 'How long would the honeymoon last'. I could not resist and spontaneously answered, 'Two weeks'. 'Out, out, out, Mc Niffe', was Dan's response to my light-heartedness, much to the merriment of the entire class. I hung around outside beside the dead-end alleyway between the new flat classrooms and the assembly hall, waiting for Dan to emerge at the end of class. When he did I approached and apologised but he was having none of it and brushed me aside. He was obviously under immense pressure for the upcoming book launch and celebrations, but I was taken aback. This was my Leaving Cert year and I did not want to continue my History education in an alleyway. The next day, Thursday, I approached him on his way into class but was told to 'get out of my sight'. I did not go to the study hall to revise as I thought he might relent and send someone out to tell me I could return. As a result I kept the alley occupied not only for Thursday but also Friday. All of this 'history' between Dan and I went through my mind as I approached his table. However he was perfectly civil and called me 'Liam', a good sign.

There were speeches by numerous notables going on for a long time[22]. President Childers stressed the needs of youth stating that 'young people were living in a storm of technological and social change' and mistakenly believed that 'the acquisition of more material consumer goods... with every group watching to see how they fared compared with others... would automatically bring personal happiness'[23]. There were speeches by Bishop Mc Kiernan, Cardinal Conway, Minister for Education, Dick Burke, college president, Fr. Mallon, the Past Pupils' president, J.J. Smith, and finally Michael Gilheany, a former P.P.U. president and Assistant Registrar National University Dublin. Following the luncheon Fr. Mallon formally launched the college history. I bought a copy and Dan signed it, 'Le deá ghuí an údair'.
Evening tea was provided for all boarders in some other location in the school but I was not at it, as I spent the entire evening from about 5.pm until 10.30 pm. helping in the kitchen. It was great, the excitement and the food. I got on a-bomb with everyone as there was a great buzz. Sr. Immaculata, a nun who taught me in first class in primary, was there from Belturbet Convent helping all day. She was amazed that another lad from Ballinamore whom she had taught only six years previously studiously avoided her. He was only a First Year and obviously embarrassed that she had known him as a six year old. We spent the evening washing up and tidying the kitchen. At the end of the work Sr. Kathleen told me to take with me as much turkey and ham as I wanted, which she wrapped in tin foil for me.
The musical 'Carousel' was staged for the first time that night in the assembly hall. President and Mrs. Childers stayed for the performance as did the Minister for Lands and a few other dignitaries. The general public was also in attendance. The Celt the following Friday stated:
'The panoply of the centenary celebrations have taken nothing from the highly polished performance of the St. Patrick's Musical Society fifth annual show'[24]. Years later speaking to one of the adults involved in producing the show, she would tend to disagree with this claim by the Celt, in so far as that first night was concerned[25]. The general dislocation caused by the centenary commemorations, coupled with one or two central characters not actually knowing their songs or lines fully, caused dismay, sheer terror and cold sweat amongst those in charge who stood in the wings, mouthing and practically shouting the lines in to some performers. The fact that the president of Ireland and his wife were in the audience added to their horror. In reality it was not bad for a first night, just not up to its usual polished standard. The Head Prefect Cathal Maguire presented a copy of the college history to the president and the youngest pupil in the school, Kevin O' Connor (Cavan)

presented Mrs. Childers with a Cavan Crystal salad bowl.
The next morning, the three national daily papers, *The Irish Independent, The Irish Press* and *The Irish Times*, all carried fairly large pieces, accompanied by photos, of the college celebrations.
As far as I remember, that Monday was a day of rest for everyone to draw their breath and to prepare for the remainder of the week's activities. There was no class, so only boarders were on the premises. Mass was a little later that Monday morning, but I was still exhausted. When Fr. Heerey was round ensuring everyone was getting up I asked could I have a lie in as I had been helping the previous day. He agreed. It was great as I had a fantastic sleep in, not needing to get up for breakfast as I had my stash of turkey and ham that provided my brunch (although I did not know the term at the time) later that morning. I did not eat any of the regular meals that day, but feasted on turkey and ham. Study was as usual that evening.
Tuesday 12 March was the exact centenary of the college opening. Consequently it was designated 'Students' Day'. Class started as usual, but then all boarders and day-pupils attended a mid-morning Mass in the cathedral. An historic photograph of all pupils was taken on the steps outside. We all returned to the college where a centenary young oak tree was appropriately planted by the local T.D. and Minister for Lands, Tom Fitzpatrick. During his speech, he asked to be excused for using the occasion to condemn the assassination that very morning of Senator Billy Fox from neighbouring County Monaghan[26].
In the early afternoon the day-boys were first treated to a special dinner in the boarders' refectory. Some of us boarders felt slightly peeved that the day-boys, who got lovely meals at home every day, were getting a beautiful meal. Had they really earned it? However our small mindedness disappeared when our turn came and we were treated to a similarly lovely meal that afternoon. Normal study was held that evening. The musical was performed that night for pupils from the other Cavan second level schools[27].
On Wednesday we had a half day's class. Dan would still not allow me return to History. The day-boys went home at lunch time and we had free time until study at 5.30. A few of the Cavan town day-boys hung around, playing soccer with us. There were table tennis tables in the basement. I learned to play that week and it was a must for an hour or so each afternoon. John Boyd (Belturbet) and Martin Coogan (Cavan) were terrific players. When playing against either of them, they would initially play at a little above my level, then increase the tempo and eventually, like a cat finishing off a mouse, annihilate me with a display that was awesome in my eyes. There was a festive feeling

around the whole college, with half days, relaxed atmosphere, and the St. Patrick's Day weekend coming up. Wednesday night was an Oíche Ghaelach, with an Irish concert open to the public.
On Thursday Dan allowed me back to class, after four days in the alley. That day was designated parents' day, with the musical for them that night.
On Friday night all pupils were allowed home after the show and I got a lift with Barry Reilly's parents who were from Ballinamore.
The festivities continued for the weekend after us boarders had gone home. The lads in the musical had to return for performances on Saturday and Sunday as those days were devoted to past pupils. Saturday was set aside for those who had attended the college since 1963, beginning with a football match between the All-Ireland winning team of 1972 versus the college's present team. This was followed by a buffet and the musical 'Carousel'. Sunday was for the pre-1963 pupils. There was also a week long exhibition of college historical items, photographs, roll books, flags and documents dating back to 1839, as well as projects presented by pupils who were still attending the school[28].
I really enjoyed the centenary celebrations, the buzz, the half-days of class, followed by long recreational periods, the sense of historic occasion on Sunday in particular, when a veritable who's who of Church and State were in attendance, the banquet that day where I was in the thick of it helping, Tuesday's pupils' banquets, the stash of lovely turkey and ham that lasted two days, and the thought of going home Friday night. It made a lasting impression on me. Looking back it was incredibly well organised and expertly executed. It must have been a nightmare for the dean, Fr. Heerey, with the normal fairly tight routine abandoned and so many events, involving the public and the pupils, taking place, both in the college and out in the cathedral. However I do not remember any untoward incidents occurring. Nowadays it would require an army of supervisors and specific policies in place.
We boarders who were not involved in the musical were free from Friday night. All boarders returned the following Tuesday evening, after the St. Patrick's Day weekend.
While Bishop Frank Mc Kiernan had flagged that finance was required to meet the expenditure for the improvements carried out in the college in the few years preceding the centenary, I do not remember much about the actual fundraising. Fr. Fintan Mc Kiernan was heavily involved in organising auctions in various towns in the diocese to raise funds. A number of Fourth Year pupils accompanied him to their home towns to help in this venture. One such auction was held in the Slieve an Iarainn Hotel in Ballinamore on

Wednesday 20 March and my mother attended it[29].

The following Sunday afternoon I got a phone call from my mother to say that my aunt Breda who lived in London was seriously ill. A few hours later I phoned home to hear that she had died[30]. Breda had won a scholarship to Loreto in Cavan and then another to U.C.D.[31]. She was single and only fifty when she died. Her remains arrived to Dublin airport from London on the following Thursday, accompanied by my uncle Seán, and headed out on the hundred mile journey to Ballinamore. I walked out from the college and waited at Tractamotors to meet the cortege as arranged. It was a lovely sunny spring evening. I returned the next day, after the requiem Mass. Breda's death did not really affect me at all. All of my aunts and uncles lived within a ten mile radius of Ballinamore, except Seán in Shercock and Fr. Micheál in Bailieborough. Breda lived most of her life in England. I remember when she was home on holidays, she was very lady-like and spoke with a very precise English accent. Since Dad's death, funerals and death affected me differently. In one sense his death increased my empathy with the bereaved as I now had some idea of what they were going through. In another sense I could not be hurt any more than I had been when Dad died and so the death of Auntie Breda did not greatly upset me. If this was true of me, I think it applied a hundred times more to Mam. She was very sorry her sister who was so young had died, but there was very little of my mother's heart left to break. I didn't realise this at the time and was worried that Mam had been dealt another death in thirteen months. As a result she decided to call up to see me in St. Pat's to allay my fears. My friend and first cousin, Raymond Mc Hugh, came up with her on the following Sunday for a few hours[32].

We got our Easter holidays on Spy Wednesday 10 April. There had been a spell of very good weather for the previous two weeks or so and this continued over the twelve day break[33]. I dug the small vegetable plot in the back garden where we planted lettuce, scallions, rhubarb and carrots. I did some study over the Easter, a few hours a day beginning on the following Monday. I was very conscious I was heading back to St. Pat's for the last term before the Leaving Cert. What I didn't realise is that the relatively short term would be etched forever in my memory for events other than the Leaving.

Centenary reception in college refectory, 1974

President Childers speaking at Centenary lunch March 1974
L-R. Mrs. Rita Childers, Bishop Francis Mc Kiernan, President Childers, Cardinal William Conway, Minister for Education Dick Burke and Bishop Cathal B. Daly of Ardagh and Clonmacnoise.

Faces in the crowd at Centenary tree planting

Includes back row (L-R) George Cartwright, Myles Mc Gourty (partly hidden), Michael Faulkner, Jim Mc Donnell (Vice- Principal), Minister for Lands Tom Fitzpatrick, President Fr. Mallon, Jimmy Nugent, Thomas Mc Tague (at back) and Kevin Kilduff (with bag at front).

Carousel cast, 1974

ST. PATRICK'S COLLEGE, CAVAN
CENTENARY CELEBRATIONS
The President and Staff of the College
request the company of

Mrs W. McNiffe

at a performance of

CAROUSEL

by THE STUDENTS MUSICAL SOCIETY
on ~~Thursday~~ Friday, ~~14~~ 15 March, 1974
at 8.30 p.m. in
THE COLLEGE AUDITORIUM

R.S.V.P. Very Rev. President, St. Patrick's College, Cavan.

Author's mother's ticket for Carousel

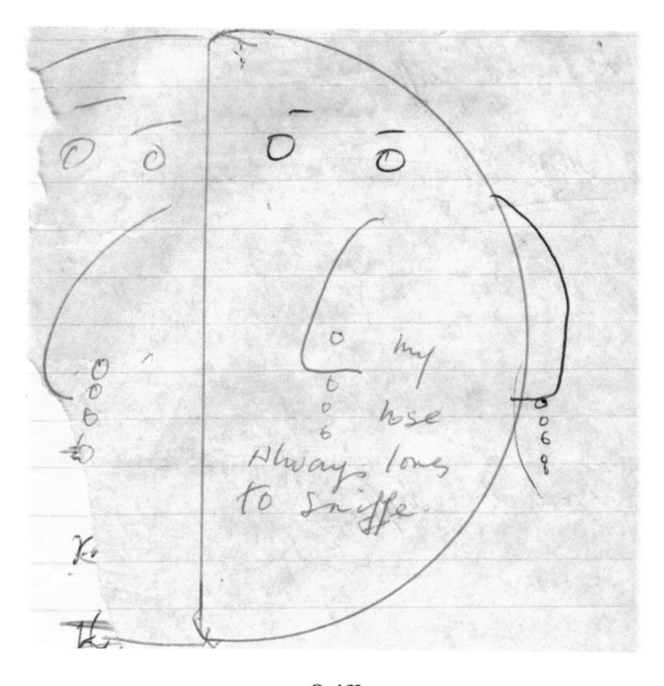

Sniffe
Unknown classmate's caricature of author with nickname

Pupils after centenary Mass in Cathedral, 1974

Book shop boy 1974
Cathal Mc Cabe serving in college bookshop

Is the dean coming? 1974
Vincent Coyle on the lookout from his room

The boys from Ballinamore 1974
Standing tall - Liam Mc Niffe, Thomas Mc Tague and Leo Plunkett

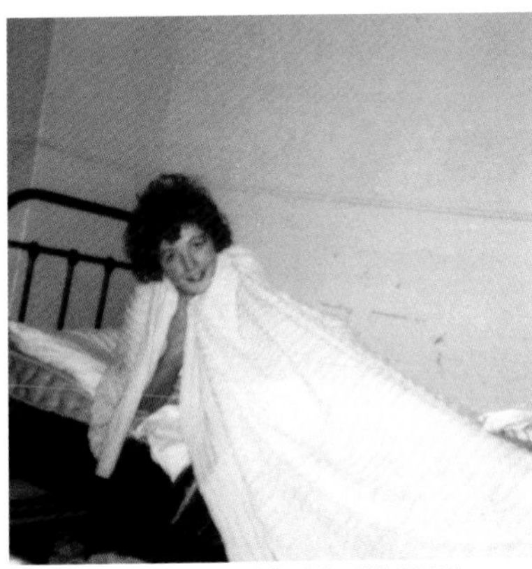

It can't be third bell! 1974

I have him by throat
Dermot Prior and Vincent Coyle

Chapter 11

Bombs, London, Leaving

Easter to June 1974

All boarders returned to St. Pat's on Monday evening, 22 April, 1974. Fr. Micheál gave me a lift back on his way to Bailieborough. The beautiful weather continued and the college was bathed in April sunshine as we remade our beds and settled back into our rooms for the last term before the summer holidays. For us Leaving Certs this term had an added significance. While the summer beckoned, the fact that we had to get through the Leaving Cert was foremost in our minds. A few of us were chatting on the top corridor as we were settling in, and the talk turned to this being our last term ever in the college. It was probably as near as we ever got to being sentimental in any of our conversations in my two years there.

There was serious study to be done before June. Fr. Ray Brady suggested to me that as I was doing honours Geography in what was a pass class, I might benefit more by studying on my own, while he was revising the ordinary level course. It was a great idea and I was now spending two class periods daily (Physics and Chemistry, and Geography) revising in the reception room on the red-tiled corridor. In total six subjects had to be passed, with honours in at least two to get to university. I was aiming for four honours and a university grant. However I had badly neglected Maths and if I failed it, I could not matriculate, irrespective of how many honours I achieved. Maths should not have been a problem for me. I had done honours for Inter Cert and this covered a fair amount of the ordinary Leaving Cert course. However I was not naturally gifted at the subject. Mental arithmetic and compound interest were fine but algebra, vectors etc. did not come easily to me. In addition because the Maths teacher, Torlac, adopted a laissez-faire attitude in class, I sometimes did my Geography homework, or more frequently acted the eejit. While Dermot Prior and sometimes Thomas Mc Tague used to help me with my Maths homework, I allocated only fifteen minutes during recreation after tea time to 'do the Maths', rather than trying to work them out properly. At one stage after Easter I told Fr. Dan about my worry about failing Maths, but I knew he thought I was exaggerating. I should have panicked but fortunately for some reason I more or less ignored the problem.

Career Guidance was in its infancy in Irish second level schools at this time. In September 1973, a staff member, Ray Dunne, had gone training full-time in Dublin to be a Career Guidance Teacher. The school was lucky that it would soon have a professional in this important area. Unfortunately until his return in September 1974 there was no formal career guidance. I do remember Fr. Dan spending a class one Friday afternoon devoted to careers in general. He talked about university and other areas as well as a religious vocation. To be fair he just mentioned the latter among a number of possible careers for us. There was no central application office, we simply applied to any university we thought we were interested in. I think I got the forms from Fr. Dan. Prior to 1970, any Catholic wishing to attend Trinity College had to first get the permission of the Catholic hierarchy[1]. While this ban had been removed, Trinity was never in the mix for most of us. U.C.D, Maynooth, the teacher training colleges and the Regional Colleges were of interest to those of us who intended going to Third Level[2]. (It was not called Third Level or college at this time, simply university, national teaching or the Regional). I remember filling out a form for Social Science in U.C.D., actually finishing it on the sill of the window opposite Class 1 on the green-tiled corridor, one Saturday afternoon. (Considering my 'unique' style of handwriting it is amazing that I got accepted anywhere). I chose Social Science because I wanted to do something that would help people. I had only heard of this course through Fionnuala, my brother's girlfriend (later wife), whose friend, Annette Mc Cabe, had started it a year or two previously in U.C.D. (The irony was that the previous year I had frequently raced to the one phone in the college, ahead of her boyfriend (future husband) Brian Brady, as he went to phone her in UCD.). I never spoke to Annette, had no idea as to the duration of the course or the career opportunities when finished. It sounded modern and exciting.

While I toyed with this course, my main interest was still English and History. I applied to Maynooth University for Arts. You were not required to specify at this stage what subjects you intended pursuing. By today's standards, the application process seems incredibly lax. It was even more so, in the sense that by 1976, some students upon receiving their Leaving Certificate results, only then made their first contact with universities and were duly accepted[3]. The fact that my uncle had attended Maynooth thirty years before, had no real influence on me as he had been a clerical student and became a priest. However I had two first cousins, Frankie and Liam Kelly there as clerical students at this time, so I was somewhat au fait with that college. From the late sixties, Maynooth had opened to lay students, albeit few at first attended, but this dramatically increased as the seventies progressed. What had a major influence on me was that my cousin Raymond and two other lads, Padraig Leydon, and Tommy Mc Manus, from Ballinamore school, had gone there

the previous year to study Science (B.Sc.).
In early May the weather remained idyllic. Fr. Colm Hurley and Fr. Ray Brady, sporting colourful red and yellow jumpers were seen some afternoons heading out to play golf. Beautiful music used emanate from Fr. Hurley's room. As he was a French teacher I assumed it was French music. In any case it exuded class, sophistication and culture. The Sunday following our return after Easter was my seventeenth birthday. My sister Valerie who had started her training as a nurse, decided 'to blow' Mam, Christopher and myself a meal in the Farnham hotel that evening[4]. I really enjoyed the celebration. Joey Mc Govern as usual covered my study and Fr. Heerey had told me to enjoy myself. A few days later the fantastic weather broke. The Oral Irish exam was on around this time. The lads doing honours were under a lot of pressure, those of us doing pass, much less so. Class went on as normal and when it came near our turn, we went up to the red-tiled corridor, waiting outside the reception room to be called. I just remember it being fine and the examiner being very nice. When finished we returned immediately to class, with lads asking what we were asked and how did it go. We all wore our good clothes for the exam. One quiet lad from Co. Louth returned during Ray Brady's English class, sporting a very fashionable, flamboyant pair of bright tartan, bell bottomed trousers. As he returned to his seat Ray just raised his eyebrows in amazement.
There was a diocesan formal-type Religion exam for all pupils in May. The old style course of religious instruction, called Christine Doctrine, based on reading of the Gospels, accompanied by a scheme of doctrinal and moral instruction was outdated following Vatican Two [5]. However a root and branch change of religious instruction did not follow for years. (By the late 1970's, Fr. Ray Brady was to head up a group in Mount Oliver in Dundalk to devise new religious text books). In the meantime the quality of instruction depended very much on the textbook chosen. In Fourth Year, I used sometimes go over my Geography work during Fr. Mallon's C.D. class. We were using a very boring text book, 'Christ in his Church'. Incredibly in Ireland, an overwhelmingly Catholic country, we were studying a textbook written by an English Jesuit, for Grammar Schools students, from ages eleven to sixteen. First published in 1961, it had none of the liberating Vatican Two influences. It was divided into four sections broadly covering the history of the Church: The Old Testament, the New Testament, The Church throughout the Ages and the last section titled 'The Church Today'. The sub- headings of this last section did not excite the imagination: The Organisation of the Church, The Church Teaches, The Church Sanctifies, The Church Rules,

The Church is One, The Church is Holy and The Church is Catholic. In addition the style of writing was somewhat archaic, even by the standards of the time. Some of the questions at the end of chapter were very English orientated (albeit we did not have to attempt them):

> 'Find out, if you do not already know, what idea of the Church is held by your non-Catholic friends'.

For a start practically none of us had non-Catholic friends. I worked with a lad in Logan's shop who was Church of Ireland. However he would tell me where to go if I had asked him what he thought about the Catholic Church. At that time you certainly did not start discussing religion with anyone of a different persuasion. Another suggestion at the end of a chapter was to 'read through the Mass of the Dead'. Even allowing for the fact that we are talking about over forty years ago, we as pupils at that time found the textbook boring and out of date. In Leaving Cert as already explained, we had Fr. Heerey twice per week and Fr. Kearns once per week. They encouraged discussion, but I remember the text book that year as being nondescript. I have a feeling that the scripts of us Leaving Cert pupils in the formal Religion exam in May were corrected by priests in the diocese.

Prizes were awarded at the end of the year for those who excelled in these exams. Noel Barrett, an absolute gentleman who was very bright, and who 'half claimed' to be an atheist won first prize in our class. The morning of the prize-giving, I was in the dean's room where the medals were laid out according to class and name of winner. One senior pupil, whom many knew had copied the exam, had got first prize in his class. I was disgusted. I quickly ran to a friend, got him to write out, 'the cogging paid off', followed by the culprit's name (so my handwriting would not be recognised) and then surreptitiously hid the note behind the medal in the plastic cover. Only the recipient would see the accusation. To be fair to the fellow who cogged, that afternoon he approached another who should have got the medal and offered it to him, saying he did not deserve it as he had cheated.

The toilets in St. Pat's were not attractive. They were old, used by hundreds of pupils and for many lads there seemed to be an unwritten rule, that if you were urinating, on no account should you first lift up the toilet seat. There was nothing malicious, it was just young lads in a hurry and not worried about the next user. The toilet paper was that hard, grease proof type that came in small sheets. Sometimes there was none left, and it was a golden rule to check before you sat that there was an adequate supply. The back of the toilet door on the top corridor was covered with former and present pupils' names. The earliest I could discover was one belonging to the mid-fifties[6].

The day-boys' toilets were on the green-tiled corridor and below at the back of the assembly hall. Some rock fan had burned 'Thin Lizzy' with a cigarette lighter onto the ceiling of the former. Despite this inspired graffiti, the day-boys' toilets, if anything, were worse than what we boarders were used to. That acrid, sharp smell of urine caught you in the throat as you approached. To be fair, the house staff did their best to keep all the toilets clean, with Jeyes fluid liberally used, but with four hundred fellows in the building, it was a losing battle. I was always a stickler for cleanliness, partly as a result of my mother being a nurse and insisting on very high standards of hygiene. As a result I detested the toilets in the college. As a Leaving Cert however I discovered a solution. While individual priests' rooms were dotted along pupil corridors, there were toilets for them a short distance away. One such toilet was on the 'forbidden' top corridor, thirty feet from my room. It had a toilet, hand basin, and bath next door. It was small, very basic, and old fashioned, but clean. I was able to work out when the priest in question (only one used it) was teaching either Leaving Cert or Fourth Years. You could say I got my movements to coincide with his absences for most of the year. I was never caught and as the year progressed I became bolder. On one occasion I was not able to avail of the normal weekly showers for pupils. Instead one morning during my free Latin class, I treated myself to a bath in the priest's bathroom. Dermot Prior knew I was doing this and somehow managed to leave class, knock on the bathroom door and scared the living day lights out of me. No more baths!.

I also pushed the boundaries a bit far with regard to my authorised access to the infirmary after ten at night. Occasionally as the last term came to an end, there might be a salad for tea for all us boarders in the main ref. It was a good meal. One Sunday evening, in the middle of May, I was very disappointed to discover the bag of crisps for evening tea. I quietly slipped out of the ref. and up to the infirmary to make myself tea and toast. Sr. Margaret Mary was usually away on a Sunday evening. As I was just ready to eat, the good Sister arrived back. From the next room to the kitchen, she asked in a perfectly innocent voice, 'Liam, were you late for ordinary tea in the ref?'. The time was just ten past seven at this stage and tea was really only beginning in the ref. I went through the floor in the kitchen and replied, 'Yes, Sister, I was late arriving'. It was obvious to both of us that I was lying. I was mortified. To be fair she did not run me.

The sub-dean, Fr. Pete Casey was on duty each Tuesday, the dean's day off. One Tuesday night he caught me out of my room late or acting the eejit on the corridor and told me I had to sleep that night in the First Year dorm. This was humiliation for a prefect, but no amount of arguing would change his mind. I made the best of a bad lot. I got into my pyjamas in my own room, hopped next door to the dormitory with my bed clothes and made up one of the spare beds in a cubicle of its own. Most of the First Years were already in bed. The following morning I jumped up at the first bell and there was no sign of me in the dorm by the time most of the First Years got up. To be fair, while I was annoyed at the time, I had to admire Fr. Casey not showing any favouritism towards prefects.

I usually finished my own study about eleven and returned to my room in darkness. One night I hit my head off a metal object as I entered my room. It was my own bed that had been 'wrecked' and put on end beside the door. I was in foul humour as I had to find the bedclothes and make it up in the dark. While my roommate, Peter Mc Caffrey, probably was not responsible for it, he did not hide the fact that he really enjoyed the prank. I secretly swore vengeance. The next afternoon, I used my key for the First Year dorm to gain access to it. I then moved Peter's bed into it, so that when he would come to his room that night he would have no idea where his bed had gone. However later that evening I had second thoughts. I was not happy that I had abused my position as prefect to get even with someone and I also was afraid the dean might hear of it and I did not want to let him down. So I went back up and replaced the bed. Peter actually returned to his room and found me doing so. I lied telling him that someone had moved his bed and that I was returning it for him. He was easy going and passed no remarks.

Around this time, two Leaving Cert boarders were caught having sneaked out to a dance. There was very little information pertaining to the escapade, as the lads involved seemed to have decided that the least said the better, and the authorities were certainly not going to enlighten us curious fellow pupils. The reaction of most of us Leaving Cert boarders was that while we admired the 'brave act' element, we didn't really see the point. You still had to be up the next day and the Leaving was approaching and we could go to all the dances we liked in a few weeks. I don't know what punishment was given, but the incident was a one or two day wonder.

Apart from being inconsolable after my father's death, my mother had a great deal on her plate at this time. The garage Dad had started was finally wound up, but there was still a number of issues to be resolved. She was worried about where she would get the money to send me to university, if I did not get the four honours and a grant, She had decided to go back nursing, after a twenty three year gap (apart from two six-week summer stints in St. Felim's in 1969-70). She did an interview in Sligo, including a small oral Irish element, a language she had not used in over thirty years. In addition she had just resumed driving, after a twenty two year break. Mam got a position in Manorhamilton Hospital. Night duty was all she could accept as Christopher was only eight years old and had to be looked after. She left him out with my uncle Thomas Patrick and his wife Bridgie in Drumgowna, four miles outside Ballinamore. She then had to drive the forty miles to Manorhamilton, work twelve hours, drive home and try to get a few hours rest before Christopher returned from school and start all over again. Her first night nursing was Wednesday 15 May. To add to my mother's worry, on that very day, the Ulster Workers' Council Strike began in Northern Ireland, called by hard-line Loyalists and Unionists opposed to the Sunningdale Power Sharing Executive. During this very menacing time, roads were blocked by Loyalist paramilitaries, workers intimidated and electricity supply became highly unreliable[7]. The economic and social life of Northern Ireland came to a complete halt. Valerie was training in Newtownards outside Belfast. Prior to this she used take the Ulster bus to Enniskillen and get collected there for home. Now however there was no public transport. Christopher had medical check-ups in Dublin on Friday of that week. Valerie had promised to accompany Mam and him on the train to Dublin. True to her word she arrived home on Thursday, having hitched through road blocks all the way from 'Ards'. She had been advised to wear her nurse's uniform which she did. On that Thursday evening the three of them got the bus to Dromad and train to Dublin as Christopher's first appointment was at 8.30 in Crumlin hospital the next morning.

While I phoned Mam every evening and knew of her worries, I was 'high' about going to London that Friday. For perhaps the first time ever, the college had organised a trip abroad. The tour was originally priced £15 (€204). A few days before we travelled the organisers apologised that it had to be increased by 50p (€6.80). In an era before cheap flights and cheap travel, £15.50 was very reasonable. It included the bus to Dublin, ferry to Liverpool, train to London, one night's accommodation including breakfast in a very modern hotel, guided tour of London, including entrance to Madame Tussauds and the Planetarium. I remember Leo Plunkett being surprised that I was sacrificing the weekend's study with only a few weeks to go to the Leaving, but I didn't care. I was mad to travel, had the money from my summer work and was not going to miss the opportunity. While few Leaving Certs were travelling, my friend Joey Mc Govern (Ballyconnell) and other fellows I knew fairly well, like Michael Maguire (Cavan) and James Ryan (Cavan) were going. Forty two pupils accompanied by teachers, Jim Hannon and Fr. John Murphy, left on Friday afternoon shortly before class finished at 4 pm. John Brennan who had joined the teaching staff the previous September got a lift with us to Dublin on his way home to Wicklow[8]. A photo of the group prior to departure appeared in the following week's Celt. Both Fr. Murphy and Jim Hannon frequently mentioned how fortunate we were to be making this journey as an educational trip for a weekend, in contrast to the hundreds of thousands of Irish who had been forced to take the emigration boat. It was only years later that I was to realise the wisdom of their pointing this out, at the time it seemed irrelevant.

I was sitting near the front of the bus. As we entered the outskirts of Dublin, probably just before six o' clock we were stopped at traffic lights. A cyclist wrapped on the door, and when the driver opened it, the cyclist exclaimed, 'there's bombs gone off in the city'. (They had gone off at 5.28, 5.30 and 5.32 pm.[9]). We had no idea how serious the situation was. To compound matters there was a bus strike in Dublin, so the traffic, even for a Friday evening, was unusually heavy. When we reached Busáras, we were to be met by another bus to bring us the few miles to the North wall. However it didn't turn up, possibly due to the chaos caused by the explosions[10]. We walked to the North Wall where we would get the Liverpool ferry. As we left Busáras I remember seeing ambulances and an area cordoned off up a street from where we were. I assume that it was the aftermath of the bomb that had gone off in Talbot Street, near the intersection with Lower Gardiner Street[11]. We had still no idea what exactly had happened. We walked what seemed an incredibly long journey to the ferry. When on board, news of the enormity of what happened filtered through. We sailed around 9 pm. We had T.V reception before we sailed and for a short time afterwards. Three bombs had gone off in the city centre, without warning, and there was extensive loss of life. We then discovered that a bomb had gone off in Monaghan at 7 pm. with more loss of life.

I was not in any way in shock. While conscious of the loss of life, I was young and excited by being in the middle of these, albeit catastrophic events. I was however concerned that my mother would be very worried about me. This was an era before mobile phones. The manual telephone exchanges meant that it took ages before you could get in contact with someone down the country. The teachers soon informed us that they had managed to phone back to the college to allay parents' fears as to our whereabouts when the bombs exploded. I do not remember being worried about my family, although I should have been. As it happened my entire family was in Dublin that fateful day. Mam and Valerie were in Crumlin Hospital with Christopher for an appointment regarding his galactosemia at 8.30 that morning, followed by an eye appointment at 11.30. They were to return by train in the afternoon. It never struck me that they could have been caught in one of the blasts. In fact they were lucky. I didn't know it at the time but they got the 2.15 train home from Connolly Station[12]. The second bomb that went off three hours later was in Talbot Street, on the main route from the city centre to Connolly Station[13]. I just assumed that they had gone home and did not know the geography of Dublin well enough to realise they might as well have been heading for the later train at the time of the explosion. In addition Micheál had recently moved to Dublin.

I was determined to enjoy the weekend. Soon after we left Dublin, I went for something to eat, not in the ordinary buffet area of the boat, but in the formal dining room, with waiters and lovely white starched table cloths and napkins. I horsed into a big meal and then did not feel so great before I finished it. Michael Ryan (I think) who was sitting on the opposite side of the table to me, casually asked was I ok. To which I replied, 'why do you ask?', and he says, 'You look kinda green'. Fortunately it passed. It was a nine hour trip and we had no cabins. However I had planned in advance how to arrive in Liverpool refreshed so as to enjoy to-the-full the next day. My mother had been prescribed sleeping tablets for a while after Dad died. I had taken the liberty of bringing two with me. While the rest of the lads tried to sleep on the seats, I secured a bunch of discarded newspapers, put them on the ground at a clear space near the seating area and, fortified with one sleeping tablet, got a good night's sleep. We disembarked and were brought by coach through part of Liverpool to a station where we caught the train to London.

This was only my fifth time ever on a train, as we always had a car. The two hour journey to London was very educational. All my Economic Geography about England suddenly came alive. The back of large industrial towns and cities seemed endless, only interrupted occasionally by the green countryside, in direct contrast to Ireland. The endless small red/brownish houses, with their aerials, small garden sheds and little back gardens conveyed a world of urbanisation and industrialisation foreign to me. I was not able to articulate it at the time, but it all looked 'tired' to me.

London was certainly not tired, it buzzed with excitement, traffic, different nationalities and lovely weather. We booked into our hotel, luxurious beyond what I expected. Occasionally I had stayed in hotels in Ireland while on holidays with my family. However this was a step above what I was used to. Four were assigned to each room. Wanting to show how au-fait I was with hotels and not fazed with my new surroundings I enquired as to what floor we were on of the porter who accompanied us in the lift. Michael Ryan diplomatically pointed out to me that as our room number started with the numeral 2, we were going to be on the second floor. The room was very spacious, and had an en-suite, the latter was certainly the exception in accommodation at that time. We couldn't believe our luck. We were told to be down in the foyer by 1.30. The three boys left, but as I was feeling a little groggy, I decided to have a shower and said I'd follow. As I am drying myself, and thinking that this is the life, the phone rings. An understated, low, calm voice says, 'Liam, we are all waiting'. It was Fr. Murphy from the foyer. I quickly realised we were following English time keeping and raced down, to be met by a round of good natured applause when I got on the bus.

We saw the usual sights, including the Houses of Parliament, London Tower, Buckingham Palace and St. Paul's. We returned to the hotel that evening. I decided to phone home, and of course ostentatiously showing my natural confidence, I rang reception from the room and they put the call through for me. I spoke to Mam for over ten minutes. In the wake of the bombings she was particularly pleased to hear me. She had been very worried about Micheál as there had been no word from him since the bombing. However a first cousin had managed that morning (Saturday) to contact her brother in Dublin and realised that Micheál was fine. Mam had also been worried about Valerie who had to hitch back to Newtownards, but had arrived safely, although she now had no water due to the Loyalist strike[14]. It had been an unpleasantly eventful few days for my mother, but at least we were all safe. Not so lucky the victims of the no-warning bombs. As we watched the news on T.V. in the hotel room in London that night, the sheer scale of the carnage sunk in. A total of 35 people were killed, (including a full-term unborn baby, and a still-birth a few weeks later), 28 in Dublin and 7 in Monaghan[15]. In addition almost three hundred people were injured.

I don't know about all the other St. Pat's lads on the tour, but I don't think anyone went off drinking or anything like that. Some of us walked a short distance in the precincts of the hotel and that was it. We returned to the room, talked and someone had managed to procure a 'dirty magazine' with topless girls, which was passed around a few rooms. While I was mad to see it, at the same time I had to feign nonchalance, as if I was used to seeing a lot more exciting magazines on a daily basis.

We went to Mass in a nearby Church the next morning. We then went on a visit to Madame Tussauds. As we were looking at King Henry and his numerous wives, there was a big shout and the flash of a camera. It transpired that one of the mainstream British tabloids had got an actress to stand perfectly still, dressed as one of Henry's wives, a seventh, when there should only have been six. The photographer had waited until some member of the public had twigged what was going on and a young lady had just done so. I was absolutely fuming. I had missed the golden opportunity to appear in a British newspaper (albeit tabloid), my cred back in Pat's would have been great. As it was, I didn't know how many wives poor Henry was supposed to have, nor did I realise that 'one' of them was real. We then went into the Planetarium next door to Madame Tussauds. The interior roof became the sky at night and we sat back on reclining type chairs to see the world of constellations. It was so real that I fell asleep for almost all of it. We then had a short time for shopping. I bought a new pair of terracotta trousers for £6 (€81), expensive, especially when I discovered later that summer that in fact they were too big. I paid my phone call bill at reception, £2.25 (€30), and could not tell anyone that I thought it would be considerably less. We headed back to the train station.

When we arrived in Liverpool the bus bringing us from the train station to the ferry terminal gave us a quick tour of the city. I remember seeing one of its cathedrals, the Catholic Liverpool Metropolitan, and hearing how World War Two had interrupted its construction and also radically changed its eventual design. We were all much less lively on our return boat trip and I did not indulge in a big meal. I got a good night's sleep, courtesy of another sleeping tablet. We arrived into a very quiet and somewhat desolate North Wall around seven or so on Monday morning. The bus bringing us back to Cavan, stopped briefly in Navan and I phoned Mam to tell her I was back safely[16]. On the last leg of the journey I used the microphone to thank our two teachers for organising the tour and we gave them three cheers. That is all they got, so much for the gratitude of youth!

We arrived in the college just as the morning break was commencing. We boarders raced up to our rooms, threw in our bags and were in class for 11.15. It was a very quick return to normality and then the terrible tiredness hit. We had Fr. Murphy for Irish, and as he walked around the class, looking at his shoes, he quietly says to me, 'Yid miss the shoe polisher'. Outside each lift in the hotel there had been an electric shoe polisher and we pupils returned with shoes shining like never before. By lunchtime we were out of it, so I asked the dean, Fr. Heerey, could those who were on the trip have a half-day and go to bed. He agreed and I retired around 2.30 and slept solidly until the next morning. The tour was a fantastic experience. Unlike my previous forays into photography in Lourdes and during the centenary, my London photos 'came out' quite well.

In general the weather was good that May. At lunchtime on one glorious day, someone had the bright idea that we prefects would ask the president for a half day, just because it was good weather. The 'pros' always walked up and down the section of the front avenue, from where it divided, to the front door, at lunch time during good weather. We four prefects approached Fr. Mallon and other priests and put forward spurious reasons for a half day, like we needed a break before the pressure of the Leaving, etc. etc. To our delight it was granted. We walked briskly towards the front door and once out of view ran like lunatics, shouting down the corridors at the top of our voices' half day, half day, half day'. By this time it was after two o' clock and some teachers were already back in class. There was a great sense that we prefects 'had swung it' securing a half day. My euphoria and I were stopped in our tracks, with the emergence of one non-too happy Fintan Mc Kiernan, who stood in front of me and demanded in no uncertain terms as to what all the rumpus was about. When I explained he did not congratulate me on my diplomatic skills. Apparently he had been teaching a double class of Physics and Chemistry to his Leaving Certs and was very keen to get work done. In retrospect I realise we were pushing an open door with the president and other priests, like Fr. Dan, when requesting a half day. They would have known Fintan's determination to make full use of his double class that afternoon, and their willingness to grant our half day may have been to annoy him. Those were innocent times, no worries about informing parents in advance, arranging lifts, coordinating buses, informing other schools. A school simply decided and the pupils thumbed home.

On the following Friday, my first cousin Frankie, who was being ordained a priest for Kilmore Diocese in two weeks' time, called in to see me. We chatted in his car, parked just outside the college library. When the bell went for evening study he asked did I not need to go, but I was enjoying the conversation so much I stayed, conscious as I was that my twenty four First Years were on their own in study. As it happened they were fine, doing no study no doubt, but doing no harm either, for the one and a half hours. Later that night I phoned Mam and told her I was broke, in the sense that I had no more money with me in the college. London extravagance had caught up. She sent back clean laundry and money via Barry Reilly's parents who came to visit him on the Sunday[17].

The following Tuesday 28 May, the strong arm tactics of the Loyalists succeeded, the Power Sharing Executive collapsed and the strike was no longer necessary. At least Mam no longer had to worry so much about Valerie. By this stage my mother had sensibly realised that night- duty nursing in Manorhamilton was not feasible and discontinued it. My world was getting narrower and narrower, current affairs and family affairs were being forced to take a back seat as the Leaving bore down on me and on everyone else in my year.

The college Annual Sports Day took place on Sunday June 2[18]. It didn't feature largely in my diary. Parents, pupils and visitors attended. The highlight was a novel soccer competition, with a team from each class, ensuring great rivalry. The final was between Class 5 (Fourth Years) and Class 7 (Inter Certs). Normal time saw a two all draw and extra time did not break the deadlock. A penalty shoot-out saw the younger Inter Cert pupils win. There were also competitions in track and field events, handball, table tennis and basketball. The same cohort of pupils triumphed in many athletic events. John Feehan (Corlough) notched three firsts and a second, to win the Best First Year Athlete Award. The Fifth Year winning relay team was made up of Bernard Donohoe (Laragh), Cathal Maguire (Bawnboy), John Clarke (Ardee) and John Boyd (Belturbet). The senior basketball title was won by Class 4 of Fourth Year, comprising Paddy Mc Govern (Belturbet), John Mc Gurk (Ballyjamesduff), Robbie Mc Dermott (Ballinagh), Francis Maguire (Lisduff), Thomas Mc Tague (Ballinamore) and Eamonn Gaffney (Carrickaboy).

Our Leaving did not begin until well into June, Wednesday 12 to be precise. Nowadays Leaving Cert students discontinue normal classes two weeks before the actual exams in order to revise. We, on the other hand, had class as usual until the Friday before, while the non-exam classes did their summer house-exams. Despite the emphasis on exams that last week of normal term had a festive atmosphere. Sports Day set the scene the previous Sunday and then there was the dean's day off. Each week the sub-dean was on duty for most of Tuesday. Traditionally the last Tuesday of term was noted for hi-jinks. Nothing untoward happened for most of the day. The First Years who were in my study raced after me en masse to 'stuff me' with grass from the newly mown senior pitch, good natured, but I was certainly determined to escape. They tracked me all around outside and then I bolted down the steps at the side of the new flat roofed classrooms towards the study hall. As I rounded the corner in full-flight, I left sprawling an unsuspecting First Year, Patrick Mc Hugh (Glenties) who happened to be standing there. Without stopping I shouted apologies and ran on[19]. Eventually I ran out of steam and the First Years caught up with me, but I persuaded them not to 'stuff me' and they didn't. This was all during evening tea time recreation. Mitchie Flanagan, whom I knew from Drumreilly Lower outside Ballinamore, was visiting his son Martin at the same time. What I didn't know is that there was a serious fight in full swing between two pupils right beside where he was talking to

Martin. The next day the authorities were trying to work out exactly what the fight was about and were concerned what Mitchie would have thought seeing such a spectacle. I thought they need not have worried, as my uncles had played football with Mitchie and he would not have been too worried about 'gasuns' having a bit of a scuffle.

On Friday 7 June summer holidays began for all but the exam classes. There was prize-giving and a half day. Traditionally the Inter Cert and Leaving Cert boarders also went home to get a break before the exams, returning the next night, Saturday. In effect the college emptied by 2 pm. I was due to attend my cousin Frankie's ordination on Sunday and his first Mass on Monday evening and so decided to stay in St. Pat's and study until Saturday evening. It was an eerie feeling. I went to bed on Friday afternoon, got up that evening, and made myself tea and toast in the infirmary. During the forthcoming exam period there would be no supervised study, with pupils studying, two to a room, in their own bedrooms, with desks brought up from one of the classrooms. I brought a desk up and studied for a few hours that night. Fr. Heerey asked me would I mind going around and switching off all the lights in the rooms, when he turned on the main switch which I duly did. I will never forget the feeling as I went around individually to seventy rooms. Teenage lads are not instinctively tidy and St. Pat's lads were no exception. Many rooms had an abandoned look, as anything that was not deemed necessary to bring home was discarded on the floors. Beds were bereft of bedclothes, the small cupboards were flung open. The place looked desolate, coupled with the fact (as far as I know) that I was the only boarder there for the next twenty four hours. Schools are meant to be full of students and noise and activity. On Saturday I studied most of the day in the weird environment. That evening the exam boarders started to stream back. I did not want to be meeting them and then heading off, so Fr. Dan allowed me to stay in his room until he returned and was ready to give me a lift to Ballinamore that night, as he too was attending the ordination.

I arrived home late and next morning the entire family went to Frankie's ordination. It was a massive event, in the sense that Ireland still regarded priesthood as a very special and sacred calling. Ordinations had begun to take place in the native parish of the priest to be ordained, rather than en masse in Maynooth College as had happened previously. Aughawillan parish, outside Ballinamore was Frankie's native parish, and the ordaining bishop was the fairly recently consecrated, Frank Mc Kiernan, a native of Aughawillan. Frankie and I were double -first cousins, (Kelly-Mc Niffe) so all his relatives were my relatives. As a result everyone knew practically everyone else. For my grandmother it was very special. A woman of great-goodness and great faith, to see her grandson ordained to the priesthood in her native parish, by a bishop whom she had seen grow up as a near neighbour, was an incredible event.

After the ceremony I returned home and studied for the evening. On Monday I studied and that evening all my family attended Frankie's first Mass in Drumcong Church, half way between Ballinamore and Carrick-on-Shannon. (In 1962 Frankie's family had moved from their native Aughawillan to Laheen Keshcarrigan in Ardagh and Clonmacnoise Diocese). I was very impressed that when Frankie was giving me his first blessing he remembered to wish me good luck on Wednesday. We all returned to 'Laheen' for refreshments and my uncle Seán and auntie Margaret gave me a lift back to St. Pat's en route to their home in Shercock. Margaret used the occasion to see the president, Fr. Mallon, and get her 'spoke in' regarding her youngest son, Niall, who was coming as a boarder the following September. She requested that he be able to share a room with another cousin, Ciarán Martin from Swanlinbar, rather than having to be in the First Year dormitory. My uncle Seán was looking around his surroundings as he was a past boarder himself.

Tuesday had a quiet and nervous tension about it. All boarders in the college were either Inter or Leaving Certs waiting for the exams to get started the next day. As was usual, a number of day-boys came in as boarders for the duration of the exams, allowing them to study uninterrupted and to dispense with bus travel etc. Among these were Tom Fitzpatrick (Ballyhaise) and Luke Flynn (Butlersbridge).

We started with Irish on Wednesday, both papers. As I was doing pass it was an easy start. During lunch Sr. Rosarii saw me, enquired about the paper and told me I looked pale. She brought me to the infirmary and got me a cup of hot Horlicks to drink. While I was very appreciative, I hated Horlicks and was convinced the milk was sour in it, so when she was gone out of the room, I discreetly dumped it down the sink. Thursday was Corpus Christi, a holy day of obligation. Consequently there were no state exams. It suited us perfectly. We had all of Thursday to revise for honours English the next day. I loved the exam, both papers. I knew the five or six turgid prescribed prose extracts, such as The Superannuated Man by Charles Lamb, inside out. The composition I chose was 'Fanatics'. Being somewhat of a fanatic myself I was in my element. I talked about historical fanatics such as Hitler and Mussolini, and Fascism itself as being a form of fanaticism. I knew a lady at home who was obsessed with caring for and talking about her teeth, at a time when dental care for most people meant getting a tooth out or getting dentures in.

I tried to analyse why people were fanatics, was there something lacking in their make-up? In the second paper I was happy with my answers on Shakespeare's play 'Coriolanus' and on George Eliot's novel 'Silas Marner'. In poetry I answered Milton's 'Lycidas', helped immensely by Ray Brady's dictated notes from the critic Tillyard. The final question I did was on the modern novel, and I included Orwell's 'Animal Farm', Steinbeck's 'The Pearl' and Fitzgerald's 'The Great Gatsby'.

Saturday and Sunday were spent studying. In one way the worst was over in that we had begun the exams and yet in another sense the worst had still to come for me. I had left myself in the stupid situation where I might scupper my chances by failing pass Maths. I had bucked up a bit in the previous few weeks. I now had a small hard backed notebook with the dozen or so theorems on our course, done out in uncharacteristically clear handwriting and diagrams.

> 'Theorem 1:
> A line parallel to the base of a triangle divides the other two sides proportionally'.

Maths paper one on Monday was a disaster. We had to do six questions and I only attempted three. I simply had no idea of how to start the others. I knew I had made a fair attempt on the three, but that left a lot of work to be done for the second leg the next morning. Latin went quite well that afternoon. Virgil's Aeneid was simple as I was able to translate it perfectly. The Roman history was similarly easy as I loved history. The translation of the unseen from Latin to English was o.k. in the sense that I had a good vocabulary, but my understanding of the grammar would have let me down. The core of the course and paper, translating English into Latin was my Achilles heel, as I was very poor at this. Fortunately I knew that the four sections carried equal marks and so I hoped to get the honour (C) without actually being able to write Latin. Micheál called briefly that afternoon and as we sat in the car, I think he was horrified that I had only attempted three questions in Maths, but sensibly did not dwell on same. We had Maths paper two on Tuesday. Monday night was totally devoted to trying to salvage what I could the next day. Dermot Prior as usual was helpful and explained vectors. It actually made sense but was there enough time? Luke Flynn, an absolute and unassuming gentleman, who was unflappable, helped me with other parts of the course. A new coffee vending machine had just been installed a few days before. I went down to the green-tiled corridor to get coffee for Luke and myself. Despite the pressure and the fact that he was helping me, I could not resist the possibility of a prank. I filled an empty coffee paper cup with hot water from the tap, and transferred the froth from a genuine coffee I had got for myself to the top of the hot water cup. For all intents and purposes it looked like an ordinary cup of coffee. Luke was not fooled however and nicely insisted that we swap cups. I then went back and got proper coffee for him. When I think of it, he spent significant amounts of time helping me with my Maths on the eve of his own Maths exam[20]. I suppose the only reason I did not 'freak out' that night considering the dilemma I had left myself in was because of the help of Luke and Dermot Prior.

Maths paper two was better, in the sense that I attempted all questions and it was the part of the course I was more comfortable with. That afternoon and evening was spent preparing for the following morning's Geography exam.

Most of my class were seated well apart in the study hall for our Leaving Cert. There was a story doing the rounds that a few years earlier, the then president, Terry Mc Manus, was passing the study hall window and saw a pupil attempting to copy. He immediately went in to the supervisor and alerted him. The pupil received a stern warning on that occasion. As our exams progressed the supervisor in our centre became a little more relaxed. Instead of individually giving out the papers, we frequently got up from our seats, went up to his desk and got our exam paper. One Leaving Cert pupil (from West Cavan) purposely did not turn up for the exam that morning. Instead one of his friends who was doing Geography told the supervisor that his friend was sick and hoped to come in as soon as possible. Meanwhile another friend who was also doing the exam secured an extra exam paper due to the manner in which they were given out. He then slipped it between the opening in the double doors at the back of the study hall, before innocently returning to his assigned seat. As prearranged another lad who was not doing Geography collected the paper and flew up upstairs with it. There the fellow who should have been in the exam poured over it, with the aid of textbooks and helped by two other non-Geography pupils. At 9.55, the pupil turned up to the exam, citing sickness as his reason for being late. In reality he was always very pale and looked so sickly, that the supervisor got him a cup of tea. He had to finish the exam at the same time as everyone else. It was an ingenious plan, perfectly executed. I was quite happy with my exam.

However at lunch time a rumour was rife that we might have to re-sit the exam. A few years earlier a Leaving Cert Maths paper had been leaked and pupils had to redo that exam, so it was not inconceivable. What appeared to have happened was that on some few Maths papers in one school the day before, a small section of the upcoming Geography paper had been printed by accident. Some of the newspapers had carried the story, and that is how the rumour gained currency. For an hour or so those of us who had just completed the Geography paper were fairly anxious that we might have to re-sit it. It was then discovered that it was the pass not the honours paper that was affected, so I selfishly stopped worrying and went to bed for a few hours. I got up that evening and started in earnest revising for my last and final paper, History. I studied until about 10 pm. when the dean, Fr. Heerey, called in to tell me that the president, Fr. Mallon wished to see me. I rather ungenerously thought to myself, 'of all the nights, doesn't he know I have History in the morning'. I went over to his room, and we chatted for a while about the exams. I was still wondering the purpose of the call until he finally said, 'have you any thoughts about what you are doing next year?'. Now I realised he was gently checking had I thought about the priesthood. In reality at that exact time I was thinking much more about the past, than the future. Any thoughts about the Church were confined to the Kulturkampf, the bitter struggle in the 1870s between Bismarck and the German Church. I just replied that I had not thought of the future as of yet. I returned to my room and studied until 1.40, when I went to bed.

I had brought an alarm clock with me and got up at 5.40 to study again. It was the last exam and all I needed to do was to make it to midday. At 8 a.m. I attended Mass as we all did, had breakfast and headed to the exam. The problem with the History exam was time management. There were five essay style questions to be done. In reality each deserved forty five minutes. However the exam was only three hours long, so the maximum time for each question was about 35 minutes. This only left five minutes for deciding what questions to do. I was very pleased with the paper, including doing one question on Parnell.

Finishing the Leaving was an anti-climax as it is for many people. It was particularly true for me as I think I was the first person of my year to be finished all exams. I was not doing Physics and Chemistry that was scheduled for that Thursday afternoon. Being conscious that the rest of my class were heading into another exam, I made no fuss of being finished or heading home. I didn't eat dinner in the ref. as I just wanted to get home. I said good luck to Dermot Prior and a few other friends. I hopped up to my room and threw all my stuff into the big russet case that I had arrived with two years earlier. By this time the exams had restarted and the corridors were totally quiet and empty. I carried out the case which took up most of the back seat in Mam's Mini car. My bundles of books were put in the small boot. As I was making my last journey between my room and Mam's car I noticed the photos of us Leaving Certs, pinned to the noticeboard beside the book shop.

I made a mental note not to forget to purchase one[21].
Fr. Heerey was sitting on the steps to the front door, reading his breviary as I said good-bye to him. It was a dry sunny day, and Mam allowed me to drive the car down the main avenue to the front gate. Despite there being no fanfare for me completing my Leaving, I was very conscious that I was going home, down the same avenue that I had come up two years earlier, but this time without Dad. Nothing was said but I think Mam and I were both very conscious of his absence. I made full use of my chance of driving on a private avenue, and only changed over when we were just outside the main entrance gates.
I was obviously exhausted. However as we drove home, I realised a great burden had been lifted from my shoulders. Summer work and football beckoned. I was excited as a new phase was about to open up in my life. I didn't know the phrase at the time, but I definitely felt that the 'world was my oyster'. It was over, but it was all about to begin. I was happy about how the exams had gone, the only worry was would I pass Maths and did I get the honour in Latin. However the die was cast and there was nothing I could do. I didn't realise it at the time, but a return journey up that same college avenue, a few weeks later (before the results were out) was to change my life for at least the next three years.

Bishop's house, 1974

Letting in the light
College chapel windows

School tour to London, some faces in the group
Back row nearest bus (L-R) Third-in: Joey Mc Govern, Liam Mc Niffe and Tony Caffrey (against bus), *Row immediately in front (L-R)* Francis Duffy (now Bishop of Ardagh and Clonmacnoise), Sean Kilkenny, J.J. Byrne, Jim Mc Morrow, Paul Kelly, (behind him) Jim Ryan and Michael Maguire. *New row, (starting in front of Sean Kilkenny)* Myles Mc Gourty, ----- -----, Vincent Coyle, ----- -----, Seamus Henry. Teachers, Jim Hannon and Fr. John Murphy.
Very front row, second-in: Rory Hayden, and *extreme right:* Mel Bouchier.

EXAMINATION IN RELIGIOUS KNOWLEDGE

COURSE C.

(Christ our Life).

Tuesday, 2nd May, 1972 — 10 a.m. to 12 noon.

Examiner: Rev. Thomas McKiernan, D.I.

(Five Questions to be answered).

1. Christ said "Love your enemies". Why should we try to love someone who hates or injures us ? In fact is this really possible ?
2. "Thou shalt not steal". This seems to be one of the least observed commandments in Ireland today, especially where public property is concerned. Please comment (approx. 150 words).
3. What is conscience ? What are the different influences that shape our conscience ? If the Church says something is wrong, then there is no need for conscience, is there ?
4. Why is every individual entitled to our respect regardless of such things as his wealth, position, popularity, conduct, etc. ? Do some people deserve more respect than others ?
5. Christ said "the poor you have always with you". Can this excuse us from facing up to the problem of poverty ? Is a poverty-free world an impossible dream ?
6. One—perhaps the most important responsibility of a teenage boy or girl is to play a part in creating a happy home. Write between 100—150 words on this topic.
7. "They fell in love, completely, utterly, suddenly". What do you think of "Love at first sight". What are the marks of genuine love? Does "love at first sight" measure up to these?
8. Write notes on the following: Drunkeness; Mortal Sin; Self-Sacrifice; Religious Prejudice.
9. What are the principal non-christian religions ? Discuss their value. Write a short note on any one of them.

Diocesan senior examination in religious knowledge

Chapter 12

Vocation?

Summer 1974

Having arrived home that afternoon, I called down to Logan's shop as soon as I had finished my dinner. My usual check-in and told them I'd be starting work the next morning. No two weeks holidays in Ibiza or even a few days lie in! I took it for granted this was the way it should be. The summer progressed much as I had anticipated. Work five days per week, finishing at 11 pm on a Saturday night and going to the dance in the Slieve an Iarainn hotel every second Saturday night or so. Sundays meant a lie in, attending football matches and going to 7.30 evening Mass. Monday was now a day off, instead of a half-day Wednesday.

Football was central. The senior team was doing very well which had a great knock-on effect on us Minors, as we trained and played football with them. No quarter was taken or given. Official training was on Tuesday and Thursday evenings, and it was frequently dusk by the time I cycled home from it. Many of us also went to 'the park' (football pitch) on Wednesday for a kick around. We progressed well in the Minor championship and were in the semi-final stage by late July.

A Leaving Cert dinner-dance was arranged for a Thursday in late June, when the exams were all finished. It was an incredibly low-key affair compared to the razzmatazz of a 'Debs' nowadays. Not all lads bothered attending. Few brought girls. A number of the priests attended. Fr. Fintan Mc Kiernan had given a pep talk to those of us who intended attending. He simply pointed out that there was no problem with lads drinking, but that if he saw anyone overdoing it, he would drain their pint (no one thought of spirits) down the sink, as he had done the previous year. I hoped to bring some girl to the night out but I had only arrived home the previous Thursday after almost eight weeks away. I mentioned my dilemma to Marie Glancy who was a few years older than I was and worked with me in Logans. On the actual day of the dinner- dance, I decided to take the bull by the horns and ask a girl I knew if she would accompany me. Marie advised me against it as it was not fair to the girl with such short notice. However during my lunch break, I called to the girl's house. Just imagine the scene. The girl is having her lunch, before returning in half an hour to school to do Accounting, her final Leaving Cert exam. I knock on the door and ask would she like to accompany me this very evening to my school's dinner dance. Unbelievably she agrees, most graciously. I return to work, leave one hour early and Fr. Dan collects the girl and myself. We drive up the forty five miles or so to the Park Hotel in Virginia. The meal was fine, possibly only half of the full year turned out and there were only a handful out dancing. It was a very tame affair. We returned home about 1.30 in the morning, with a drunk pedestrian half-staggering out in front of Dan's green Volkswagen Beetle en route home. I was up for work as normal the next morning.

I hoped to go to Maynooth doing Arts. I awaited the Leaving Cert results, they were due out sometime in August. I hated the term 'vocation'. It conjured up images of 'Mammy's boy' in a black suit, a Holy Joe, who certainly had no impure thoughts and was not mad about girls, a good person but not living life to the full in my estimation. We had been given an essay in English class the previous February on 'The Problem of Choosing a Career'. I had opened my essay with: 'Ah, Johnny 'ill be a priest, please God'... I am by no means anti-clerical, but I do believe that a happy good living Catholic is a greater asset to the Church than an unhappy priest'[1]. While most of my essay was concerned with how to approach choosing a university course or deciding what career one would like to pursue, I did return briefly to the vocation idea: 'So many priests visit schools to enlighten the students to the possibility of their following the vocation of the Church, it seems like conscripting for an army. As a result many Leaving Certificate students are inclined to regard a clerical vocation rather cynically... and many never seriously consider this possibility. Every boy and girl should consider the idea of God calling them however unlikely it may seem'.

Looking back from this perspective, there were a number of subtle factors that influenced me to consider becoming a priest. Today it is almost impossible to convey to anyone under forty years of age, the esteem in which the Catholic Church was held in the early 1970s. While its power and influence were beginning to be questioned, and in some small instances beginning to wane, it still occupied a central position in Irish society and was treated with great respect. A look at the coverage of Catholic Church affairs in the 1972-74 period by the local Cavan newspaper, *The Anglo-Celt*, gives some indication of the position of the Church in society at that time. What is interesting is not just the extensive coverage accorded to Church affairs and Church men, but the language and terminology used that show how pervasive clerical influence was in ordinary life. The Celt, always incredibly popular and with almost biblical status locally, was merely reflecting what its readers expected.

In September 1972, its front page carried a large photo of the Bishop of Meath who was visiting Kingscourt Church on the occasion of its centenary. Inside carried a full page of photos and text devoted to the event, despite the fact that Kingscourt was the only Cavan parish in Meath Diocese and Bishop Mac Cormack was not known throughout the rest of Cavan or Leitrim[2]. When

Frank Mc Kiernan was appointed the new Bishop of Kilmore in October, the Celt gave extensive coverage to the announcement[3]. When he was consecrated bishop on 10 December of that year, its front page was dominated by a large photo and news of the event[4]. A further three pages inside were full of photos and detailed reporting, including a summary of every speech delivered on the occasion. The fact that the Taoiseach of the day, Jack Lynch, not only attended but was accorded the honour of reading the First Lesson, in Irish, at the Mass, indicated the close relationship between Church and State. (Bishop Mc Kiernan's Maynooth classmate Bishop Eamonn Casey read the Gospel). In January 1973 the then president of the college, Fr. Terry Mc Manus, gave a very comprehensive review of the previous year's achievements of St. Pat's to the Past Pupils Union at the annual dinner[5]. His entire speech was reported verbatim with a large photo of the dignitaries in attendance. When Terry was replaced by Fr. Paddy Mallon, this news was put on the front page of the Celt, accompanying a photo of the two men. What is particularly significant is the language used in part of the heading: 'Diocesan changes'. In other words, the news is seen in the context of a society where 'clerical changes', i.e. where priests take up new appointments, is news, not the fact that a major second level school is to get a new principal[6]. The following month saw the front page with a massive heading informing readers that the De La Salle Brothers were withdrawing from St. Felim's school in Cavan town[7]. A sub-heading was titled, 'Shock for people of Cavan'. The paper then gave verbatim and long glowing tributes from various organisations, including Fr. Mallon on behalf of St. Pat's, extolling the virtues of the Brothers and their contribution to education in Cavan for the previous thirty one years. In May, the Kilmore Diocesan pilgrimage to Lourdes was recorded with a massive front page photo of all three hundred and forty pilgrims. In addition one inside page was completely given over to the pilgrimage[8].

While it was only proper to expect that the centenary celebrations of a major educational establishment like St. Pat's be reported, what is significant, and typical of the era, is not only the great extent of that coverage, but the language in which it is couched. Everything is viewed from the perspective of the prominence enjoyed by the Catholic Church in Irish society. In October 1973, a large article and accompanying photo, titled, 'Bishop of Kilmore launches college Centenary appeal', was carried by the Celt[9]. For three weeks before the actual centenary, in very large bold type, the approaching activities were announced. The first instalment of a synopsis of the forthcoming book on the history of the college, carried the sub-heading, 'Notable Occasion in Diocese of Kilmore'[10]. The next two weeks' serialisation of the book was likewise accorded great prominence[11]. Interestingly each had a sub-title referring to the diocese, 'prominent Kilmore Institution' and

Prominent Kilmore Educational Establishment'. Numerous full pages, including nineteen photos (some very large) and much text gave almost saturation coverage of the actual week's activities[12].The sermon delivered at the cathedral Mass and the exact speech of each dignitary was reported in full. Of the seven speeches, four were given by prominent ecclesiastics.

From the setting up of 'The Free State' in 1922, Ireland in effect was a Catholic state for a Catholic people, just as Northern Ireland was a Protestant state for a Protestant people. Things were gradually beginning to change. In December 1972 the electorate in the Republic had voted to remove from the constitution the special position accorded to the Catholic Church. However the vast majority of rural Ireland had no major objections to the position enjoyed by the Catholic Church in education and most other spheres of life. That was all soon to change. In the meantime the influence of the Church was just there, you accepted it. The centrality of faith in ordinary life was shared by those of different faiths. President Childers, a Church of Ireland man, used the centenary occasion in St. Pat's to state his Christian beliefs and more importantly his views as to Church involvement in education when he stated:

> There are people calling for complete secularisation of education and the barring of clergy from the schools...recently I have been challenged to answer ...did I believe in the oppressive authoritarian influence of the Catholic Church?...to which I replied that all Churches had to face the cynical questioning scepticism of many young people and should continually seek new ways to inspire them[13].

His entire speech was concerned with young people giving Christian service. Although I was part of Irish society where clerical power and influence were pervasive, it does not fully account for why I might have thought of being a priest, as every other seventeen year old lad in Ireland lived in the same milieu.

St.Pat's definitely had a major influence on my thinking. The idea of becoming a priest never entered my mind, and was not part of my decision to change schools after Inter Cert. However had I remained at school in Ballinamore, priesthood would never have been on the radar. It was no accident that St. Pat's put the idea of a 'vocation' as a possible choice. 'This is a minor seminary', the college president, Terry Mc Manus, stated in an address to us pupils in 1972. Many did not know what a seminary was, let alone how St. Pat's was a minor one. However Terry was correct, in that one of the main purposes of St. Pat's was to produce students to go on to study for the priesthood in Maynooth or another major seminary. From 1914 to 1940 the percentage recruitment to clerical colleges (not all remained until ordination) from each senior class rarely fell below 45% and was often as high as 75%[14]. In the 1956-62 period, St. Pat's had the second largest percentage recruitment of all the diocesan colleges in the country[15]. The following table shows the number of St. Pat's pupils, in the thirty year period before 1973, who were actually ordained priests[16].

St. Pat's Pupils, 1944-73 Period, who were Ordained Priests.			
Year Entered College	Number who Completed L. Cert	Number ordained	% ordained
1944	29	9	31
1945	33	8	24
1946	30	7	23
1947	35	7	20
1948	32	7	22
1949	28	8	29
1950	37	5	14
1951	21	4	19
1952	30	10	33
1953	34	12	35
1954	37	12	32
1955	33	8	24
1956	46	9	20
1957	41	5	12
1958	50	7	14
1959	61	4	7
1960	41	4	10
1961	50	6	12
1962	60	2	3
1963	43	1	2
1964	48	3	6
1965	49	2	4
1966	56	3	5
1967	62	2	3
1968	58	1	1.75
1969	52	2	4
1970	77	3	4
1971	72	2	3
1972	74	3	4
1973	76	0	0
Totals	No. of pupils	No. of priests	Priests as % of pupils
1944-73 (inclusive)	1,395	156	11

The overwhelming majority of young men (from the area covered by the Kilmore Diocese) who became priests, either for home or foreign dioceses, were educated in St. Pat's. A marked decline in vocations is evident in the thirty years covered by the above table: 1944-53 had 25% of the total Leaving Cert class becoming priests, 1954-63 had 12% and 1964-73 had just over 3%[17]. However St. Pat's was still the cradle of vocations. In June 1973 five priests were ordained for the Kilmore diocese, all ex-St. Pat's pupils. In September of that year, three Leaving Cert pupils headed off for the seminary, two going to Maynooth for the Kilmore Diocese, Tom Flynn (Killinkere) and Charlie O'Gorman (Cavan) and Gerry O 'Brien (Kilmainhamwood) going to the Holy Ghost seminary.

While the vast majority of pupils in my time there never thought of being priests, life in the college for boarders was based on the Minor Seminary idea: compulsory daily Mass and night prayer, public Grace before and after meals and annual three day official silence retreats. While the latter was for the day-pupils as well, we boarders had to continue the retreat all evening until bedtime. To be fair, the silence was more honoured in the breach than in the observance. When the president, Terry Mc Manus, was giving his address to the P.P.U. (already alluded to) he devoted over half of it to the importance of Christian training, the centrality of Religious Education in the college curriculum and the scourge of the growing materialistic culture[18].

The atmosphere as a boarder in the college was certainly conducive to fostering a vocation to the priesthood. All my teachers were priests. Dan Gallogly, Seán Brady, Ray Brady, John Murphy and Charlie Heerey were all energetic young men, under thirty five years of age at the time I entered the college. They were all excellent teachers and very good Christians in every sense. They were fair, hardworking, obviously loved their job, had a sense of humour and inspired me. As boarders we lived our full day, week, month and term in the college, alongside these priests, to whom it was also home.

I had not entertained any idea of becoming a priest, because it seemed old fashioned and outdated. The cultural revolution of the sixties (more loosely defined than the actual decade), began around 1963 and ended in 1974[19]. The upheaval in social norms about clothing, music, drugs, sexuality, formalities and schooling inevitably influenced my contemporaries and me. Politically, left wing politics including social reform had become fashionable, especially among the young. Thirty two African countries had gained independence from their European colonial rulers between 1960 and 1970. Vatican Two had charted a brave new world for the Catholic Church. Change was in the air, the old ways were seen to be totally inadequate to someone young like me. The former French Prime Minister, Aristide Briand, had stated that a person who wasn't a socialist at twenty had no heart, but one who remained a socialist at forty had no head. I was seventeen and had a heart. I didn't articulate these views, but they were part of me all the same.

I wanted to be a modern person, at home in the fast changing world, but making a difference. I had the beginning of a social conscience. The priests who were my teachers in St. Pat's were good role models for me. Although Dan was quite traditional in his views, (he used to say about himself half-jokingly, 'I'm fifty years behind the times and proud of it') he did influence me. He was a man of integrity, passion, a great mind and yet had the common touch, and he was very human. John Murphy was unflappable, calm, humorous and very decent. Seán Brady was a total gentleman, concerned for his pupils, very keen on football, never sarcastic, humble and unassuming. Ray Brady was energetic, very tuned in to the changing world, and showed a great understanding of human nature in his teaching of English literature. Charlie Heerey showed great common sense, empathy and decency in his job as dean. He was progressive but did not court popularity. Of course in my idealistic young mind there was none of these men who combined all the characteristics of the totally perfect priest I might hope to be (youthful arrogance!). However their humanity and goodness certainly had a major impact on me.

Two events happened in May that moved my thinking forward. Fergus Clarke, a recently ordained priest was on the college staff from the previous September. He and another priest brought a few of us up to Maynooth College one Saturday afternoon. It was open to anyone who wished to see the college to travel. Two car loads went up. We met the lads there who were studying for the priesthood from Kilmore Diocese. I met my cousin Liam and a few others I knew. It was a lovely afternoon and evening, the lads were as ordinary as you could get and I got a good feel for the place. We went at one stage to the beautiful college 'Gun' Chapel in the French Gothic style of the fourteenth century, with its magnificent west-facing Rose window filtering the sunlight[20]. It was peaceful and spiritual.

Also in May, Leaving Certs had a one day retreat specifically for them. I don't remember much of the proceedings of the day, but I do remember having some free time at the end and a number of us were sitting on the grass at the top of the ramp at senior pitch. Dermot Prior and I were talking when Dermot told me that he intended going for the priesthood. I was a little surprised as Dermot was no Holy Joe and not my usual idea of a priest. He was very surprised that I had not thought about it myself and intimidated that it was staring me in the face. Maybe I was in denial, I don't know, but that was the first time I thought I might study to be a priest. However the pressure of the Leaving Cert was too real, to allow me to devote any time to such an idea.

During that summer, thoughts about studying to be a priest were at the back of my mind. I remember feeling the need to be convinced that you could lead a fully human and fulfilled life as a priest. Of course there was the fact that priests were not allowed marry. I don't think it was the sex that bothered me too much (although I had a very healthy sexual appetite at the time). I was not sacrificing something that was already part of my life (apart from my thoughts) but something I was hoping to enjoy in the future, if I got married. What concerned me was the idea of not being able to look forward to going to films with a girl, to walk hand in hand, to eventually have a life-long friend, with whom I could share everything. I suppose the example of my mother and father was there somewhere in my sub-conscious.

The last three generations of my family (on the Kelly side) had produced priests for the Kilmore Diocese. My grand uncle, Monsignor Michael Kelly had ended his days as Parish Priest in Ballinamore and I remember him as an old man. My uncle, Father Micheál Kelly, was C.C. in Bailieborough at this time and frequently visited our house. My double first cousin (Mc Niffe and Kelly) Frankie Kelly, as previously stated, was ordained in June. His brother Liam was a clerical student in Maynooth, having just completed his degree there. It was only at this stage in my life that I was getting to know both Frankie and Liam as they were respectively seven and five years older than me, a considerable difference when you are seventeen. Both were very normal, worked on the farm, played football and were very good lads. I didn't think at the time that I was from a family with a strong tradition of priests but it obviously influenced me nonetheless.

Like most Irish families at the time, religion was an integral part of family life. We went to Mass every Sunday and said the rosary every night. I do not think we were particularly religious, we certainly were not pious. Like many of our neighbours we 'did the First Fridays', i.e. the tradition of going to Mass on the first Friday of each month for nine consecutive months. We weren't ever told by Mam or Dad to go to confessions, we just went when we wanted to. In fact as a young fellow religion added a great social dimension to my life. During Lent many people attended evening Mass. Dad was always late home from work and so he could not make it. Mam was minding Christopher who was quite young, but I went to Mass nearly every evening during Lent. However it was social, not religious motivation. It was the only way I'd be allowed down the town in the evening and I met my friends after Mass and straggled home afterwards. Like most of the lads in my national school, I served Mass for three years while in fourth, fifth and sixth class. This entailed 8 am. daily Mass for one week and a Sunday morning Mass, two weeks in four. Put simply, religious observance was an integral part of the social fabric of life at the time.

A number of events from when I was six did have an effect on my family and its faith. In 1963 Mam had told us she was expecting a baby (the term pregnant was not usually used until years later). We were overjoyed and full of anticipation. Mam was very sick during the pregnancy and we all prayed that everything would be ok. Elizabeth was born on 3 June 1964, to great rejoicing. Exactly one week later she died. There was no warning and the entire family was devastated. I was only seven but remember the little white coffin, the private burial, and the terrible grief of my mother in particular. She enrolled us in the Green Scapular devotion to Our Lady. This was not unusual. The scapular consisted of a simple piece of green cloth, rectangular in shape, hanging from a green string around the neck. Those who wore it and said the simple daily prayer were supposed to benefit in physical health and peace of mind.

Mam and Dad had wanted another baby, so by the end of that year, Mam was pregnant again. We all prayed at the nightly rosary that everything would be alright. Christopher was born the following August, but spent the second three months of his life in Crumlin hospital. At first we thought he would die and as a family we placed all our hope in God and Our Lady. Normally the rosary took ten minutes but we added trimmings especially for Christopher. The night that Dad and Mam returned, having first left Christopher in Crumlin, Dad told us that he had promised to go to Lourdes. Christopher got better and returned home to us in January 1966. Dad went to Lourdes at Easter that year. By today's standards we may seem to have been a very religious family, but by the norms of mid-1960s Ireland we were not particularly so. Undoubtedly, the death of Elizabeth and Christopher's serious illness did bring us closer to God.

As a young lad growing up in Ballinamore I was pious and a bit wild. A few points will illustrate this dichotomy. Josie Gilheaney, who worked in a local shop told Dad to take the bike off me as a nine year old, or I would kill myself. Kielan Logan and I had tried to pass cars coming down High Street in Ballinamore as a dare. On two occasions in national school I fell off my bicycle and was concussed for the rest of the day. I broke Maloney's front window (possibly the biggest in Church Street at that time) with Noel Mc Tague's new ball. Such was the enormity of the crime that I completely put it out of my ten year old mind, until that evening when Micheál wondered aloud in our house what eejit had broken Maloney's window. Then I confessed to Dad that it was me. He was fuming with the dishonesty. I broke Mc Carthy's window as well, but at least owned up immediately. I also broke our own windows on at least three occasions, all with footballs. I was boasting how strong I was in sixth class, and as a result three fifth class fellows challenged me to a fight, three against one. It took place after school outside the nearest local shop, the 'Candy Store'. There was no reason for the fight, no animosity, just my hubris. It did not go on for long, as someone noticed the principal of our school, Paddy Joyce, looking down in horror as he made a courtesy call on the school Manager, the local P.P. whose house overlooked the shop. Another time Danny Mullen and I got a spool of thread, tied it to Jimmy Clyne's light door knocker one Halloween night and kept knocking. He'd come out, we'd wait another ten minutes and do so again. I was about thirteen at the time. The fun stopped when he ran out by us, hunched and hidden as we were behind his garden wall. Luckily he did not see us, but we saw him go straight down to the Garda Barracks.

However I was pious, or maybe it was superstition, at the same time. I never went to school from I was about seven, without rosary beads in my pocket. One morning in third class I was half way to school, when I realised I had forgotten them and returned home to retrieve them. I was then late for school but would dare not tell the teacher, Mrs. Gannon, the real reason. I usually said a Memorare and an Act of Contrition on my way to school each morning. Nobody, either class mates or teachers would know this. As far as I know my siblings were not like this. This continued as I progressed to St. Felim's Secondary School. I never intended becoming a priest, I just felt wrong if I did not pray a bit each day.

When I went to St. Pat's I certainly would not have been seen as a Holy Joe. I did not cause trouble and was quite mature, but was not seen as pious or religious. I continued with my three or four formal prayers each day, usually said during Mass, and I suppose I learned to talk to God (I was never a great one for listening) in my own words. Even when Dermot Prior and I went for the two days in December of Fourth Year to the Holy Ghost Fathers in Kimmage, I had no intention of going to be a priest. Studying to be a priest never entered my mind, despite the fact that I went on the pilgrimage to Lourdes six months later.

Dad's death probably was the major factor in me deciding to become a priest. As I stated earlier, I was fortunate that his untimely death did not shake my faith in God but actually increased it. I now had Dad in Heaven to intercede and look after my family and me. Before study each evening I took out the last letter/note he had written to me and prayed to him to help me study. It was on a yellow little 'post it' sheet, a few lines asking how I was, had I enough money, hoped all was well, and signed off with 'Dad'. I prayed every morning and every night to him, in effect talked to him. His death made me mature more quickly. It made me want to do something good and positive with my life. Every day during lunchtime, I used go to the college chapel to pray for five minutes. I would not risk being seen entering the chapel, but like Joseph of Arimathea, was a secret disciple. I went up to the second floor to the gallery of the chapel, kneeling between the organ and the wall, so that even anyone below in the church would not know I was there. I was obviously keen on my personal prayer as I remember writing in the Religion exam we had in Leaving Cert regarding my attitude to Mass, that I did not think there was sufficient time for personal prayer. On another occasion there was confession available while Mass was on. When I returned to Mass having been to Confession, Communion had finished. I always thought Mass was empty without it and so asked Fr. Heerey, the celebrant who was still in the sacristy, could he give me Communion which he readily did. I was a strange mixture. This was the religious me. Yet a year earlier, I had seen Confession as a chance for a prank.

Two of us Fourth Years, were allowed out of study to look up *Leaders and Men of the Easter Rising* in the library, for our study of Irish history[21]. Visiting priests who came into the college to hear Confession, usually did so behind a kneeler and grill in the library. On this occasion Confessions were someplace else, but my friend and I decided to try and fool some Second Years who were outside the library waiting for Confession. My friend told them the priest was ready and I was seated in semi-darkness behind the grill. However the lad who came 'to confession' knew well what was up and if five per cent of what he started telling me was true he would have been jailed for life.

My decision to go to Maynooth to study for the priesthood in a sense grew on me as the summer progressed. There was no flash of inspiration, but a realisation that I had no good reason for not going. This did not stop the avalanche of what were famously called 'impure thoughts' streaming into my mind, as they no doubt did into the minds of many of my footballing friends in Ballinamore. One evening at football training, my cousin Liam Kelly who was a clerical student in Maynooth arrived at the pitch as we were nearly finished. He had come to talk to me. We returned to my house where he chatted about what I intended doing after the results were out. I am not exactly sure what I said, but it was another signpost on my road to Maynooth. By late July I had come round to the idea that I would study to be a priest. There was a sense of freedom once I had made up my mind, I told nobody. Anyone who has done the Leaving, will remember being bombarded by well-meaning people with the famous question, 'what do you intend doing?' I stated that I hoped to do Arts in Maynooth, no mention of going as a clerical student. My uncle Fr. Micheál, on a visit to our house, quietly asked me the same question. I told him I was hoping to go as a clerical student. He advised me to contact the president of St. Pat's so that an appointment would be made for me to see the bishop. To be fair to Fr. Micheál, he had never put any pressure on, or even suggested to, me that I should consider the priesthood.

I phoned Fr. Mallon and a meeting was arranged with the bishop for Saturday 10 August[22]. About a week before this, I was drying dishes that Mam was washing and she expressed concern as to what would happen if I did not get the four honours and the university grant. I told her not to worry that I had decided to go as a clerical student and the diocese would pay for me even if I did not get the grant. She was taken aback, as she had no idea I was thinking along those lines. I now realised I had a new problem. I was incredibly independent and tetchy, even at that stage in life, if anyone questioned my motivation for anything. More than ever I now hoped I would get the four honours and the grant so that nobody could accuse me of looking for a free education paid by Kilmore Diocese, if I ever left after I had gotten my degree.

This was the summer that Watergate, the major political scandal in the United States, reached its climax. The Nixon administration's attempted cover-up of its involvement in the 1972 break-in at the Democratic National Committee headquarters at the Watergate office complex in Washington, resulted in Nixon being eventually forced to resign. I got up in the early hours of Friday 9 August (8 August U.S.) to listen to his resignation speech to the nation.

A day later, on the morning of Saturday 10 August, Micheál drove me through the familiar college gates, but this time we swung right where the avenue divided and drove to the bishop's house. The official purpose of my visit was to see would I be accepted as a clerical student for the Kilmore Diocese. I regarded it as a formality, which it turned out to be. While the house was right beside St. Pat's College, I had never been inside it before. In fact it used to be called the bishop's palace, especially by older people. I remember a fairly large house, like a good land agent's home from the late nineteenth century. The Bishop, Frank Mc Kiernan had been in the same class as my father in national school in Derrada, Corraleehan outside Ballinamore. In addition he had been in Maynooth, four years behind my uncle, Fr. Micheál and from the same parish. I had been a pupil of St. Felim's, for three years, the school of which he was not only president, but had set up from scratch in 1962. So we knew each other well.

Frank was friendly, enquiring about my mother whom he knew well and my hopes in the Leaving. After discussing many aspects of me going to Maynooth, he then proceeded to tell me that there were many girls around Ballinamore who, no doubt were interested in me. Even though this was a serious occasion, I thought to myself, where have they been for the last three or four years? Uncharacteristically I stayed silent. He then talked about celibacy, and the next sentence almost caused me to burst out laughing. 'You know Liam, you can't ride two horses at the same time'. To seventeen year old me 'ride' meant one thing, and it didn't involve any horse. To be fair to Frank, he was a gentleman, genuine and learned with a great innovative mind regarding education. He had given us sex education lessons in Ballinamore, very progressive for the time. However I thought to myself as I left the 'palace', what am I letting myself in for when my future leader does not know the sexual connotation of 'ride'.

Later I told my uncle, Fr. Micheál, who laughed heartily at the bishop's use of the term. He also used the conversation to advise me to go out with girls, while I was home on holidays from Maynooth for the first three or so years. I thought it was very sensible and liberal advice. However it did not solve the problem of finding out where were all these girls around Ballinamore who were apparently dying to go with me.

The following week started off normally enough. It was the annual Ballinamore Festival. Monday was my day-off, so I thumbed to Cavan to visit the dentist. A temporary crown, that had been implanted when I was six after I had smashed my front tooth on the footpath, was acting up. Arriving at the door of my usual dentist, Hickey, I was taken aback to see a black notice informing me that he had died a day or so previously. I then went to another dentist, called King. I was dying to point out to him the pun on his name and my need for a new crown but I desisted. I was becoming very (alarmingly) mature.

I thumbed home and went to work as usual the next morning in Logan's. It was the agricultural show day. That evening I went to football training as normal. It was the end of normality for about three days. I woke in excruciating pain that night. My jaw had swollen like a boxer's and Dispirin tablets were absolutely useless. I will never forget the toothache. Mam stayed up all night and eventually I got a few hours' sleep after 8 am. An old abscess under the crown had reignited with the probing by the dentist the previous Monday. By that afternoon I had a bad infection, still had pain and was now on antibiotics. What is more I was supposed to be playing in the Minor county final the following Sunday.

Our seniors had been so successful for a good number of years that what we in Ballinamore pejoratively called 'The League of Nations', was formed to counter their dominance of Leitrim club football. Three clubs, Carrick-on-Shannon, Kiltubrid and Fenagh amalgamated to form Sheemore Gaels. They beat Ballinamore by one point in the senior semi-final, played in perfect conditions in Carrick- on-Shannon. (My cousin Liam Kelly was on the victorious team that went on to win the county final). We were in the Minor semi-final, directly after the senior game. I will never forget the fact that the defeated and dispirited senior players remained for our game and urged us on. We needed it. Garadice (Aughawillan/Drumreilly) were our opponents and had a wonderful group of players. We were playing against lads whom we had sat beside in school in St. Felim's Ballinamore. In a very free-flowing open game we came out on top, 1.8- 0.7. No other win ever gave me the same satisfaction. We defeated a very talented team with sheer effort, belief and passion. We felt we kept the flag flying on what had been a bad day for the seniors. The final was fixed for Sunday 18 August. I just had to be right for it, and three days in bed with a tooth infection was not my idea of preparation.

On Friday morning more drama. I was still in bed when Valerie came running home from down the town, shouting that the Leaving results were out. Those were different times, no exact and reliable date was ever issued by the Department of Education as to when to expect the results. I immediately phoned St. Pat's and Fr. Mallon told me I had gotten four honours. I double checked that I had passed Maths, which he assured me I had. (At this stage only the number of honours and passes were told. The exact grades would issue by post from the college to arrive Monday). I was ecstatic. I felt my work had paid off. I would now get the university scholarship grant and could go as a clerical student to Maynooth, without anyone saying I was just there for a free education.

That afternoon I was still in bed when Valerie rushed up to my room, with a little slip of paper. Frankie, now Fr. Frankie, had called into St. Pat's for something that afternoon, and the president had given him the details of my results to pass on to me. I was amazed. I had gotten three B's in honours papers, English, History and Geography and a C in honours Latin, as well as a B in pass Irish. My fears regarding Maths had been well founded in that I just got the minimum D, in the pass paper.

As well as working in Logan's supermarket, I had worked half a dozen nights that summer in Paddy Dolan's bar at the top of the town. Ballinamore had a population of about nine hundred at this time and the grand total of twenty two pubs. Dolan's and Prior's (Dermot's father) were possibly the two largest, with modern lounge bars. During the Festival the pub was thronged, so much so that sometimes people didn't get in the front door and drinks were handed out to them. That Friday night I was able to return to work in Dolan's from 9 pm. until 1.30. It was Wrenboys competition night in the Festival and so there was a total of thirteen working there all that night.

The next morning I was back again working in Logan's and finished that night around 10.45. Next day was the final, so no Slieve dancing that night. Our opposition was Kiltubrid, championship winners for the two previous years. I had my place as right half back on the team as normal and despite my three days of infection, felt fine. I played my usual, unspectacular reliable game, glued to my man. We won the game, 1.8 to 1.4. To be fair the few other seventeen year old age lads (Thomas Mc Tague, Michael Reynolds, Frank Maxwell, Michael Mc Girl, Leo Plunkett) and myself were greatly bolstered by a number of very good eighteen year olds, Seán Crossan, Leo Logan and Michael Plunkett, as well as a great crop of up-and-coming lads a year or two younger than us, like Brian Gallogly, Hugh Murphy, Gerry Logan, Colm Reynolds, Patrick 'Beezer' Mc Kiernan and Gay Darcy. I now had a County Minor Medal, for a fairly mediocre player it was a great feeling to think I was part of the best Under Eighteen team in Leitrim.

That Sunday night will forever be etched in my memory. We returned victorious to Ballinamore, stopping just outside the town so as to organise the triumphant cavalcade. It was nearly dusk and the town was experiencing its greatest crowds and buzz of the entire year. It was the closing night of the Festival and people appeared to be under the impression that they would have to wait for next year's Festival to ever drink or socialise again. I was in the leading vehicle, a minibus, with players half out every window, the yellow and green jerseys streaming behind them, the cup on the front bonnet held precariously by other members of the team. We crawled through the crowded town, the horns of all cars in the procession blaring and we all shouting at the top of our voices. I was strategically positioned standing with another lad in the very back of the minibus, roaring my head off with the two back doors tied open.

Different times. A few of the team went to the pub, but the vast majority of us did not. I was still a Pioneer at the time, as were most of my age group. I went to the Festival dance in the marquee on the Swanlinbar road, where Evelyn and the Envoys provided the music. The very popular Carpenters' song of the time played, and its lyrics suited my mood perfectly that night:

'I'm on top of the world lookin' down on creation'.

I had four honours, a Minor medal and knew what I was going to do with my life.

A week or so later I had to go to Cavan shopping and so I called out to St. Pat's to collect a reference from the president that I required for Maynooth. The college was obviously very quiet with only Fr. Mallon present. Another Leaving Cert pupil happened to be there at the same time, also looking for a reference. Fr. Mallon apologised and asked us to wait while he rushed out to the Post Office with letters. While waiting, the other lad suggested that we go up to Fr. Mallon's office and see if the results were there. Like Adam in the Garden of Eden, I had no problem with this suggestion. Sure enough he was correct, there were the results of all our classmates open on Fr. Mallon's desk. We quickly poured over them, totally immoral and unethical, especially for me going to be a priest, but nevertheless very satisfying.

In the Leaving of the previous year, 1973, eighteen students had got a minimum of four honours. In 1974, 76 of us did the Leaving Cert of whom 6 were repeats, who were only doing two or three subjects each. The following table refers to the seventy who did a full Leaving Cert in 1974[23].

1974 Overall Leaving Cert Results

Results	Number	% of Total
Total No. students 70	70 Passed (at least 5 subjects)	100
No. getting 1 honour	10	14
No. getting 2 hons.	9	13
No. gettting 3 hons.	6	9
No. getting 4 hons.	7	10
No. getting 5 hons.	5	7
No. getting 6 hons.	2	2.8
No. getting 7 hons.	1	1.4

Every pupil doing the Leaving Cert in my year in St. Pat's passed, an incredible achievement when the normal failure rate nationally among boys was in the mid 20% range. Over 42% could go to university having gained at least two honours. In addition eighteen pupils qualified for the university grant (subject to means test), three helped by having an honour in higher level Irish that counted as two honours for grant qualification. Six honours was the maximum possible in St. Pat's at that time as those doing honours Maths did a maximum of six subjects. However one lad managed seven honours. He did Geography outside of class in his own time and secured an honour in it, some achievement!
In 1974 an A grade in a honours paper was nearly unheard up and a B grade was a rarity as the following table illustrates[24]:

1974 Leaving Cert Results in Subjects at Honours Level								
Subject	**Total no. doing subject**	**Total no. doing Honours**	**% doing Hons**	**Number of Grades in Honours**				
				A	**B**	**C**	**D**	**E**
Irish	70	17	24%		2	13	2	
English	70	30	43%		4	15	10	1
Maths	70	7	10%	2	2	1	2	
History	37	34	92%		5	12	17	
Geography	35	15	43%		1	2	12	
Latin	36	26	72%		2	10	11	3
French	54	36	67%	1	5	24	6	
Phys. & Chem.	43	30	70%		5	11	12	2
Accounting	10	1						1
Business Organisation	6	1					1	
Art	16							
Ag. Sc.	11	1					1	

Far fewer students attempted honours compared to the present. Accounting, Business Organisation, Art and Agricultural Science were only offered to the Third Stream class and usually at pass level. Pupils, parents and teachers usually talked in terms of honours achieved, not grades awarded. There were only 3 'A's and 26 'B's awarded among the entire 70 Leaving Cert students.

Grade inflation is striking over the forty year period, 1974-2014, as shown by the following national table[25]:

A and B Grades Awarded Nationally in Higher Level Papers in Leaving Cert 2014		
Subject	**% As**	**% Bs**
Irish	14.2	25.7
English	9.3	13.8
Maths	10.2	17.7
History	13.0	20.3
Geography	9.1	18.0
Latin (108 total students)	26.8	26.9
French	12.0	17.4
Physics	19.7	18.1
Chemistry	20.5	20.0
Accounting	19.8	26.4
Business	10.7	17.9
Art	4.7	19.4
Ag. Sc.	10.6	17.0

Over 41% of the Leaving Cert class of '74 went on to either university or a Regional college. UC.D. accounted for half of those going to Third level, as shown by the following table[26]:

Third Level Colleges and Courses Chosen		
College	**Course**	**No. of pupils**
U.C.D.	B. Comm.	4
U.C.D.	Engineering	4
U.C.D.	Arts	4
U.C.D.	Ag. Sc.	1
U.C.D.	Soc. Sc	1
Maynooth	Clerical	3
Maynooth	Arts	2
St. Pat's Drumcondra	Primary Teaching	2
T.C.D.	B. Comm.	1
N.C.P.E. (Limerick)	P.E.	1
Regional College	Business	1
Regional College	Lab. technician	1
Regional College	Not known	4

Two lads who did Arts in U.C.D. and one who did Social Science there, subsequently did the conversion course for Primary teaching, so in effect five of the '74 class ended up as Primary teachers. Two pupils joined the Garda Síochána.

The following table shows the occupations of those who went straight into employment:

Immediate Employment	
Occupation	**No. of individuals**
Family business	5
Killeshandra Co-op.	3
Farming	2
Nursing	2

The following occupations each attracted one pupil:

Jackson's garage, Mc Carren Meats, Bank, Army, Commercial traveller, Co. Council, E.S.B., Health Board, Posts and Telegraph. Three emigrated to England and elsewhere[27]. In addition four pupils went back to repeat so as to improve their results[28].

I got an excellent education, academic, extra-curricular and character formation. It was traditional, tough if viewed by the standards of today, and boarding school was certainly not suited to everyone. Fr. Dan in his centenary history of the college stated that since 1874 'whenever the staff was young, energetic and enthusiastic, these same characteristics were reflected in the life of the college'[29]. In that sense I was very lucky, a new talented and hardworking group of teachers, lay and clerical, had recently joined the staff prior to my arrival. The academic education I received was fantastic and it influenced my entire life. I got a great love of learning that my years in university in Maynooth nurtured. Ray Brady prepared us for the Leaving, but he did not just teach to the exam. We did the entire course, including two plays, the modern novels and all the prescribed poetry. We got a liberal education. In fact in my First Arts exam in Maynooth, I relied extensively on the notes Ray had given us by the critic Tillyard on Milton's poem, Lycidas. Two of the text books that Dan used for History, F.S.L. Lyons, *Ireland since the Famine* and D. Thompson's *Europe since Napoleon* were the standard text books for the first year history course at university. History is about trying to be as objective as possible. Dan's natural sympathies were Republican. It was no accident that years later it was he who was asked to celebrate the funeral Mass of his fellow Ballinamore man, John Joe Mc Girl, the Vice-

President of Sinn Féin. In his sermon Dan referred to him as an unbroken and unbreakable Fenian[30]. And yet this was the same Dan who prescribed for us the most scholarly and most recent history book, written by the F.S.L. Lyons, Professor of Modern History in Kent and later the Provost of Trinity College. Furthermore it emphasised the importance of the parliamentary tradition, rather than any Republican agenda. That was real teaching. It showed me what striving for objectivity really meant. My love of History and English was greatly enhanced by teachers like Dan and Ray. I taught these two subjects for my entire teaching career and they are still central pillars of my life.

On Thursday 5 September 1974, Dad's birthday, and two years to the day from when I first entered St. Pat's, my cousin, Liam Kelly, drove me to another St. Patrick's College, this time in Maynooth. Thirty one years later, in September 2005, I was to find myself driving up the front avenue of St. Pat's Cavan once again, this time as the new principal, but that's another story.

Praying
College chapel 1973

Leaving Cert Class 1975 - 76

Back standing (L-R) B. Mc Mahon, G. Tivenan, T. Mc Mahon, S. Brady, J. Greene, S. Wilson and B. Seagrave. *Front seated (L-R)* M. Briody, L. Lynch, V. Matthews, J. Sheridan and J. F. Smith.

Back standing (L-R) G. Curran, J. Mc Dermott, G. Mc Cabe, T. Flanagan, D. Condon, N. Dinneny, P. Mc Govern, P. O'Sullivan, P. Flynn and S. O'Callaghan. *Front seated (L-R)* M. O'Brien, F. O'Reilly, G. Soden, S. Galligan, T. Sheridan, M. Mc Gourty, D. Kilduff, P. Murphy and P. Phair.

Leaving Cert Class 1975 - 76

Back standing (L-R) P. Meehan, B. Fox, L. Smith, D. Donohoe, C. Dolan, P. Martin, G. Bennett, S. Murphy, P. Tackney, P. Duggan, H. Reilly and S. Henry.
Front seated (L-R) R. Caslin, D. Young, F. Corr, S. Lennon, A. Daly, G. Gallagher and J. Reilly.

Back standing (L-R) M. Mc Cabe, P. Foynes, P. Mc Cormick, T. Mc Dermott, P. Corr, D. Rawle, R. Cullivan, M. Cusack, G. Clarke and J. O'Callaghan.
Front (L-R) S. Flanagan, D. Flaherty, S. Mc Loughlin, B. Waters, J. Donoghue, L. Connerton, P. Seagrave, P. Mc Evoy and S. Carolan.

Leaving Cert Class 1976 - 77

Back standing (L-R) B. Mc Evoy, M. Farrell, J. Mc Weeney, P. O' Donnell, S. Carolan, N. Lovett, H. O'Kane, M. Sorohan, M. Gaffney and S. Mc Cormick.
Front seated (L-R) B. Smith, M. Bouchier, S. Mc Tague, S. O'Kane, T. Quealy, S. Carolan, M. Flanagan and C. Lindon.

Back standing (L-R) P. Flynn, K. Mc Clarey, J. Olwill, D. Feeley, S. Prior, K. Boyle and J. Mc Mahon.
Front seated (L-R) D. Corcoran, P. Reilly, M. Brady, P. Denning, S. Boyle and S. Linehan.

Leaving Cert Class 1976 - 77

Back standing (L-R) D. Maguire, P. Callaghan, M. Thompson, T. Lynch, P. Murphy, T. Brady, D. Cullen, D. O'Brien, T. Curley, S. Devine and D. O'Brien.
Front seated (L-R) S. Smith, J. Deane, M. Shankey- Smith, H. Quigley, N. Mc Loughlin, H. Brady and M. Mc Keon.

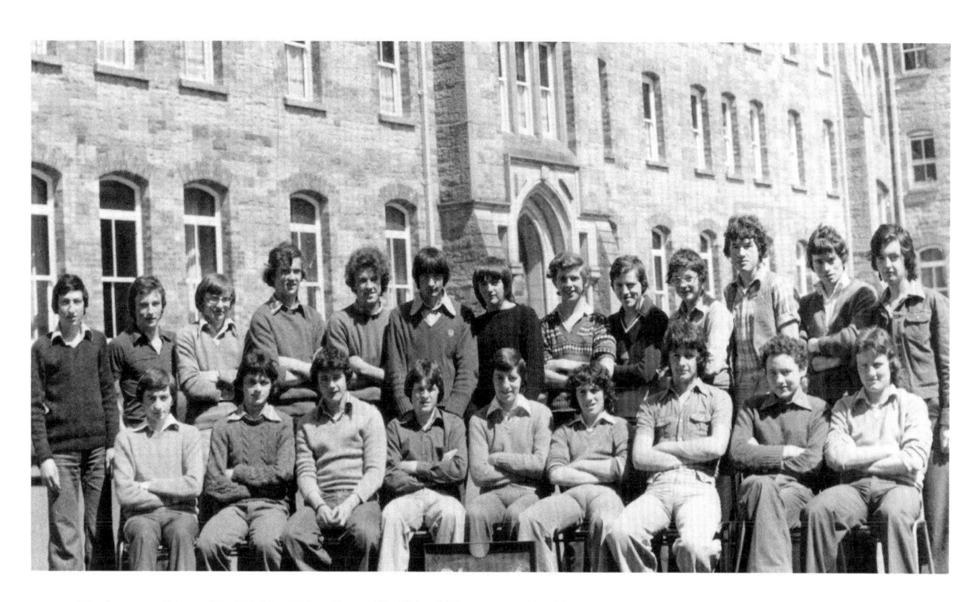

Back standing (L-R) R. Hayden, S. Mc Kiernan, G. Fortune, F. Brodie, H. King, J. Lynch, J. Kelly, T. Costello, C. Smith, B. Sherlock, S. Reilly, F. Mc Donagh and P. Smith.
Front seated (L-R) J. Smith, F. Flynn, P. Hayes, B. Murray, J. Gilhooly, P. Brady, M. Dolan, F. Smyth and P. Mc Manus.

Leaving Cert Class 1977-78

Back standing (L-R) P.J. Madden, D. Smith, O. Honeyman, J. Reilly, K. Sexton, M. Faulkner, B. Smith, P. Brady, B. Sherlock, T. Mc Manus, M. Gaffney, J. Tierney, H. Fitzpatrick, J. Kelly, E. Thompson, T. Coyle, A. Smith, ----- -----, K. Brennan, J. Clarke, T. O'Reilly and G. Kerin.
Middle standing (L-R) V. Tierney, H. O'Donnell, P. Hayes, B. Tierney, C. Lynch, T. Martin, M. Keaney, T. Mc Govern, M. Tierney, M.J. Martin. E. Mc Partlan, P. Brody, G. Mc Partlan, J. Cullen, M. Mc Nally, G. Daly and T. Gaffney, ----- -----, ----- -----, ----- ----- .
Seated (L-R) T. Maguire, H. King, B. Boyd, E. O'Callaghan, D. Dolan, D. Mc Carthy, T. Mc Manus, H. Farrell, T. Mc Hugh, P. Mc Govern, E. Smith, M. Tierney, S. Lavery and E. Conaty, ----- -----.
Front (L-R) M. O'Rourke, T. Costello, K. Reilly, D. Reilly, P. O'Donnell, J. Feehan, S. Mc Gahern, E. Reilly, B. O'Grady, M. Mc Kiernan, B. Reilly, T. Leonard and C. Murray.

References

Chapter 1
Life before St. Pat's

1. Peter and I were together in national school, secondary school (St. Felim's and St. Pat's); a very affable fellow he died when only forty four years old on 12 August 2001 R.I.P.
2. *The Anglo-Celt* 28 February 1969, Johnston Central Library, Cavan town.
3. Prior to this the annual fee for pupils in the day school, St. Felim's College Ballinamore, was £20 in 1965 (€394 in today's terms). To give some indication of the relative cost, the top price for the best three year old bullock in Drumshanbo fair in the early 1960s was £60, (€1,184) information from Frankie Kelly, pupil of St. Pat's 1962-67.
4. Irish Central Statistics Office, August 1972, compared to January 2013.
5. The 'Primary Cert.', that pupils leaving national school had previously undertaken, had been abolished by the government in 1967.
6. Diary of Elizabeth Mc Niffe (author's mother), Friday 14 March 1969.
7. The shoes were slip-ons that I had bought in Frank O' Brien's the previous August, for £2 (€33) and £1.10 shillings (€25) respectively.
8. Tony Plunkett boarded from 1934-40, Mac Kiernan & Dunne, *The College Boys* (Breifne, 2008).
9. I am not sure of exact numbers, 108 entered the college the following September, but many, like me, just did the exam and did not enrol, Mac Kiernan and Dunne.
10. St. Felim's College Ballinamore, had been set up by the Diocese of Kilmore in 1962 as a day school for boys. In 1968 a very ambitious model of cooperation was begun, when St. Felim's, the local V.E.C. school and the local Meán Scoil Fatima (Mercy girls' secondary school) all pooled their resources to provide a very comprehensive range of subjects for pupils.
11. The Group Certificate and the Intermediate Certificate were abolished and the New Junior Certificate was introduced in 1989 and first examined in 1992.
12. At that time many pupils were older arriving to St. Pat's and only spent four years there, Mac Kiernan & Dunne.
13. His spinster sister, Bessie, persuaded the bishop, Patrick Finegan, to send him out to a parish, so that she could become his housekeeper, as the priest for whom she was housekeeper had recently died.
14. Seán Kelly (1933-7) and Micheál Kelly (1934-40): An older brother of theirs, Thomas, did the entrance exam in 1929, but never attended, Thomas Kelly in conversation 27 Oct. 2006.
15. My first cousin, Frankie Kelly (1962-7), had won a half County Council scholarship to St. Pat's. County Councils had a certain amount of money to grant scholarships for secondary school, based on a competitive exam, before free second level education was introduced. Sometimes they halved the amount among two candidates, in this case worth £30 (€394) per annum for three years: Frankie Kelly email, 12 Feb.2014. His brother Liam completed Fourth and Fifth year there (1969-71). Two other first cousins, sons of Seán, also attended the college, Anthony Kelly (1967-72) and his brother Micheál (1968-73) who was still attending at this time.
16. Of course this also meant that we would no longer have the new car to which we were accustomed.
17. *The Anglo-Celt*, 1 Sept 1972. Date for Belturbet dance not fully legible on advertisement.
18. He was a far-out relation of mine.
19. En.wikipedia.org, 1970s in fashion,

accessed 3 March 2014.
20. *The Anglo-Celt*, 2 March 1973.
21. En.wikipedia.org, 1970s in fashion, accessed 3 March 2014.
22. *The Anglo-Celt*, 2 March 1973.
23. Ferriter, *Ambiguous Republic Ireland in the 1970s*, (Great Britain 2012), p.295; although the 1970's saw many homes getting televisions, by November 1977, 15% of homes still had no T.V.
24. Ibid, approximately only 20% of T.V. homes had colour sets by November 1977.
25. *The Anglo-Celt*, 15 September 1972.
26. Ibid.
27. Raidió na Gaeltachta had just been set up in April 1972.
28. Original receipt of payment for 1972-73 boarding, in author's possession.
29. We did not get home for weekends, there was no midterm in February and only ten days off at Easter.
30. *The Anglo-Celt*, 2 March 1973.
31. Equal pay for the same work did not come into law until the late 1970s; approximate figures given based on A.S.T.I. Yearbook 1970/71, courtesy of Gerry Brady, friend and former teacher in St. Felim's College, who dropped dead five days after sending me these figures. R.I.P.
32. *The Anglo-Celt*, 13 Oct.1972.

Chapter 2
Daily Routine

1. Later that day, all the hostages and all but three of the terrorists were killed.
2. Kielan Logan who had also done that entrance exam was now going as a boarder to St. Mel's in Longford.
3. Details pertaining to addresses of pupils are from Mac Kiernan & Dunne.
4. Tom and I were both clerical students in Maynooth and then we both ended up teaching in different schools in Kells. Tom's voluntary work in parishes, (Mullagh and later Nobber, Co. Meath), as well as his passion for sport, especially G.A.A. and basketball coaching, was incredible. I lost a true friend, a real gentleman and a man of utmost faith and integrity when Tom died after a short illness in December 2006 aged fifty.
5. Figures compiled from Mac Kiernan and Dunne.
6. Information on the song is from Thomas Mc Tague.
7. Cunningham and Gallogly, *St. Patrick's College Cavan, A Centenary History*, (St. Patrick's College, 1974), p.100; Mac Kiernan and Dunne, p.254; G. Cartwright, *Breifne Abú!, Cavan GAA records 1886-2011*, p.288, (Cavan County Board GAA, 2011).
8. In 1960 there were six times as many pupils in primary schools as there were in second level, J. Coolahan, *Irish Education, History and Structure*, 2012 edition, p.79, (Institute of Public Administration 1981).
9. NCCE.org, National Centre on Education and the Economy, (NCCE), Ireland Education Report, accessed 16 April 2014.
10. Mac Kiernan and Dunne, pp 207-8, 105 entered as new pupils that year, and while at least three of these were identified as not being First Years, it is possible that a few more also were not First Years.
11. Mac Kiernan and Dunne.
12. Detailed analysis of 1972 Inter Cert results, (St. Patrick's College, archives).
13. Coolahan, p.197.
14. Information from Fr. Charlie O'Gorman.
15. E. Mc Niffe diary, 18 September 1972.
16. Ibid. 8 October 1972.
17. Cartwright, *Breifne Abú!*
18. Dan Gallogly, *Ballinamore, Seán O'Heslin's 1889-1984*, p.94, (Seán O'Heslin G.A.A. Club, 1984).
19. *The Anglo-Celt*. 29 September 1972.
20. Despite the *The Anglo-Celt* of 20 October 1972, referring to St. Pat's Third win, there is no account of the second game in the previous few weeks' editions.
21. Ibid.
22. *The Anglo-Celt*. 27 October 1972.
23. Ibid. 3 November 1972.
24. Ibid. 10 November 1972.
25. Compiled from all *The Anglo-Celt* reports of the Rannafast campaign, September - November 1972.
26. Fran died a few years after leaving St. Pat's due to cancer. He was a very decent, nice person.
27. As Principal of St. Patrick's College,

2005-2013, I can vouch for this assertion.
28. Mac Kiernan and Dunne, p.1X.

Chapter 3
Out of Routine

1. Frankie Kelly, email, 12 February 2014.
2. Augustine Martin (ed.), Patrick Kavanagh, Advent, *Soundings*, Leaving Certificate/Interim Anthology, (Gill and Macmillan, Dublin, 1969).
3. Seamus Heaney, Blackberry Picking.
4. En.wikipedia.org/wiki/List of performers on Top of the Pops, accessed 3 March 2014.
5. *The Anglo-Celt*, 17 November 1972.
6. Ibid. 24 November 1972.
7. E. Mc Niffe diary, 11 December 1972.
8. Author's homework notebook for Fourth Year, 1972-3.
9. Ballinamore school introduced it shortly after this.
10. Peter Brady, Irish Identity. com, accessed 9 May 2014.
11. Author's homework notebook for Fourth Year, 1972-3.
12. Author's English Essay copy, Fourth Year.
13. Ibid.
14. North and Hilliard, *Latin Prose Composition*, p.9.
15. Author's homework notebook 1972-3, Physics and Chemistry homework for some Wednesday in October.
16. Author's homework notebook.
17. *The Anglo-Celt* 5 January, 1973.
18. garda.ie, accessed 21 May 2014.
19. Welseyjohnston.com, Deaths in each year of the 'Troubles', 1969-1988, accessed 21 May 2014.
20. wikipedia. org, 1972 and 1973 Dublin Bombings, accessed 21 May 2014.
21. Ibid.
22. Brian Friel, *Philadelphia Here I Come*, Faber and Faber, 1985, Episode 1.
23. E. Mc Niffe diary, 5 January 1973.

Chapter 4
History of St. Pat's

1. The Synod of Raith Bressail near Borrisoleigh in Tipperary in 1111 saw the first formal establishment by a single authority of a comprehensive network of dioceses; The Synod of Kells in 1152 saw the culmination of this reorganisation, Connolly, (ed.) *The Oxford Companion to Irish History* (Oxford, 1998), p. 472, p.282.
2. Leitrim was not established as a county until 1583 and Cavan acquired county status the following year, www.leitrimtourism.com/History-of - Leitrim.aspx,
3. Connolly, p.472.
4. Originally O'Rourkes controlled all of Breifne, but by the fifteenth century West Breifne (roughly corresponding to modern County Leitrim) was held by the O'Rourkes, while East Breifne (corresponding to modern County Cavan), was under the dominance of O' Reillys, Connolly, p.419: Mac Atasney, *The Plantation of County Leitrim (1585-1670)* (Carrick-on-Shannon, 2013) pp 4-5: Gallogly, *The Diocese of Kilmore 1800-1950* (Breifne, 1999), p.XV11.
5. R.V. Comerford, Emeritus Professor of Modern History, N.U.I. Maynooth, in conversation, 2 Feb.2014.
6. Foucault, Discipline and Punish (1975), in *Literary Theory, An Anthology* (2003), eds. J. Rivkin & M. Ryan: Foucault's theories addressed the relationship between power and knowledge and how they were used as a form of social control through social institutions.
7. Comerford in conversation, 2 Feb.2014.
8. Cunningham and Gallogly, p.45.
9. Mac Kiernan & Dunne, p. XV.
10. Connolly, p. 505.
11. Ibid. hence the establishment of Irish colleges in Paris in 1578, Salamanca in 1592 and subsequently others elsewhere on the continent.
12. Ibid.
13. Mac Kiernan & Dunne, p.X1.
14. Ibid.
15. Waterford in 1807, Wexford in 1819 and Thurles in 1837, Connolly, p. 505.
16. Gallogly, p.88.
17. Cunningham and Gallogly pp 4, 39: There was no such thing as free second level education at this time.
18. Ibid. p.7.
19. Ibid. pp 18-20.
20. Ibid. p.20.
21. Gallogly, p.157.

22. Cunningham and Gallogly, p. 20.
23. Ibid. p. 39.
24. Gallogly, p.160.
25. By 1886 a total of thirty nine students had completed their theology courses in the college and were ordained priests, Mac Kiernan & Dunne, p. XV111.
26. Gallogly, p.161.
27. Mac Kiernan & Dunne, p.X1X; Gallogly, p.162.
28. Mac Kiernan & Dunne, p.X1X.
29. Ibid. 1X.
30. Frankie Kelly, Leaving Cert pupil 1966-7, email 12 Feb. 2014.
31. Some allowance has to be made also for the fact that some pupils may have left to attend other schools.
32. Figures compiled are based on Mac Kiernan and Dunne, a small degree of error has to be allowed for as not all pupils came to the school as First Years.
33. Coolohan, p.195: Mac Kiernan and Dunne.
34. Coolohan, p.195.
35. *The Anglo-Celt*, 12 Jan.1973, president's address to P.P.U.; while he does not mention Biology, Fr. Dan Gallogly does in his article, *The Anglo-Celt* 22 February 1974.
36. Figures compiled are based on Mac Kiernan and Dunne; approx. 522 entered the college in these years, over 90 had left before 1972, either not completing the Leaving Cert or having originally entered a more senior Year than First Year. All such subsequent figures have a margin of error as it is impossible to know exactly who left early and who had entered as a senior student.
37. Cunningham and Gallogly, p.82.
38. *The Anglo-Celt*, 12 Jan.1973, president's address to P.P.U.
39. These figures are based on the fact that there were approx. 180 boarders in 1972, and pupils recorded from any county other than Cavan are regarded as being boarders, with an adjustment being allowed for some day-boys who came from Carrigallen.
40. Mac Kiernan and Dunne; It was impossible to categorise correctly all the addresses, as pupils from the same area sometimes gave the nearest town instead of the parish address. Cavan town includes those areas on the immediate outskirts.
41. Cunningham and Gallogly, p.103; by 1921 the Ancient Order of Hibernians, the political machine for the Irish Parliamentary Party, was regarded as too moderate by Sinn Féin supporters.
42. Ibid.
43. *Spectrum* June 1971, Vol.VI; the irony was that the student-author in question, while born and living in Cavan, was the son of a Leitrim man.
44. Mac Kiernan and Dunne.
45. Cunningham and Gallogly, p.84.
46. Ibid., p.78.
47. *The Anglo-Celt*, 12 Jan.1973, president's address to P.P.U.
48. 16% of girls failed the Leaving Cert nationally, *The Anglo-Celt* 22 September 1972.

Chapter 5
Snow

1. *The Anglo-Celt*, 17 Nov. 1972.
2. Ibid. 24 Nov. 1972.
3. Ibid. 2 March 1972.
4. Ibid.
5. Ibid. 9 March 1972.
6. Ibid. 16 March 1973.
7. Ibid. 5 January1973.
8. Ibid. 23 February 1973.
9. Ibid. 26 January 1973.
10. Years later, on a school tour abroad, some pupils bought remote controlled cars and were racing same on the corridor of the hotel in the early hours of the morning. Undaunted, St. Rosarii emerged from her bedroom, and in one fell-swoop confiscated the offending vehicles and retired to her room. About thirty minutes later the lads, still in possession of their remote controls, from their position outside her door, activated the cars inside Rosarii's bedroom.
11. *The Anglo-Celt*, 26 January 1973.
12. Ibid.16 February 1973, major photo of snow scene and comment.
13. Mac Kiernan and Dunne, p. 1X.
14. Interview with Josie Mc Govern, 11 March 2014.

Chapter 6
Mid-Term Break

1. E. Mc Niffe diary, 19 February 1973.
2. Seamus Heaney, Mid Term Break, from *Death of a Naturalist* (1966) collection.
3. Harper Lee, *To Kill a Mockingbird*, (1997 ed.), p.307.
4. At the time of writing my mother is a widow for forty one years.
5. Told to author by Fr. Tom Mc Manus.
6. *The Anglo-Celt*, 16 March, 1973.
7. W. Wordsworth, Surprised by Joy, lines 6-9, on my Leaving Cert English course.
8. *The Anglo-Celt*, 7 March 1973.

Chapter 7
First Kiss

1. 'Spear' as a nickname appears to have been passed on to different lads from Crosserlough, having its origins in the nickname of one of the famous Crosserlough football players of the 1960s (information from Frank Cogan).
2. I can't recall what past pupil told me this story.
3. *The Anglo-Celt*, 27 April 1973, at a cost of £400,000 (€5,448,000 in today's terms): It didn't actually open until a few months after that.
4. Ibid, 1 June 1973.
5. Coolahan, p. 198.
6. *The Anglo-Celt*, 20 April, 1973.
7. Ibid, 27 April, 1973.
8. Ibid, 6 April 1973.
9. En.wikipedia 1973 FA Cup Final, accessed 12 June 2014.
10. William Wordsworth, Loud is the Vale.
11. *The Anglo-Celt*, 25 May 1973.
12. Ibid.
13. Ibid. 1 June 1973, no event recorded for the last two names.
14. Ibid.

Chapter 8
Summer work, football and ... pure thoughts

1. Ferriter, p.573.
2. *The Anglo-Celt*, 10 August 1973.
3. E. Mc Niffe diary, 3 August 1973: Mam had only recently restarted diary entries after Dad's death.
4. Ferriter, p.271.
5. Ibid. p.585.
6. Ibid. p.586.
7. Prior, *That's the Way* (Sligo,2008), p.124.

Chapter 9
Prefect

1. I don't know how word leaked out from St. Pat's.
2. Pat Bradley was a power-house of strength, giving one hundred per cent to whatever he did, sport or work. Tragically he was killed in a farm accident around Easter 2012. R.I.P.
3. Thirty five years later, I discovered that Tommy came as a worker to the college on the 6 September 1973, one day after I had arrived as a pupil. We both left the college in 2013, Tommy after forty one years of unbroken and loyal service, and me after eight years as principal.
4. *The Anglo-Celt*, 14 September 1973.
5. Ibid.
6. Ibid. 21 September 1973.
7. Ibid. 28 September 1973, 2 Nov. 1973: despite perusal of the Celt there appears to be no account of any further games by St. Pat's in the Rannafast competition that year and there is no comprehensive list of players given. (Thomas Mc Tague kindly provided me with names of players). As the 1 Dec. 1973 issue of the Celt is missing from the archives in Johnston Central Library, there is no information available for some games in late November.
8. This list may contain some errors.
9. *The Anglo-Celt*, 21 September 1973.
10. Ibid. 1 October 1973.
11. E. Mc Niffe diary, 3 November 1973.
12. *The Anglo-Celt*, 9 November 1973.
13. Ibid. 23 November 1973 (reported fixture to be played on 1 Dec.1973).
14. E. Mc Niffe diary, 21 December 1973.
15. Ibid. 30 December 1973.
16. Coolahan, p.198.

Chapter 10
Centenary

1. Connolly, p.290.
2. E. Mc Niffe diary, 29/30 January 1974.
3. Cain.ulst.ac.uk/events/Sunningdale,

accessed 29 July 2014.
4. Author's English essay copy, 1973-4.
5. *The Anglo-Celt*, 16 November 1973.
6. Ibid. 9 November 1973.
7. Ibid. 23 November 1973.
8. Ibid.
9. The *The Anglo-Celt* newspaper for 1 Dec. 1973 is missing from the archives in Johnston Central Library, hence less than full information is available for some games.
10. Ibid. 8 February 1974.
11. Ibid. 15 February 1974.
12. Ibid. 1 March 1974.
13. Ibid. 19 October 1973.
14. Ibid.
15. Ibid. 8, 15, 22 February 1974.
16. Ibid. 1 March 1974.
17. Ibid. 15 March 1974.
18. Ibid.
19. While I remember well the atmosphere of the centenary week, some details of what days were half-days etc. are a little vague.
20. *The Anglo-Celt*, 15 March 1974.
21. Member of teaching staff in conversation with author, circa 2012.
22. *The Anglo-Celt*, 15 March 1974.
23. Ibid.
24. Ibid.
25. Frances Galligan, in conversation Spring 2010.
26. *The Anglo-Celt*, 15 March 1974: The irony was lost on us at the time, but we had just met President Childers two days previously, one of a handful of Church of Ireland members who had served in the Oireachtas (representing the Monaghan constituency), and now Billy Fox, also a Church of Ireland and Oireachtas member from Monaghan had been brutally murdered by the I.R.A.
27. Ibid.
28. Ibid. 8 March 1974.
29. E. Mc Niffe diary, 20 March 1974.
30. Christened Bridie, she was later called Breda by most of her family, as that was what she was known as in England.
31. *Loreto College Cavan, 1930-2013*, Liam Kelly and Brendan Scott, Cumann Seanchais Bhreifne 2013, p.124.
32. E. Mc Niffe diary, 31 March 1974.
33. Ibid. 11 April 1974.

Chapter 11
Bombs, London, Leaving

1. Ferriter, p.639.
2. The Regional Colleges later evolved into the Institutes of Technology. They were in their infancy at this stage, and Cavan was in the catchment area of Dundalk Regional.
3. Mary Mc Niffe (nee Smith, author's wife) first applied to Maynooth College in mid-August 1976, after receiving her Leaving Cert results, and secured a place.
4. E. Mc Niffe diary, 28 April 1974.
5. Vincent Comerford, Emeritus Professor of Modern Irish History, N.U.I. Maynooth, in conversation 12 August 2014.
6. When I returned as principal to the college in 2005, I checked the door, but it had been painted over numerous times and the names were no longer legible.
7. Ulster Workers' Council Strike 1974, en wikipedia.org., accessed 14 August 2014.
8. I was not aware that John (Jack) Brennan was also on that bus to Dublin, until it came up in conversation between us almost forty years later, when I returned as principal.
9. en.m.wikipedia.org., Dublin and Monaghan Bombings, accessed 14 August 2014.
10. Rev. John Murphy in conversation, 15 August 2014.
11. en.m.wikipedia.org., Dublin and Monaghan Bombings, accessed 14 August 2014, Second Bomb.
12. E. Mc Niffe diary, 17 May 1974.
13. en.m.wikipedia.org., Dublin and Monaghan Bombings, accessed 14 August 2014.
14. E. Mc Niffe diary, 18 May 1974.
15. en.m.wikipedia.org., Dublin and Monaghan Bombings, accessed 15 August 2014.
16. E. Mc Niffe diary, 20 May 1974.
17. Ibid. 24 May 1974.
18. *The Anglo-Celt*, 7 June 1974.
19. Almost forty years later, as principal, I received an email from Patrick recalling the incident.
20. When I returned to St. Pat's as principal in 2005, Luke's son Patrick was a

student. Luke himself had not changed, as affable and unassuming as ever. I got thanking him for his help, which he did not remember. He developed cancer and died a few years later. R.I.P.

21. I forgot to purchase the photos. Fortunately when I became principal, Maureen Kelly (nee Cosgrove) found one such photo in her house (her brother Martin and I were in the same class) and kindly copied and framed it for me, which I hung in my office.

Chapter 12
Vocation

1. Author's English essay copy.
2. *The Anglo-Celt*, 1 Sept. 1972.
3. Ibid. 20 Oct. 1972.
4. Ibid. 15 Dec. 1972.
5. Ibid.12 Jan. 1973.
6. Ibid. 9 March 1973.
7. Ibid. April 6 1973.
8. Ibid. 11 May 1973.
9. Ibid. 19 Oct. 1973.
10. Ibid. 8 Feb.1974.
11. Ibid. 15, 22 Feb. 1974.
12. Ibid. 8,15 March 1974.
13. Ibid. 15 March 1974.
14. Gallogly and Cunningham p.83; while not all went on to be ordained, a very high proportion did so.
15. Ibid. citing Dr. Jeremiah Newman in *Ecclesiastical Record* July 1962.
16. Mac Kiernan and Dunne: the table is constructed on the basis of what year the pupils, who subsequently became priests, entered the college. The percentages may be slightly inaccurate for some years, as a small number of pupils only spent their two senior years in St. Pat's, and some spent six years, some seven in Maynooth and other seminaries.
17. Ibid.
18. *The Anglo-Celt*, 12 Jan. 1973.
19. Wikipedia, 1960s, accessed 29 August 2014.
20. Corish, *Maynooth College, 1795-1995*, (Dublin 1995), p.193.
21. F.X. Martin, *Leaders and Men of the Easter Rising*, Methuen 1967.
22. I am not exactly sure it was this Saturday, but it was before the results came out.
23. Analysis of 1974 Leaving Cert results in St. Patrick's College archive.
24. Ibid.
25. State Examinations Commission website, statistics, accessed, 7 Nov.2014.
26. I am indebted to George Cartwright for most of this information, whose knowledge of courses chosen and whereabouts of former pupils is very good.
27. Ibid.
28. This leaves eleven pupils not accounted for as to career choice: In addition there may be inaccuracies as to courses chosen as I am a bit hazy about some of the details.
29. Cunningham and Gallogly, p.78.
30. Echoing the epitaph he used referring to the Fenian, Thomas Clarke.

Select Bibliography

Primary Sources

Privately Held
Diaries of Elizabeth Mc Niffe (author's mother), 1969-74.
School text books, 1972-74.
Homework notebooks, 1972-74.
Exercise and essay copies 1972-74.
Spectrum June 1971, Vol. V1; June 1972, Vol. V11, College Student magazine.

St. Patrick's College, Cavan
Intermediate Certificate results, 1972.
Leaving Certificate results, 1974.

Kilmore Diocesan Archives, Bishop's House, Cullies, Cavan
Photograph albums of St. Patrick's College.

Johnston Central Library, Cavan
The Anglo-Celt, August 1972-September 1974.

Secondary Sources

1. Cartwright, George, *Breifne Abú!, Cavan GAA records 1886-2011*: Cavan County Board GAA, 2011.
2. Connolly, S.J. (ed.), *The Oxford Companion to Irish History*: Oxford University Press, 1998.
3. Coolahan, John, *Irish Education, History and Structure*, Dublin: Institute of Public Administration, 1981 (2012 edition).
4. Corish, Patrick J., *Maynooth College, 1795-1995*, Dublin: Gill and Macmillan, 1995.
5. Cunningham, Terence P. & Gallogly, Daniel, *St. Patrick's College Cavan and the Earlier Kilmore Academy, A Centenary History*, Cavan: St. Patrick's College, 1974.
6. Ferriter, Diarmaid, *Ambiguous Republic: Ireland in the 1970s*, London: Profile Books, 2012.
7. Foucault, Michel, 'Discipline and Punish', 1975 in *Literary Theory An Anthology*, 2003, eds. J. Rivkin & M. Ryan.
8. Gallogly, Daniel, *Ballinamore Seán O'Heslin's 1889-1984*: Seán O'Heslin G.A.A. Club, 1984.
9. Gallogly, Daniel, *The Diocese of Kilmore 1800-1950*: Cumann Seanchais Bhreifne, 1999.
10. Kelly, Liam & and Scott, Brendan, *Loreto College Cavan, 1930-2013*: Cumann Seanchais Bhreifne, 2013.
11. Mac Atasney, Gerard, *The Plantation of County Leitrim (1585-1670)*: Carrick-on-Shannon Heritage Group, 2013.
12. Mac Kiernan, Francis & Dunne, Raymond, *The College Boys: Students of the Kilmore Academy & St. Patrick's College, Cavan, 1839-2000.* Cumann Seanchais Bhreifne, 2008.
13. Prior, Joe, *That's the Way*, Sligo: Ben Aughlin, 2008.

Internet

Specific sites accessed are recorded in the references for each chapter.